Formatting toolbar

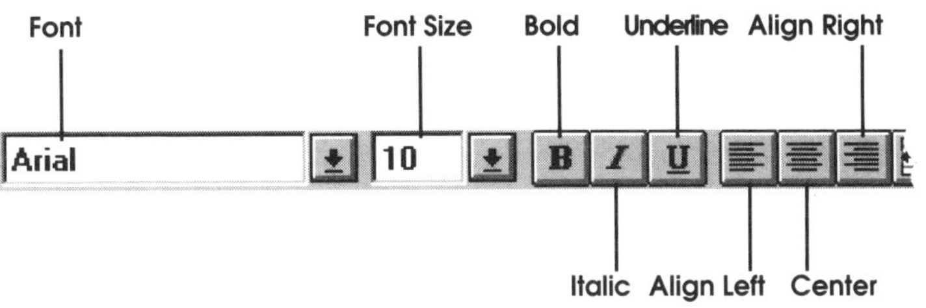

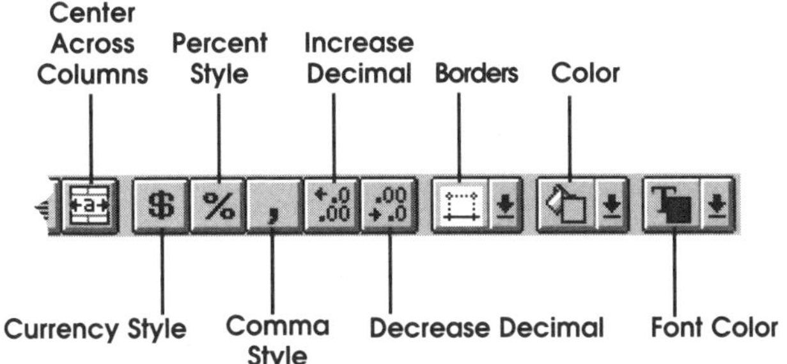

For Every Computer Question, There Is a Sybex Book That Has the Answer

Each computer user learns in a different way. Some need thorough, methodical explanations, while others are too busy for details. At Sybex we bring nearly 20 years of experience to developing the book that's right for you. Whatever your needs, we can help you get the most from your software and hardware, at a pace that's comfortable for you.

We start beginners out right. You will learn by seeing and doing with our **Quick & Easy** series: friendly, colorful guidebooks with screen-by-screen illustrations. For hardware novices, the **Your First** series offers valuable purchasing advice and installation support.

Often recognized for excellence in national book reviews, our **Mastering** and **Understanding** titles are designed for the intermediate to advanced user, without leaving the beginner behind. A **Mastering** or **Understanding** book provides the most detailed reference available. Add one of our pocket-sized **Instant Reference** titles for a complete guidance system. Programmers will find that the new **Developer's Handbook** series provides a higher-end user's perspective on developing innovative and original code.

With the breathtaking advances common in computing today comes an ever increasing demand to remain technologically up-to-date. In many of our books, we provide the added value of software, on disks or CDs. Sybex remains your source for information on software development, operating systems, networking, and every kind of desktop application. We even have books for kids. Sybex can help smooth your travels on the **Internet** and provide **Strategies and Secrets** to your favorite computer games.

As you read this book, take note of its quality. Sybex publishes books written by experts—authors chosen for their extensive topical knowledge. In fact, many are professionals working in the computer software field. In addition, each manuscript is thoroughly reviewed by our technical, editorial, and production personnel for accuracy and ease-of-use before you ever see it—our guarantee that you'll buy a quality Sybex book every time.

To manage your hardware headaches and optimize your software potential, ask for a Sybex book.

For More Information, Please Contact:

Sybex Inc.
2021 Challenger Drive
Alameda, CA 94501
Tel: (510) 523-8233 • (800) 227-2346
Fax: (510) 523-2373

Sybex is committed to using natural resources wisely to preserve and improve our environment. As a leader in the computer books publishing industry, we are aware that over 40% of America's solid waste is paper. This is why we have been printing books on recycled paper since 1982. This year our use of recycled paper will result in the saving of more than 153,000 trees. We will lower air pollution effluents by 54,000 pounds, save 6,300,000 gallons of water, and reduce landfill by 27,000 cubic yards.

In choosing a Sybex book you are not only making a choice for the best in skills and information, you are also choosing to enhance the quality of life for all of us.

Excel 5 for Windows Instant Reference

The SYBEX Instant Reference Series

Instant References are available on these topics:

1-2-3 Release 2.3 & 2.4 for DOS

1-2-3 Release 4 for Windows

1-2-3 Release 5 for Windows

AutoCAD Release 12 for DOS

AutoCAD Release 12 for Windows

AutoCAD 13

CorelDRAW 4

dBASE IV 2.0 for Programmers

DOS 6.2

Excel 5 for Windows

Harvard Graphics 3

Internet

Microsoft Access 2

Microsoft Office Professional

Norton Desktop for Windows 2.0

Norton Utilities 7

OS/2 2.1

Paradox 4.5 for DOS Users

Paradox 4.5 for Windows Users

PC Tools 8

Quattro Pro 5 for Windows

SQL

Windows 3.1

Word 6 for Windows

Word for Windows, Version 2.0

WordPerfect 5.1 for DOS

WordPerfect 6 for DOS

WordPerfect 6 for Windows

WordPerfect 6.1 for Windows

Excel 5 for Windows™ Instant Reference

Douglas Hergert

San Francisco • Paris • Düsseldorf • Soest

Acquisitions Editor: Joanne Cuthbertson
Developmental Editor: Richard Mills
Editor: Armin Brott
Project Editor: Valerie Potter
Technical Editor: Adebisi Oladipupo
Production Editor: Carolina Montilla
Production Artist: Ingrid Owen
Screen Graphics: John Corrigan
Typesetter: Stephanie Hollier
Proofreader: John Selawsky
Indexer: Liz Cunningham
Cover Designer: Archer Design
Cover Photographer: Mark Johann
Screen reproductions produced with Collage Complete.
Collage Complete is a trademark of Inner Media Inc.

Library of Congress Card Number: 93-87246

ISBN: 0-7821-1325-7

Manufactured in the United States of America

10 9 8 7 6 5

To Rudolph Langer,

with thanks for a decade of advice and friendship

Acknowledgments

I want to thank Richard Mills, Armin Brott, Adebisi Oladipupo, and Val Potter for their work on the current edition of this book; and Dianne King, James Compton, Peter Weverka, Brenda Kienan, and Maryann Brown for their work on *Excel 4 for Windows Instant Reference*. Also, sincere thanks to Claudette Moore of Moore Literary Agency.

Table of Contents

Introduction *xv*

What's New in Excel 5 for windows **1**
Add-Ins **4**
Alignment **7**
Analysis Tools **10**
Arithmetic Operations **12**
Array Formulas **14**
Auditing **16**
AutoFill **17**
AutoFormat for Charts **20**
AutoFormat for Worksheet Data **21**
Borders **23**
Centering across Columns **25**
Charting **25**
Clearing Worksheet Cells **35**
Clipboard **37**
Colors **38**
Column Widths **42**
Consolidating Data **43**
Copying Data **46**
Copying Formats **49**
Copying Formulas **51**
Custom Number Formats **53**
Customizing Excel **55**
Data Form **56**
Data Tables **60**

Database 64
Database Criteria 66
Database Functions 68
Date and Time Functions 70
Date Entries 72
Deleting 75
Deleting Files 76
Dialog Sheets 77
Directories 80
Dynamic Data Exchange (DDE) 81
Editing 84
Engineering Functions 85
Exiting Excel 86
File Formats 87
Filling Ranges 89
Filters 90
Financial Functions 95
Finding Files 97
Finding Worksheet Data 99
Fonts 100
Formatting Worksheet Cells 103
Formula Bar 104
Formulas 105
Functions 108
Goal Seek 109
Graphic Objects 111
Group Editing 115
Headers and Footers 117
Help 118
Hiding 120

Importing Files 121
Info Window 122
Information Functions 123
Inserting 124
Iteration 127
Links and 3-D References 128
Lists 134
Logical Functions 135
Lookup and Reference Functions 138
Lotus 1-2-3 Help 140
Macro 141
Macro Recording 145
Mathematical Functions 148
Moving Data 149
Names 151
Notes 156
Number Formats 159
Object Linking and Embedding (OLE) 161
Opening Files 164
Outlines 165
Page Setup 169
Panes 170
Parsing 172
Passwords 173
Patterns 175
Pivot Table 177
Point Size 183
Previewing 184
Printer Setup 185

Printing Charts	186
Printing Worksheets	188
Protecting Cells in a Worksheet	190
Protecting Workbooks	192
Query	193
Recalculation	196
References	197
Repeating Commands	201
Replacing Worksheet Data	202
Reports	204
Row Height	206
Saving Files	207
Scenarios	208
Selecting a Range	213
Series	215
Shading	219
Shortcut Menus	219
Solver	221
Sorting	225
Spelling Checks	228
Statistical Functions	229
Styles	231
Subtotals	234
Summation	236
Template	237
Text Box	239
Text Functions	242
Text Operations	243
Time Entries	244
TipWizard	246

Toolbars 247
Transposing Ranges 251
Trendlines 252
Undo 254
Views 254
Window Operations 256
Workbooks 259
Workspace 263
Wrapping Text 264
Zooming 265

Index

267

Introduction

Microsoft Excel is the popular Windows spreadsheet program that provides worksheets, charts, database and list operations, and application programming all in one software environment. In Version 5, Excel takes many important steps forward in both the simplicity of its operations and the sophistication of its features. On one hand, Microsoft has added a variety of tools designed to make your work more efficient—streamlined workbook documents; special worksheet operations such as in-cell editing, custom AutoFill, and "rich text" formatting; ease-of-use enhancements, including tear-off palettes and a new Name box on the Formula bar; and help features like the TipWizard, ToolTips, and the Function Wizard. On the other hand, you'll find many new high-end features that extend Excel's power and flexibility for calculating, organizing, and analyzing data. For programmers, Excel is the first Microsoft application to provide Visual Basic as a language option for developing macros and modules.

Excel 5 for Windows Instant Reference gives you succinct, accessible instructions for the most important tasks you'll want to accomplish in Excel. In over a hundred alphabetically arranged entries, you'll find the information you need to complete your work with accuracy and understanding. Entries provide step-by-step procedures, shortcuts, examples, notes on usage, and cross references to related tasks. The goal is to help you work more efficiently and effectively with worksheets, charts, lists, databases, and macros.

WHAT'S NEW IN EXCEL 5 FOR WINDOWS

As you begin working in Excel 5, the first major change you'll notice is the use of *workbooks* as the basic document type. A workbook is a convenient storage unit for the worksheets, charts, and macros that you develop in Excel. In one workbook you can create any number of interrelated sheets. (For more information, turn to the Workbook entry in this book. To learn how to develop specific kinds of sheets in a workbook, see the Charting, Macro, and Macro Recording entries.)

Worksheets

Because a workbook can contain any number of worksheets, you'll want to learn how to share and update data from one worksheet to another:

- Excel 5 allows you to create formulas that extend across worksheets in a book—including 3-D formulas, which you can use to summarize periodic data stored in several adjacent worksheets.
- Names that you create in the sheets of a workbook have *book-level* scope by default. This means that one worksheet can refer by name to data located on other sheets. The convenient new Name box on the Formula bar gives you a list of all the book-level names in a workbook.
- Group editing—the process of performing identical operations on multiple worksheets at once—is easier than ever before.

For more information, see Formulas, Group Editing, Links and 3-D Formulas, Names, and Workbooks.

Databases and Lists

Database features in spreadsheet programs sometimes seem like afterthoughts—but this is far from true with Excel 5. You now define a list or a database simply by entering a row of field names followed by rows of records. Once you've created a database on a worksheet, sophisticated data operations are just a mouse click away:

- With the AutoFilter feature you can examine groups of records that match conditions you select.
- You can instantly sort your database by any field simply by selecting a field and clicking a Sort button.
- You can reorganize your database and display totals and subtotals by choosing the Data ➤ Subtotals command.
- You can create dynamic, interactive pivot tables to examine the information in your database in new arrangements and combinations.

See Database, Filters, Lists, Pivot Tables, Sorting, and Subtotals for more information.

Charting

Charting has always been one of Excel's strengths, and this new release gives you even greater charting capabilities:

- The ChartWizard and the AutoFormats features provide the most convenient techniques for developing chart sheets (or embedded charts) from a selection of worksheet data.
- A great variety of options are available for making a chart look exactly the way you want it.
- The Insert ➤ Trendline command quickly adds a trendline to a chart, showing you the trends in your data.

See AutoFormat for Charts, Charting, and Trendlines for instructions and information.

Programming

Finally, Excel now includes a professional programming language known as Visual Basic for Applications:

- Programmers will use this language to devise sophisticated applications that operate within the Excel environment.
- If you're not a programmer, you can still create your own library of Visual Basic macros to streamline your work in Excel. Just turn on the Macro Recorder, work through the steps of a task, and turn the recorder off when you're finished.
- You can use the macros you create in some surprisingly versatile ways—assigning them to buttons on toolbars, creating menu commands to represent them, and assigning them to graphic objects displayed directly on worksheets.

See the Macro and Macro Recording entries for more information. Note that the traditional macro language from previous versions of Excel is also still available.

ADD-INS

An *add-in* is an Excel file that expands the scope of operations you can perform in workbooks. Excel comes with a library of add-ins designed to provide you with special-purpose functions and menu commands. For example, the Analysis Toolpak, the Report Manager, the Solver, and the View Manager are all presented as add-ins. (Each of these components is described in its own entry in this book.) Using the Tools ➤ Add-Ins command you can include an add-in as part of your Excel installation; when you do so, all the commands and functions defined in the add-in become part of Excel. Conversely, you can remove any add-in that defines features you don't use.

You can also create new add-in files, to integrate your own macros into the Excel application. Using the Tools ➤ Make Add-In command, you can save a workbook in the special add-in file format. You then use Tools ➤ Add-Ins to install your new add-in.

To Install Add-Ins

1. Choose Tools ➤ Add-Ins. The Add-ins dialog box contains a list of the available add-ins, each represented as a check-box.
2. Click the name of the add-in you want to install. An X appears in the corresponding check box. Repeat this step for any combination of add-ins in the list.
3. If an add-in you want to install is not yet in the list, click the Browse button. In the Browse dialog box, double-click the name of the directory that contains the add-in file and then select the name of the directory in the File Name list. Click OK. In the Add-ins dialog box, the name of the selected add-in now appears in the list.
4. When all the add-ins you want are checked, click OK. If the newly installed add-ins define commands, the commands now appear in the appropriate Excel menus. If the

add-ins define functions, the names of the functions appear in the Function Wizard list.

NOTES Add-in files have .XLA extensions. Although the features of an installed add-in are available for your use, you cannot view or edit the contents of an .XLA file in Excel.

When you use the Tools ➤ Add-Ins command to install an add-in, the corresponding add-in features will be available in the current session and all subsequent sessions with Excel—unless you later remove the add-in.

If a particular add-in is missing from the Add-ins Available list—and if you cannot find the add-in file by clicking the Browse button—you'll have to run Excel Setup to install the add-in on your hard disk. Double-click the Excel Setup icon (located by default in the Microsoft Office group); then click the Add/Remove button in the Microsoft Excel 5.0 Setup dialog box. In the next window, select the Add-ins check box and click the Change Option button to view the list of add-ins that can be installed.

To Open an Add-In for Use Only in the Current Session

Choose File ➤ Open and select the name of the .XLA file you want to open. Then click OK. Although the add-in macro sheet is not displayed as an open document, its features are now available for you to use.

To Remove an Add-In

1. Choose Tools ➤ Add-ins. The Add-In dialog box appears on the screen.
2. In the Add-Ins Available list, click the name of the add-in that you want to remove. The X is cleared from the corresponding check box.
3. Click OK. The next time you start Excel, the features of this add-in will be removed.

NOTES Removing an add-in does not delete it from the Add-Ins Available list. You can always reinstall the add-in by choosing Tools ➤ Add-Ins.

To Create a New Add-In

1. Open or activate the workbook from which you want to create an add-in. The workbook must contain at least one macro (on a module sheet or macro sheet).
2. Activate a module or macro sheet in the workbook, and then choose the Tools ➤ Make Add-In command.
3. In the Make Add-In dialog box, double-click the directory where you want to save the add in, and enter a file name. Notice that .XLA is the default extension for add-in files.
4. Click OK to create the add-in file on disk. Excel *compiles* your workbook into the special add-in format, resulting in a new component that will operate efficiently in the Excel environment.
5. To install the new add-in, choose Tools ➤ Add-Ins and follow the steps described at the beginning of this entry.

NOTES If you plan to create an add-in from a workbook you have developed, save the workbook in the standard .XLS format before you choose the Tools ➤ Make Add-In command. Keep in mind that you cannot edit or even view the contents of an .XLA file; the only way to revise an add-in you create is to open the original .XLS file, make the necessary changes, and then recompile it into an .XLA file.

When you save a workbook file from which you later plan to create an add-in, use the Summary Info dialog box to identify the contents of the file. Enter a name for the file in the Title text box, and a brief description of the file in the Comments box. When you create and install the add-in, these two items of information will appear in the Add-in dialog box.

See Also Analysis Tools, Customizing Excel, Macro, Macro Recording, Reports, Saving Files, Scenarios, Solver, Views.

ALIGNMENT

Excel offers a variety of horizontal and vertical alignments and orientations for displaying text and numeric entries in a cell or range. You can also change the alignment and orientation of the text displayed in a text box, the label on a button, or attached text in a chart.

To Change the Alignment of Entries in a Cell or Range

1. Select the cell or range of cells that you want to realign.
2. Choose the Format ➤ Cells command. In the Format Cells dialog box, click the Alignment tab.
3. In the Horizontal box, select the Left, Center, or Right option to change the alignment of text and numeric entries within the current column-width settings.
4. Optionally, choose Top, Center, or Bottom in the Vertical box to adjust the placement of entries within the current row height.
5. Click OK.

Shortcuts Select a cell or range and click one of the three alignment buttons in the Formatting toolbar—Align Left, Center, or Align Right. Alternatively, point to a cell or range and click the right mouse button to pull down the shortcut menu for the selection. Choose the Format Cells command; then click the Alignment tab in the Format Cells dialog box.

NOTES The General option in the Horizontal box represents the default alignment settings: left-alignment for text entries, right-alignment for numeric entries, and centering for logical and error values.

When you change the column widths or row heights, Excel adjusts the placement of entries according to the current alignment settings. For example, if you increase the column width for a range of centered entries, Excel centers the entries within the new width.

To Rotate Entries within Cells

1. Select the cell or range of cells that you want to rotate.
2. Choose Format ➤ Cells, and click the Alignment tab.
3. Select one of the samples displayed in the Orientation box— for vertically arranged text, text rotated to read from bottom to top, or text rotated to read from top to bottom.
4. Click OK.

NOTES Excel automatically adjusts the row height to accommodate the length of a rotated entry. If you later restore the default horizontal orientation, Excel restores the appropriate row height (unless you have manually changed the height yourself). To adjust a row's height to the contents of its cells, double-click the line below the corresponding row heading.

To Justify a Long Text Entry within Its Cell

1. Select the cell containing the long text entry you want to justify.
2. Choose Format ➤ Cells and click the Alignment tab.
3. Select the Justify option in the Horizontal box. Then click OK. Excel wraps the text within the cell, increasing the row height as necessary. To the extent possible, the text is aligned along the left and right sides of the cell.
4. Optionally, adjust the column width and row height at the cell's location to achieve the justified text arrangement that you want.

To Break and Realign Long Text Entries within a Range of Cells

1. Select a range consisting of a column of long text entries and the adjacent columns (to the right) within which you want to realign the text.
2. Choose Edit ➤ Fill. On the Fill submenu, choose the Justify command. Excel redistributes the text contained in the first column of the range selection, resulting in lines of text that are roughly the same length.

NOTES If the range you select is not large enough for the realignment of text entries, Excel displays the message "Text will extend below range." If you click OK, Excel increases the range by the number of rows necessary to realign the lines of text.

To Change the Text Alignment of a Text Box or a Button

1. If a macro is assigned to the text box or button, select the object by holding down the Ctrl key while you click it with the mouse. If no macro is assigned, simply click the object to select it.
2. Choose Format ➤ Object. (This command is available when a graphic object is selected.) In the Format Object dialog box, click the Alignment tab.
3. Select any combination of options for the horizontal and vertical text alignment and orientation, and click OK.

Shortcut Point to the object and click the right mouse button to select the object and pull down its shortcut menu. Choose the Format Object command from the shortcut menu and then click the Alignment tab in the Format Object dialog box.

To Change the Alignment of Titles or Labels in a Chart

In a chart window, select the title or axis containing the text that you want to realign, and choose Format ➤ Selected Chart Title, Format ➤ Selected Axis Title, or Format ➤ Selected Axis. In the resulting dialog box, click the Alignment tab, and then select any combination of alignment and orientation options. Click OK.

Shortcut Point to the text, click the right mouse button, and choose the Format command from the shortcut menu. Then click the Alignment tab in the resulting dialog box.

See Also Charting, Column Widths, Filling Ranges, Formatting Worksheet Cells, Graphic Objects, Row Height, Text Box, Toolbars, Wrapping Text.

ANALYSIS TOOLS

The Analysis ToolPak add-in supplies tools for engineering and statistical applications. Given the input of relevant worksheet data, the components of this add-in are designed to perform specific statistical and engineering analyses.

To Use a Tool from the Analysis ToolPak

1. Create or open a worksheet containing the data that you want to analyze.
2. Choose Tools ➤ Data Analysis. The Data Analysis dialog box appears on the screen.

3. Select the analysis that you want to perform and click OK. The dialog box for the corresponding analysis tool appears on the screen.
4. In the Input Range box enter a reference to the range of data to be analyzed.
5. In the Output Range text box, enter a reference to the location where you want Excel to display the results of the analysis. (You can enter a reference to a single cell to specify the upper-left corner of the output range.) Respond to the other options that appear in the dialog box. Click Help if you need more information about a particular analysis tool.
6. Click OK to perform the analysis. The results appear in the selected output range.

NOTES The following tools are available in the Analysis ToolPak:

Anova: Single-Factor produces an analysis of variance for an input range that contains two or more data samples.

Anova: Two-Factor with Replication produces an analysis of variance for two or more groups of samples.

Anova: Two-Factor without Replication produces an analysis of variance for two or more data samples.

Correlation calculates the statistical relationship between two sets of data.

Covariance calculates the statistical relationship between two sets of data.

Descriptive Statistics supplies a table of statistical measurements, including mean, standard deviation, minimum, maximum, and so on.

Exponential Smoothing implements a mathematical forecasting technique.

F-Test: Two-Sample for Variances produces a comparison of variances, given an input range containing two columns or rows of data.

Fourier Analysis calculates the coefficients of a periodic function.

Histogram calculates frequency distributions, given an input range of numeric data and a range of bins in which to perform the distribution.

Moving Average supplies a forecasting tool.

Random Number Generation produces an output range of random numbers; optionally, the numbers can match a particular distribution scheme that you specify in this tool's dialog box.

Rank and Percentile determines the ordinal and percentile rank of each value in an input range, in relation to the other values in the range.

Regression performs a linear regression analysis, calculating the best straight-line fit through a data sample.

Sampling produces a representative data sample from a larger population in the input range.

t-Test calculates the correlation between paired sets of measurements in an input range. (Three variations of this test are available.)

z-Test compares two sets of measurements in the input range.

See Also Add-Ins, Data Tables, Engineering Functions, Iteration, Scenarios, Solver, Statistical Functions.

ARITHMETIC OPERATIONS

Along with the four most familiar arithmetic operations—addition, subtraction, multiplication, and division—Excel supports exponentiation and percentage operations in arithmetic formulas.

To Write an Arithmetic Formula

Use any combination of the following operands:

+	addition
–	subtraction
*	multiplication
/	division
%	percentage
^	exponentiation

NOTES Excel offers buttons for inserting any of the six arithmetic operators into a formula. You can view these buttons in the Customize dialog box: Point to any toolbar, click the right mouse button to pull down the toolbar shortcut menu, choose the Customize command, and then select the Formula category in the resulting dialog box. The operator buttons are not initially part of a toolbar, but you can add them to any toolbar by dragging them from the Customize dialog box. See the Toolbars entry for more information.

In a formula that contains more than one arithmetic operand, Excel performs operations in this order: percentage, exponentiation, multiplication and division (left to right), addition and subtraction (left to right). Use parentheses in a formula to override this default order of operations.

EXAMPLE In the following formula, Income, Expenses, and Taxrate are names defined for three cells on the current worksheet:

=(Income–Expenses)*Taxrate%

To evaluate this formula, Excel performs the percentage operation first (dividing the value of Taxrate by 100), then the subtraction (enclosed in parentheses), and finally the multiplication.

 **See Also** Formula Bar, Formulas, Functions, Toolbars.

ARRAY FORMULAS

An array formula can be an efficient and economical way to perform an operation involving multiple rows and columns of data, or to enter the same formula into multiple cells in a range. In addition, several of Excel's built-in functions take arrays as arguments or return array results.

To Enter an Array Formula

1. Select the cell or cells where you want the formula to appear.
2. Enter the elements of the formula. To include a range as an operand in the formula, point to the range with the mouse or enter the range reference directly from the keyboard.
3. Press Ctrl-Shift-↵ to complete the formula. In response, Excel encloses the array formula in braces, { and }.

e.g. **EXAMPLE** An array formula can calculate a result from intermediate operations on a range of data. For example, suppose you've developed a worksheet in which the range B2:E2 contains four quarterly gross income amounts and B3:E3 contains the four corresponding quarterly expense amounts. Cell B4 contains an estimated tax rate. An array formula provides a quick way to calculate the estimated tax due on net income for the entire year. Begin by typing the following formula into cell B5:

=SUM((B2:E2–B3:E3)*B4%)

To enter this as an array formula press Ctrl-Shift-↵. Excel encloses the formula in braces:

{=SUM((B2:E2–B3:E3)*B4%)}

This single array formula performs two intermediate calculations on each column of quarterly data in order to compute the total year's tax amount. First, it subtracts each quarter's expense amount from the gross income to find the net income, and then it multiplies the result by the estimated quarterly tax rate. The SUM function adds these quarterly tax amounts together to produce the year's total.

NOTES You can include an *array constant* as an operand in an array formula. An array constant is a sequence of numeric or text values enclosed in braces. Within the braces, the sequence of constant values requires specific punctuation: commas to separate columns of data, and semicolons to separate rows. For example, in the following array formula, each value in the five-column by three-row range A1:E3 is multiplied by the corresponding value in a five-by-three array constant:

```
{=A1:E3*{1,2,3,4,5;2,2,2,2,2;9,8,7,6,5}}
```

When you enter this array formula into a worksheet range of the appropriate size, the result is an array consisting of five columns and three rows.

To Select the Range of an Array Formula

Select any cell within the range where the array formula is entered, and press Ctrl-/. (Alternatively, choose Edit ➤ Go To, click the Special button, and select the Current Array option in the Go To Special dialog box. Then click OK.)

To Edit an Array Formula

1. Select the entire array range or any cell within the range, and press F2. (The braces around the formula disappear.)
2. Edit the formula—either in the formula bar or in the active cell—and then press Ctrl-Shift-↵ to re-enter the array formula.

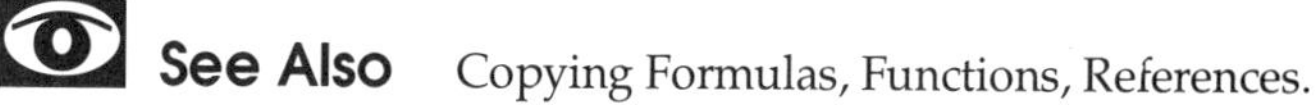

See Also Copying Formulas, Functions, References.

AUDITING

The commands in the Auditing submenu allow you to trace *precedents* and *dependents* on a worksheet. A precedent is a cell that is referenced in the formula of the active cell. A dependent is a cell containing a formula that refers to the active cell. By selecting the Trace commands in the Auditing submenu, you can visually examine a cell's precedents or dependents.

To Trace a Cell's Precedents

1. Select a cell that contains a formula referring to other cells.
2. Choose Tools ➤ Auditing and then choose Trace Precedents from the Auditing submenu. Excel displays one or more tracer arrows from the precedent cells to the active cell.

Shortcut Select a cell and click the Trace Precedents button on the Auditing toolbar. (To display this toolbar, choose Tools ➤ Auditing and then click the Show Auditing Toolbar command.)

To Trace the Cells That Refer to the Active Cell

1. Select a cell that appears in one or more formulas elsewhere on the active worksheet or another worksheet.
2. Choose Tools ➤ Auditing and then choose Trace Dependents in the Auditing submenu. Excel displays one or more tracer arrows from the active cell to its dependent cells.

Shortcut Select a cell and click the Trace Dependents button on the Auditing toolbar.

NOTES A tracer arrow that points from or to a small spreadsheet icon represents an external reference. To find the precedent or dependent of the active cell, double-click the tracer arrow itself. In response, Excel displays the Go To dialog box with a list of all the precedent or dependent references. Select a reference and click OK to activate the precedent or dependent cell.

If the active cell contains an error value, choose Tools ➤ Auditing and then choose the Trace Error command in the Auditing submenu. (Alternatively, click the Trace Error button on the Auditing toolbar.) Excel displays tracer errors from cells that may be the source of the error.

To Remove Tracer Arrows

Choose Tools ➤ Auditing and then click Remove All Arrows in the Auditing submenu.

Shortcuts Click the Remove All Arrows button in the Auditing toolbar. Alternatively, click the Remove Precedent Arrows or the Remove Dependent Arrows button to remove tracer arrows in categories.

See Also Formulas, Info Window, References.

AUTOFILL

By dragging the fill handle—the small black box at the lower-right corner of a selected cell or range—you can easily create series, copy data, or replicate formulas across rows or down columns in a worksheet.

Excel also defines built-in lists of labels that you can enter into a worksheet range by dragging the fill handle. These include the days of the week (Sunday to Saturday, or Sun to Sat) and the names of the months (January to December, or Jan to Dec). You can define your own *custom lists* of commonly used labels; when you do so, the AutoFill feature is available for entering these lists into a worksheet.

To Create a Series by Dragging the Fill Handle

1. Enter the first elements of the series in consecutive cells in a column or adjacent cells in a row, and then select the range of cells containing these entries.
2. Position the mouse pointer over the fill handle for the current selection. The pointer changes to a cross-hair shape.
3. Drag the mouse down or across to the cells where you want to extend the series. Excel fills the selection with sequential elements of the series you defined in the initial cell entries.

e.g. **EXAMPLE** To create a series of integers in column A, enter 1 in cell A1 and 2 in cell A2. Select the range A1:A2. Then drag the fill handle at the lower-right corner of cell A2 down column A to the last cell you want to fill. Excel fills the column with integers 3, 4, 5, 6, 7, and so on. Use the same technique to create numeric series with step values other than 1—for example 5, 10, 15, 20…

To enter a series of month names in column A, enter January in A1, and drag the cell's fill handle down to A12. From A2 to A12, Excel fills the column with the text entries February, March, April, and so on. Use the same technique to create a column of days (Sunday, Monday, Tuesday), quarter labels (Quarter 1, Quarter 2, Quarter 3, Quarter 4), or other numbered labels (for example, Product 1, Product 2, Product 3; or 1st, 2nd, 3rd, 4th, 5th, and so on.)

NOTES To fill a column or row with an identical sequence of entries—rather than a series—hold down the Ctrl key while you drag the fill handle. For example, imagine that you want to fill the range A1:A12 with repetitions of the labels Product 1, Product 2, and Product 3. To do so, enter these three labels into A1, A2, and A3. Then select A1:A3 and hold down the Ctrl key while you drag the fill handle from A3 to A12.

You can also drag the fill handle to copy a formula from an initial cell to consecutive cells down a column or adjacent cells across a row. If the formula contains relative references, Excel adjusts the references accordingly as it copies the formula to new positions.

Shortcut If an adjacent column is already filled with data, you can copy a formula down the equivalent range by double-clicking the fill handle. For example, suppose the range A1:A10 contains labels, and you have just entered a formula into cell B1. You can copy the formula down the range B2:B10 by simply double-clicking the fill handle in cell B1.

To Create a Custom List of AutoFill Labels

1. Choose Tools ➤ Options. In the Options dialog box, click the Custom Lists tab.
2. The NEW LIST entry is selected in the Custom Lists box. Activate the List Entries box and begin typing the labels of your custom list. Press Enter after each label in the list.
3. When you finish typing your list, click the Add button to copy the list to the Custom Lists box.
4. If you want to create an additional list, select NEW LIST in the Custom Lists box, and repeat steps 2 and 3.
5. Click OK to close the Options dialog box.

e.g. EXAMPLE Suppose you frequently need to create a column containing the names of departments in your company—for example, Editorial, Production, Art, Technical, Sales, Accounting, and Management. To streamline this common data entry task, you can create a custom list consisting of these names. After defining the list, you can enter these labels into a column by typing any one of the names and then dragging the fill handle down the column.

See Also Copying Data, Copying Formulas, Filling Ranges, References, Series, Sorting.

AUTOFORMAT FOR CHARTS

The AutoFormat command for charts provides a large variety of predefined formats that you can apply to an existing chart. This is a quick way to change the way a chart depicts your data. In addition, you can add your own *custom* formats to those available in the AutoFormat dialog box.

To Apply a Chart AutoFormat

1. Activate a chart sheet, or double-click an embedded chart on a worksheet. Then Choose Format ➤ AutoFormat. The AutoFormat dialog box gives you a choice between built-in and user-defined formats.
2. To apply a built-in format, select a chart type from the Galleries list and then click on one of the formats pictured in the Formats box. Click OK to apply your selection to the active chart.
3. To apply a user-defined format, select the User-Defined option in the Formats Used box, and then select the name of a custom format in the Formats list. A preview box shows how the active chart will look in this format. Click OK to apply the format.

Shortcut Activate a chart sheet and position the mouse pointer inside the chart area. Click the right mouse button to pull down the shortcut menu for charts, and choose the AutoFormat command. The AutoFormat dialog box appears on the screen.

To Create a Custom AutoFormat for Charts

1. Activate a chart sheet or double-click an embedded chart. Organize this chart to represent the AutoFormat you want to define: Select a chart type; add titles and labels; apply

colors, patterns, and fonts; and so on. (See *Charting* for more information.)

2. Choose Format ➤ AutoFormat. In the AutoFormat dialog box, click the User-Defined option button. Then click the Customize button. The User-Defined AutoFormats dialog box appears on the screen.
3. Click the Add button. The Add Custom AutoFormat dialog box appears. In the Format Name text box, enter a name for the AutoFormat you are creating. In the Description text box, enter a brief description of the format. Then click OK. Back in the User-Defined AutoFormats dialog box, your new custom AutoFormat appears in the Formats list.
4. Click the Close button to complete the process. The new AutoFormat will now be available for use whenever you choose the Format ➤ AutoFormat command.

NOTES You can delete a custom AutoFormat by selecting its name in the User-Defined AutoFormats dialog box and then clicking the Delete command. You cannot delete a built-in chart AutoFormat.

See Also Charting.

AUTOFORMAT FOR WORKSHEET DATA

In the AutoFormat command, Excel offers over a dozen predesigned table formats that you can choose from. These designs include specific selections from Excel's border, font, pattern, alignment, and numeric formatting options, as well as adjustments in column widths and row heights. If one of the available designs suits the data you have entered into a given worksheet, you can save time by selecting the format directly from the AutoFormat dialog box, rather than applying formats individually.

To Use the AutoFormat Feature

1. Select the table of data where you want to apply a predesigned format. (Alternatively, select a single cell within the data table, and Excel will select the contiguous table range.)
2. Choose the Format ➤ AutoFormat command. The AutoFormat dialog box appears on the screen.
3. Select the name of a predesigned table format in the Table Format list, and examine the sample of the selected format that appears in the Sample box.
4. Repeat step 3 until you find a format that suits the current data table. Then click OK to apply this format to your data.

NOTES If you wish to apply only certain parts of a predesigned format to your data table, click the Options button on the AutoFormat dialog box. In response, the dialog box expands to display six check boxes labeled Number, Border, Font, Pattern, Alignment, and Width/Height. By default, all these options are checked. Click a check box to remove the X and disable a given category of formatting.

An AutoFormat button is available for you to add to any open toolbar. (Click any toolbar with the right mouse button, and choose Customize from the shortcut menu. In the Customize dialog box, select the Formatting category. The AutoFormat button is displayed as the third selection in the second row of the Buttons box. You can drag this button from the Customize dialog box to any open toolbar.) To use the AutoFormat button, select the data table that you want to format, and click the button. By default, this button applies the last format design that you selected from the AutoFormat dialog box. Alternatively, hold down the Shift key and click the AutoFormat button repeatedly to step through all of the available format designs.

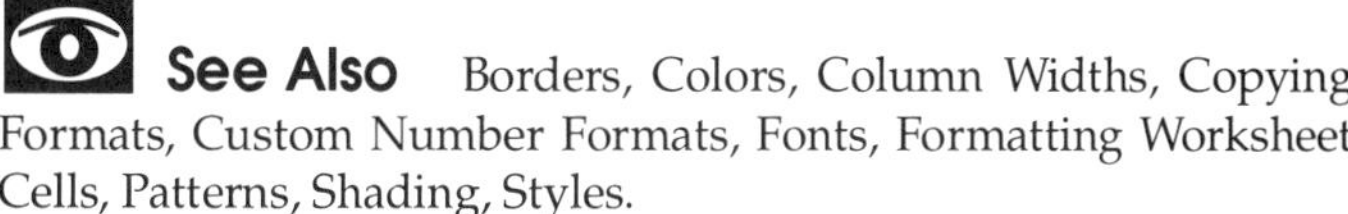

See Also Borders, Colors, Column Widths, Copying Formats, Custom Number Formats, Fonts, Formatting Worksheet Cells, Patterns, Shading, Styles.

BORDERS

Using the Borders command, you can draw a border around the perimeter of a selected range of cells in a worksheet, or around the individual cells within a range selection. Alternatively, you can draw borders along specified sides of cells in a range. You can select from a variety of border styles and colors.

To Draw Borders

1. Select the range of cells where you want to create a border.
2. Choose the Format ➤ Cells command, and then click the Border tab. The resulting dialog box contains a list of border locations and a group of available border styles.
3. From the Border options, select the location for a border you want to draw. The Outline option draws a border around the perimeter of the current range selection. The Left, Right, Top, and Bottom options apply borders to all the cells within the current range.
4. From the Style options, select a border style for the current Border location. Eight style options are available: dotted, thin, medium, thick, double, small dashed, long dashed, and none.
5. Optionally, pull down the Color list and select a color for the current border style.
6. Repeat steps 3 to 5 for each additional location where you want to apply a border. Note that you can apply different border styles and colors to particular locations within the current range of cells.
7. Click OK to apply the borders you have selected.

Shortcuts Select a range of cells, press the right mouse button, and choose the Format Cells command from the resulting shortcut menu, then click the Border tab on the Format Cells dialog box. Alternatively, select a range of cells and click the down-arrow next to the Borders button on the Formatting toolbar. Make a selection from the palette of border options that appears beneath the button. (This is a *tear-off palette*—you can drag it away from the button and keep it on the screen if you want to apply borders to several ranges on a worksheet.)

NOTES Excel has several additional border buttons that are not initially displayed on any of the toolbars. To see these buttons, point to any toolbar, click the right mouse button, and choose Customize from the resulting shortcut menu. Then click the Formatting option in the Categories box. The border buttons are displayed in the first row of the Buttons box. You can drag any combination of these buttons to any open toolbar. (See Toolbars for more information.)

To Remove a Border

1. Select the range of cells that contain the border you want to remove.
2. Choose Format ➤ Cells and then click the Border tab.
3. In the Style frame, select the no-border option. Then, in the Border frame, select each of the locations where you want to remove the border.
4. Click OK.

Shortcut Select the range of cells where you want to remove the borders, and press Ctrl-Shift-hyphen(-) to remove all borders from the range, or click the down-arrow next to the Border button and select the no-border option from the Border palette.

See Also AutoFormat for Worksheet Data, Patterns, Shading.

CENTERING ACROSS COLUMNS

Worksheet titles and other text or numeric entries can be centered across a horizontal range of cells.

To Center an Entry across a Range of Columns

1. Starting from the cell that contains a text or numeric entry, select a horizontal range of cells. The selected cells to the right of the entry should be blank.
2. Choose Format ➤ Cells and click the Alignment tab. In the list of Horizontal options, choose Center across selection. Then click OK. Excel centers the entry across the range you have selected.

Shortcut Select a range of cells and click the Center Across Columns button on the Formatting toolbar.

NOTES For editing and formatting purposes, a centered entry is stored in the cell where you originally entered it.

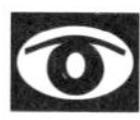

See Also Alignment.

CHARTING

A chart in Excel is created from—and linked to—a table of worksheet data. You can create a chart as an embedded graphic object in a worksheet, or you can work with a chart in a separate sheet in a workbook. Either way, Excel offers a great variety of chart types and formats to choose from. The first step in creating a chart is to select a target range of worksheet data. Then a special feature called the ChartWizard will guide you through the steps of creating the new chart.

To Create an Embedded Chart

1. Select the worksheet data from which you want to create the chart. If you want Excel to copy labels to the chart from your worksheet, include a row and/or column of text entries in your range selection.
2. Choose Insert ➤ Chart and then choose On This Sheet from the Chart submenu.
3. Move the mouse pointer back to the worksheet; the pointer appears as a cross-hair next to a small chart icon. Click the mouse button anywhere in the worksheet; Excel will set the initial size of the chart object. (If you want to size the object yourself, drag the mouse pointer over the worksheet area where you want to display the chart. Optionally, hold down the Shift key while you drag to create a square chart box, or hold down the Alt key to create a chart box that is aligned with the worksheet grid. Release the mouse button when you have defined an area for the chart object.)
4. The first ChartWizard dialog box appears on the screen. To create a chart in the default format, click the Finish button. Alternatively, to create a chart in some other format, respond to each of the five ChartWizard dialog boxes as they appear on the screen. (The steps are described later in this entry.)

Shortcut Select the worksheet data, click the ChartWizard button on the standard toolbar, and then click anywhere on your worksheet. The first ChartWizard dialog box appears; click Finish for a chart in the default format.

NOTES The default chart format is a column chart with a legend. If you do not select a specific chart type, this is the format that Excel applies to a new chart. You can apply the default format to any existing chart by activating the chart and clicking the Default Chart button on the Chart toolbar. (You can also change the default format, as described later in this entry.)

Most typically, you create a chart from a single contiguous range, but Excel can also create a chart from nonadjacent ranges—as long as the range dimensions together form a usable data table. See Selecting a Range to learn how to select nonadjacent cells.

Select an embedded chart by clicking it once with the mouse. When you do so, Excel displays handles—small black squares—around the perimeter of the chart box. (Excel also normally displays the Chart toolbar when an embedded chart is selected.) You can change the size of the embedded chart by dragging one of its selection handles, or you can move the chart to a new position in the worksheet by dragging the entire chart object with the mouse. Deselect an embedded chart by clicking elsewhere in the worksheet. Delete an embedded chart by selecting it and pressing the Del key. (See Graphic Objects for more information about working with objects on a worksheet.)

To Create a New Chart Sheet

1. In the source worksheet, select the range of data from which you want to create a new chart.
2. Choose Insert ➤ Chart. In the Chart submenu, choose As New Sheet.
3. The first ChartWizard dialog box appears on the screen. Click Finish to produce a chart in the default format, or work through all five ChartWizard steps as they appear on the screen. (The steps are described later in this entry.) Excel inserts the chart sheet into the active workbook, just to the left of the active worksheet.

Shortcut Select the range of data on the active worksheet, and then position the mouse pointer over the sheet tab at the bottom of the workbook. Click the right mouse button to view the shortcut menu for the sheet. Choose the Insert command. In the resulting Insert dialog box, select Chart and click OK. The first ChartWizard dialog box appears on the screen.

NOTES The ChartWizard is Excel's step-by-step guide through the process of creating a chart—either an embedded chart or a new chart sheet. Using the ChartWizard you can easily make specific decisions about the type, format, and structure of your chart, and about the link between the chart and the source data. You can also add elements such as a title, axis labels, and a legend during the ChartWizard procedure. Many Excel users find the ChartWizard the most efficient and effective way to create charts.

To Use the ChartWizard

1. Carry out the initial steps for creating a chart, as outlined above: Select the worksheet data from which you want to create a chart, and choose Insert ➤ Chart. Choose On This Sheet for an embedded chart, or As New Sheet for a new chart sheet. For an embedded chart, click the worksheet at the location where you want the chart object to appear.
2. Excel displays the first of five dialog boxes, this one named *ChartWizard–Step 1 of 5*. In the Range text box you can change or confirm the source data range for the chart. If the range reference is correct, click the Next button.
3. In the second ChartWizard dialog box, Excel displays icons representing the fifteen available chart types. Select one of these icons and click the Next button.
4. In the third dialog box, Excel displays icons representing a variety of formats (or *subtypes*) for the chart type you have selected. Select a format and click Next to continue.
5. In the fourth ChartWizard dialog box, you make decisions that will affect the link between the worksheet data and the chart. First, select Rows or Columns to specify whether the data series for the chart should be read from the rows or the columns of the source data table. Then specify whether the first column and first row of the data table contain entries that should be used as labels or as

data points in the chart. Study the Sample Chart box to see if the resulting chart is the one you want to create. Click Next to continue.

6. Finally, the fifth dialog box gives you options for including a legend, a chart title, and axis titles. Enter the titles in the appropriate text boxes, and study the sample chart to confirm that your entries are correct.
7. Click Finish. Excel creates a chart, following the specifications you have supplied in the five ChartWizard dialog boxes.

NOTES In addition to Next and Finish, the ChartWizard dialog box has a Back button that allows you to backtrack to the previous dialog box, and a Cancel button that closes the ChartWizard without creating a chart.

The fifteen chart types available in Step 2 of the ChartWizard are the area chart, bar chart, column chart, line chart, pie chart, doughnut chart, radar chart, X-Y (scatter) chart, combination chart (column chart overlaid by line chart), 3-D area chart, 3-D bar chart, 3-D column chart, 3-D line chart, 3-D pie chart, and 3-D surface chart. Toolbar buttons are available for all of these chart types, in the Charting category of the Customize dialog box. (See the Toolbars entry for information about adding any of these buttons to a toolbar.) If you develop a toolbar that contains a selection of these buttons, you can use them to create an embedded chart: Select a range of worksheet data, click a chart-type button, and then click the worksheet. Excel creates a chart in the format represented by the button you have clicked.

After you have created a chart, you can click the ChartWizard button again to revise the chart's structure. In this case, the ChartWizard has only two steps. In the first step you can revise the range of worksheet data from which the chart is created. In the second step, you can change the row/column orientation of the resulting data series.

To Edit and Format a Chart

1. Activate the chart:
   - To activate an embedded chart, double-click the chart object. In response, Excel displays a thick border around the chart. (If the chart object is too large to appear on the screen, Excel instead copies the chart to a temporary window; the name of this window is the name of the source worksheet followed by a generic chart name such as Chart 1, Chart 2, and so on.)
   - To activate a chart sheet, click the sheet's tab in the active workbook.
2. When a chart is active, a number of chart-related commands are available in the Excel menus. Choose commands from the Insert and Format menus to make changes in the appearance of the chart:
   - The Insert menu allows you to add new items to your chart, including titles, labels, a legend, and gridlines.
   - The Format menu contains commands for changing the appearance of the entire chart (Chart Type and AutoFormat) or of selected items in the chart.

NOTES In an active chart you can select individual items or areas of the chart for editing. To do so, click the item or area with the mouse; Excel displays selection handles around or within the element that you select. For example, you can select the entire chart area, the plot area, a series, an axis, the legend, a label, or the chart title. After selecting an item in the chart, pull down the Format menu and choose the Selected command (Selected Chart Area, Selected Plot Area, Selected Series, and so on); the resulting tabbed dialog box shows the relevant formatting commands.

Alternatively, point to a chart item and press the right mouse button to view a shortcut menu of commands that apply to the selection. Or double-click any chart item to view the Format dialog box for the item.

When you select a series in the chart—that is, the chart markers representing a particular range of numbers from the source worksheet range—the formula bar shows the series formula that links the series to the corresponding worksheet range. The series formula consists of a call to Excel's built-in SERIES function.

To delete a series from a chart, select the series and press the Delete key. To insert a new series into an embedded chart, select the range of worksheet data for the new series, and drag the range to the chart object. To insert a series into a chart sheet, choose Insert ➤ New Data. In the New Data dialog box, enter the worksheet range into the Range box (or point to the range in the source worksheet) and click OK.

Finally, you can select an individual data marker—that is, a single bar, point, wedge, or other chart item that represents one numeric value on the source worksheet table. To select a data marker, click it once to select the entire series to which it belongs, and then click it again to select the individual marker. Excel displays selection handles around the perimeter of the marker. In some chart formats—for example, column charts, bar charts, and line charts—you can drag a black selection handle to change the value that the marker represents. When you do so, Excel automatically changes the corresponding value in the source worksheet table.

e.g. EXAMPLES In Figure C.1, the embedded chart in the worksheet is a column chart created from the data in the range A1:E3. Notice that Excel displays the entries from row 1 as labels along the x-axis; these are known as the category names. The entries from column A appear as labels in the legend; these are the series names. The y-axis shows a scale of values appropriate to the range of data that the graph represents.

To add a title to this chart, double-click the chart object to activate it. Then choose Insert ➤ Titles, select the Chart Title option, and click OK. The initial title text is simply *Title*. To change this, type a new entry into the formula bar and press Enter. The new title appears at the top of the chart object. You can use the same process to add titles to the horizontal x-axis and the vertical y-axis. The position of a title is not fixed in Excel 5; you can then drag a title to any position in the chart area. To change the font, pattern, or alignment

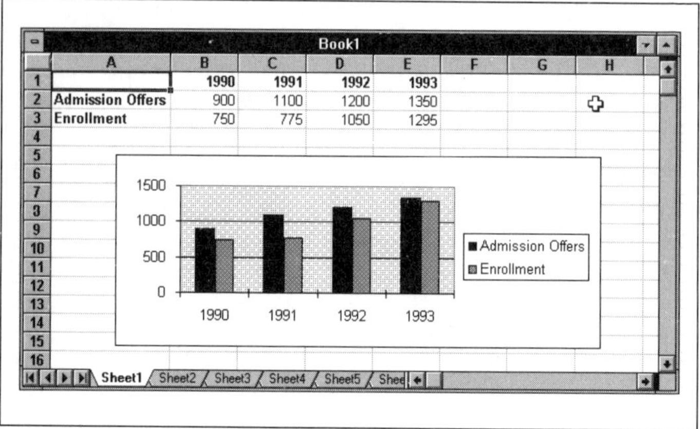

Figure C.1: An embedded chart

of text in a chart, double-click the text, and select options in the resulting Format dialog box.

This chart contains two data series. The first series, shown here as a set of dark columns, represents the data in row 2 of the worksheet table. The second, shown as a set of gray columns, represents the data in row 3. Each data series contains four data markers, representing the four years of data. Here are the SERIES functions for these two series:

=SERIES(Sheet1!$A$2,Sheet1!$B$1:$E$1,Sheet1!$B$2:$E$2,1)

=SERIES(Sheet1!$A$3,Sheet1!$B$1:$E$1,Sheet1!$B$3:$E$3,2)

As you can see, the SERIES function takes four arguments. Here the arguments are references representing the series name, the category names, the series data, and the series number.

In this example, the chart series are plotted from rows of data. You can easily change this arrangement using the ChartWizard. (See the next section of this entry for details.)

To change the chart type itself, you can click the arrow next to the Chart Type button in the Chart toolbar, and then click the icon representing the chart type of your choice. You can use these icons to apply a type to the entire chart or to one selected series. For example, in the worksheet in Figure C.2, the chart has been changed to a

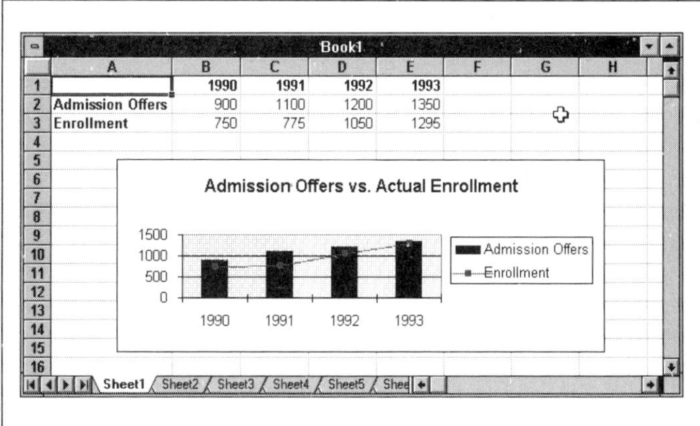

Figure C.2: Changing the chart type

combination chart. To accomplish this, select the second series in the chart, click the arrow next to the Chart Type button, and click the line chart icon. (Alternatively, choose Format ➤ Chart Type or Format ➤ AutoFormat.)

To Change Series from Rows to Columns or Columns to Rows

1. Activate the chart.
2. Click the ChartWizard button on the Standard toolbar or the Chart toolbar. (Notice that the same tool appears on both toolbars.)
3. In the first dialog box, which is named *ChartWizard–Step 1 of 2*, click the Next button.
4. In the second dialog box, select an option under the Data Series in label. If the current selection is Rows, click Columns; conversely, if Columns is selected, click Rows. Notice the resulting change in the Sample Chart box.
5. Click OK to apply this new arrangement to the active chart.

EXAMPLE In the chart in Figure C.3, the series are formed from four columns of worksheet data—columns B, C, D, and E. As you can see, the four series names displayed in the legend are now taken from row 1 of the worksheet. The category names, displayed along the x-axis, are from column A of the worksheet.

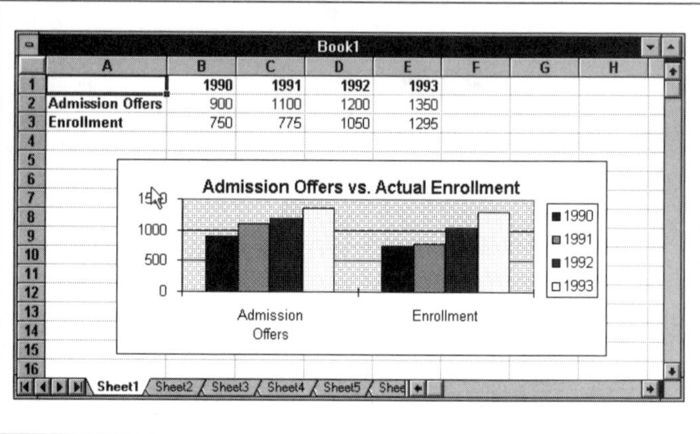

Figure C.3: Changing the series from rows to columns

NOTES When a chart window is active, you can print the chart by choosing File ➤ Print or by clicking the Print button in the Standard toolbar. (See Printing Charts for more information.)

To Change the Default Chart Format

1. Activate a chart that contains the format that you want to make the default.
2. Choose Tools ➤ Options and click the Chart tab in the Options dialog box.
3. In the Default Chart Format group, click the Use the Current Chart button.
4. The Add Custom AutoFormat dialog box appears on the screen. Enter a name for the new default format, and click OK.

5. Click OK on the Options dialog box.

NOTES To change any chart to the default format, click the Default chart button in the Chart toolbar.

To Create an Embedded Chart from a Chart Sheet

1. Activate the chart sheet and choose the Edit ➤ Copy command (or press Ctrl-C). A moving border appears around the chart.
2. Activate the worksheet where you want to copy the chart object, and select the worksheet location where you want to place the embedded chart.
3. Choose Edit ➤ Paste (or press Ctrl-V).

See Also AutoFormat for Charts, Colors, Graphic Objects, Printing Charts, References, Text Box, Toolbars, Trendlines.

CLEARING WORKSHEET CELLS

The Edit ➤ Clear command allows you to clear the contents, formatting, or notes in a range of worksheet cells.

To Clear Data with the Edit ➤ Clear Command

1. Select the range of worksheet data that you want to clear.
2. Choose Edit ➤ Clear, and select one of the four options from the Clear submenu:
   - All removes all entries, formats, and notes;

- Formats removes formatting only;
- Contents removes text, numbers, and formula entries;
- Notes removes any notes you have saved in the worksheet range.

Shortcuts Select the worksheet range and press the Del key to clear the contents of the range. Alternatively, click the right mouse button and choose the Clear Contents command from the shortcut menu.

The Edit category in the Customize dialog box contains Clear Contents and Clear Formats buttons that you can add to any toolbar. (See Toolbars for more information.)

NOTES To undo an inadvertent Clear operation, choose Edit ➤ Undo Clear or press Ctrl-Z immediately after the clear. Alternatively, click the Undo button on the Standard toolbar.

Clearing data is not the same as deleting cells. See Deleting for details.

To Use the Dragging Technique for Clearing Data

1. Select the range of data that you want to clear.
2. Position the mouse pointer over the fill handle, the small black square located at the lower-right corner of the selection. The mouse pointer is displayed as a cross-hair shape.
3. Drag the fill handle up or to the left, over the data that you want to delete. (Optionally, hold down the Ctrl key while you drag if you want to delete data, formats, and notes.) The range that you drag over is displayed in gray.
4. Release the mouse button. Excel clears the data from the range.

See Also AutoFill, Deleting, Formatting Worksheet Cells, Notes.

CLIPBOARD

The Clipboard is a storage area that Windows applications use during cut-and-paste and copy-and-paste operations.

To Copy a Range of Worksheet Data to the Clipboard

Select the data and choose the Edit ➤ Copy command, or press Ctrl-C.

To Copy a Picture of Data to the Clipboard

1. Select a worksheet range.
2. Hold down the Shift key, and choose the Edit ➤ Copy Picture command. (This command appears in the Edit menu only when you hold down the Shift key.)
3. In the Copy Picture dialog box, select options to specify the type of picture you want to copy. Then click OK.

NOTES The Copy Picture command creates a worksheet picture that you can insert into a document as a graphic object.

To View the Clipboard

Switch to the Program Manager, and double-click the Clipboard Viewer icon in the Main group.

NOTES The Clipboard window does not need to be open during cut-and-paste and copy-and-paste operations.

See Also Copying Data, Moving Data.

COLORS

Several formatting commands in Excel provide color palettes or color lists from which you can select the display colors for worksheets and charts. For worksheets, the color selections appear in the Font, Patterns, and Border tabs of the Format ➤ Cells command. For charts, color selections are available on the Patterns tab (and where appropriate, the Font tab) of the Format ➤ Selected commands—for example, Format ➤ Selected Chart Area, Format ➤ Selected Plot Area, Format ➤ Selected Series, and so on. You can use the Color tab of the Tools ➤ Options command to customize the color palette for a given workbook.

Excel 5 provides some convenient shortcuts for selecting colors. The Color and Font Color buttons on the Formatting toolbar provide color palettes with large selections of colors. These are "tear-off" palettes that you can drag into the Excel work area and use for making several color changes in sequence.

To Display Worksheet Entries in Color

1. Select the range of worksheet data and choose the Format ➤ Cells command. Click the Font tab in the Format Cells dialog box.
2. Click the arrow at the right side of the Color box to view the list of available colors.
3. Select a color and click OK.

NOTES When you select a range on the worksheet, the colors change due to the selection highlight. To view the actual colors, deselect the range.

Shortcuts Select a range of data and then click the down-arrow next to the Font Color button on the Formatting toolbar. A color palette appears on the screen. Click any color to change the display of the current worksheet selection. If you want to change several colors in a row, you can drag this palette off the toolbar and place it at any convenient position on the screen. The palette remains visible until you close it by clicking its control-menu box.

To Change the Cell Color (Foreground) of a Worksheet Range

1. Select the worksheet range and choose the Format ➤ Cells command. Click the Patterns tab in the Format Cells dialog box.
2. Select a color in the Color palette.
3. Optionally, click the down-arrow next to the Pattern box and make a new selection in the resulting palette. The Sample box shows what your combined color and pattern selections will look like.
4. Click OK to apply these selections to the current range.

NOTES You can use the options in the Patterns tab to apply a solid or patterned color to a selected range of cells.

Shortcuts Select a range of cells, and then click the down arrow next to the Color button on the Formatting toolbar. Click a color to change the color of the selected cells. If you want to change several colors in a row, you can drag this palette off the toolbar and place it at any convenient position on the screen. The palette remains visible until you close it by clicking its control-menu box.

To Change the Border Color in a Worksheet Selection

1. Select the worksheet range and choose Format ➤ Cells. Then click the Border tab.
2. Click the arrow at the right of the Color box and select a color for the border.
3. Select a border location and style. (See the Border entry for details.) Then click OK.

Shortcuts Select a range, click the right mouse button, and choose the *Format Cells* command from the shortcut menu. Then click the Border tab, and make selections for the color, location, and style.

To Change the Color of Gridlines

1. Activate a worksheet, macro sheet, or dialog sheet in a workbook.
2. Choose the Tools ➤ Options command. Then click the View tab.
3. Click the arrow at the right side of the Color box, just beneath the Gridlines check box.
4. Select a color. (Make sure the Gridlines option is checked.) Then click OK.

NOTES The gridline color applies only to the active sheet. Each sheet in a workbook can have its own gridline color.

To Change the Color of a Text Item in a Chart

1. In a chart window, select a text item (a title, label, axis, legend, or text box).
2. Choose the appropriate Format ➤ Selected command (Selected Chart Title, Selected Data Labels, Selected Axis Title, and so on). Click the Font tab.
3. Select a color from the Color list, and then click OK.

Shortcuts Click the arrow next to the Font Color button on the Formatting toolbar. Then make a color selection from the palette that drops down from the toolbar. If you want to make several color changes in a row, you can drag this palette away from the toolbar and place it at any convenient position on the screen.

Alternatively, double-click the text item on the chart to open the Format dialog box, or click the item with the right mouse button and choose the Format command from the resulting shortcut menu.

To Change the Color of a Chart Area or Chart Item

1. In a chart window, select the chart area, plot area, series, or other item whose color you want to change, and choose the corresponding Format ➤ Selected command. Click the Patterns tab on the Format dialog box.
2. On the Patterns dialog box, choose a color from the palette or Color list and click OK.

Shortcuts Click the arrow next to the Color button on the Formatting toolbar, and make a selection from the resulting color palette.

To Customize a Color in a Workbook's Color Palette

1. Switch to the workbook in which you want to customize the color.
2. Choose the Tools ➤ Options command, and then click the Color tab in the Options dialog box.
3. In any one of the color categories, select the color that you want to customize. Then click the Modify button. The Color Picker dialog box appears.
4. Adjust the selected color by clicking inside the color box and the brightness bar. When the color appears as you want it, click OK in the Color Picker dialog box.
5. Repeat steps 3 and 4 to change any other colors in the palette for the active document.
6. Click OK in the Color Palette dialog box to apply the new color palette to the document.

NOTES Changes in the color palette apply to all the sheets in the active workbook. To copy a customized color palette from an open workbook to the active workbook, select a workbook name from the Copy Colors list in the Color tab. To revert to the default color palette, click the Reset button in the Color tab.

See Also Borders, Charting, Copying Formats, Customizing Excel, Fonts, Graphic Objects, Patterns, Shading, Styles.

COLUMN WIDTHS

Adjusting the widths of worksheet columns allows you to display large amounts of data as effectively as possible.

To Change the Width of a Single Column

1. Select a cell in the column, or click the column heading to select the entire column.
2. Choose Format ➤ Column. Then choose the Width command from the Column submenu.
3. Enter a new value in the Column Width text box. (This value is the width of the column in characters, in the standard font and point size.) Then click OK.

Shortcuts Position the mouse pointer over the line located just to the right of the column's heading, and drag the line to the right for a wider column, or the left for a narrower one. Double-click the line to adjust the column width to the *best fit* for the current contents (or choose Format ➤ Column and then choose AutoFit Selection from the Column submenu). Alternatively, point to the column heading, press the right mouse button, and choose Column Width from the shortcut menu to view the Column Width dialog box.

NOTES To change the widths of a group of columns, select the columns and choose Format ➤ Column. Then choose Width from the Column submenu.

The standard column width for a worksheet is the width of all columns that you have not adjusted individually. To change the standard width setting, choose Format ➤ Column and then choose Standard Width from the Column submenu. Enter a new value in the Standard Column Width text box, and click OK.

See Also Alignment, Hiding, Row Height.

CONSOLIDATING DATA

The Data ➤ Consolidate command provides flexible techniques for combining data from multiple worksheet sources in a single destination worksheet. By default, the Consolidate command uses the SUM function to combine the corresponding values from source worksheets; but you can choose from eleven different functions—including AVERAGE, MAX, MIN, and others—to perform the consolidation. Optionally, you can create links between the source worksheets and the destination worksheet, so that the destination is updated whenever the data changes in any one of the sources.

To Consolidate Data from Multiple Source Worksheets

1. Activate the destination worksheet and select the location where you want to consolidate data. You can specify the destination area by selecting the upper-left corner cell, the top-row range, the left-column range, or the entire range. (During the consolidation process, Excel expands the destination area accordingly.)
2. Choose Data ➤ Consolidate. The Consolidate dialog box contains boxes labeled Function, Reference, and All References, along with several buttons and check boxes. The Reference text box is active initially.
3. Optionally, click the Browse button if your source workbooks are not currently open. In the resulting dialog box,

find and select the name of a source workbook, and click OK. Back in the Consolidate dialog box, Excel enters a reference to the source workbook in the form NAME.XLS!. (Alternatively, you can type this worksheet reference directly into the Reference text box, without using the Browse facility.)

4. If the source area is not on the same worksheet as the destination area, type the name of the worksheet followed by an exclamation point. Then type a range name or range reference identifying the data that you want to consolidate from the source worksheet. (If the source worksheet is in the active workbook or another open workbook, you can select the source area with the mouse or the keyboard. Excel enters a reference to your selection in the Reference text box.) The source area may contain numeric entries alone, from a worksheet range that matches the size and shape of other source areas you are including in the consolidation; in this case, Excel consolidates by position. Alternatively, the source area may include an identifying row and/or column of labels, and the data may be arranged differently in other source areas; in this case, Excel consolidates by category. (See the "Notes" section below for more information about this distinction.)
5. Click the Add button. Excel adds the current source area reference to the All References list, and reactivates the Reference text box.
6. Repeat steps 3, 4, and 5 for all the source areas that you want to include in the consolidation.
7. If you are performing a consolidation by category, click one or both of the Use Labels In options: Top Row if the category labels are at the top of each source area; Left Column if the category labels are at the left side of each source area. (In response, Excel will copy the selected category labels to the destination area.)
8. Optionally, pull down the Functions list and select an entry other than the default SUM function.

9. Optionally, select the Create Links to Source Data check box, if you want Excel to create external references to the source.
10. Click OK. Excel consolidates the data and displays it in the destination area you have selected.

NOTES You can consolidate as many as 255 source worksheets into a destination worksheet.

If you have created the source worksheets in a consistent format—placing the source data in the same rectangular arrangement in each worksheet—you can consolidate the data by position. (See Group Editing for information about entering data into more than one worksheet at a time.) When you consolidate by position, Excel does not copy labels from the source worksheets to the destination area. You should therefore begin your work by entering any necessary labels at the top row or left column of the destination area, and formatting the area appropriately.

On the other hand, if you are consolidating data from diverse arrangements in the source worksheets, the source areas should include consistent category labels that identify particular rows or columns of data. When you consolidate by category, Excel copies the category labels from the source to the destination.

The Function list in the Consolidation dialog box offers the following eleven functions:

FUNCTION	DESCRIPTION
Average	Calculates the average of corresponding values in thc source areas.
Count	Counts the corresponding entries in the source areas.
Count Nums	Produces a count of the corresponding numeric entries in the source areas.
Max	Selects the largest among corresponding values in the source areas.

FUNCTION	DESCRIPTION
Min	Selects the smallest among corresponding values in the source areas.
Product	Multiplies corresponding values together.
StdDev and StdDevp	Calculate standard deviations of corresponding values.
Sum	Finds the sum of corresponding values in the source areas.
Var and Varp	Calculate the variances of corresponding values.

If you select the Create Links to Source Data option, Excel reorganizes the destination area as an outline, and inserts rows into the area for external references to the source data. You can then expand the outline to view the source data along with the consolidated data, or collapse the outline to view the consolidated data alone.

The consolidation references reappear in the Consolidate dialog box for the destination worksheet, whether or not you choose to link the source worksheets. You can revise the consolidation at any time—adding new source areas, deleting source areas, or changing the references to source areas—by activating the destination worksheet and choosing Data ➤ Consolidate again.

See Also Group Editing, Names, Outlines, References, Statistical Functions.

COPYING DATA

Along with the familiar Copy and Paste commands available in most Windows applications, Excel has a simple drag-and-drop operation that you can use to copy a range of data from one worksheet area to another.

To Copy Data Using the Copy and Paste Commands

1. Select the range of data that you want to copy, and choose Edit ➤ Copy. Excel displays a moving border around the range, and copies the data to the Clipboard.
2. Select a cell or range for the destination, and choose Edit ➤ Paste. Excel copies the data to the paste range.

Shortcuts To copy the selected data to the Clipboard, press Ctrl-C or Ctrl-Ins, or click the Copy button on the Standard toolbar. To paste the data, press Ctrl-V or Shift-Ins, or click the Paste button on the Standard toolbar. Note that the Copy and Paste commands are also available on the shortcut menu for worksheet cells. (See Shortcut Menus.)

NOTES If you select a paste area that already contains data, the Paste command overwrites the previous data entries with the copied data.

To Insert Data During a Copy-and-Paste Operation

1. Select the range of data that you want to copy, and choose Edit ➤ Copy.
2. Select a cell or range for the destination, and choose the Insert ➤ Copied Cells command. (This command is available only when a source copy range is marked with a moving border.)
3. In the Insert Paste dialog box, select the Shift Cells Right or Shift Cells Down option and click OK. Excel pastes the data and moves existing entries into the cells to the right or the cells below the paste area.

To Copy a Selection to Multiple Locations

1. Select the copy range and choose Edit ➤ Copy.
2. Select the first paste range, then hold down the Ctrl key as you select each additional range.
3. Choose Edit ➤ Paste. Excel copies the data to all of the paste ranges at once.

NOTES If the copy range contains hidden cells, or collapsed outline rows, the Copy and Paste commands normally produce a copy of the entire copy range, including the hidden or collapsed ranges.

To Copy Only the Cells That Are Visible

1. Select a range of cells that includes hidden or collapsed ranges.
2. Choose the Edit ➤ Go To command, and click the Special button on the Go To dialog box.
3. In the Go To Special dialog box, select the Visible Cells Only option, and click OK. This step results in a multiple range selection consisting of the visible cells.
4. Choose Edit ➤ Copy. A moving border appears around the copy range.
5. Select a cell or range for the paste area, and choose Edit ➤ Paste.

To Copy Data Using the Drag-and-Drop Technique

1. Select the range of data that you want to copy.
2. Position the mouse pointer along the border of the selection. The pointer shape changes to a white arrow.
3. Hold down the Ctrl key and drag the mouse pointer to the location where you want to paste the data. A small plus sign appears next to the arrow pointer when you hold

down the Ctrl key. A gray frame representing the copy area follows the mouse pointer as you drag.

4. Release the mouse button, and then release the Ctrl key. Excel copies the data from the copy range to the paste range.

To Insert a Copy Range Using the Drag-and-Drop Technique

1. Select the range of data that you want to copy and insert.
2. Position the mouse pointer along the border of the selection. The pointer shape changes to a white arrow.
3. Hold down the Ctrl key and the Shift key together. Then drag the mouse pointer to the location where you want to insert the copy range. A horizontal or vertical insertion bar follows the mouse pointer as you drag. To switch between a horizontal and vertical insertion, drag the pointer toward a row or column gridline.
4. Release the mouse button, then release the Ctrl and Shift keys. Excel copies the data from the copy range to the paste range and shifts existing entries down or to the right.

See Also AutoFill, Copying Formats, Copying Formulas, Deleting, Filling Ranges, Hiding, Inserting, Moving Data, Outlines, Selecting a Range.

COPYING FORMATS

You can use the Edit ➤ Paste Special command—or the Format Painter button—to copy formatting from one worksheet range to another without changing the data values in the paste range. This operation copies alignments, fonts, borders, colors, patterns, and number formats.

To Copy Formats from One Range to Another

1. Select the range from which you want to copy the formats, and choose Edit ➤ Copy. A moving border appears around the copy range.
2. Select a cell or range to which you want to copy the formatting from the copy range.
3. Choose Edit ➤ Paste Special. In the Paste Special dialog box, select the Formats option and click OK. In response, Excel applies all the formats from the copy range to the paste range.

To Copy Formats Using the Format Painter Button

1. Select the range that contains the formats you want to copy.
2. Click the Format Painter button in the Standard toolbar. When you move the mouse pointer into the worksheet area, the pointer appears as a cross with a paintbrush icon.
3. Select the area that you want to format, or simply click the upper-left corner cell of the area. Excel copies the formats from the source range to the destination.

NOTES If you want to copy the formats to more than one range, double-click the Format Painter button. Then select each of the destination ranges in turn. When you are finished copying formats, click the Format Painter button once to turn the feature off.

To Clear Formats from a Range

1. Select the range from which you want to clear the formats.
2. Choose Edit ➤ Clear, and then choose Formats from the Clear submenu. Excel clears all formats from the range you have selected.

See Also Alignment, AutoFormat for Worksheet Data, Borders, Clearing Data, Colors, Custom Number Formats, Fonts, Formatting Worksheet Cells, Number Formats, Patterns, Point Size, Shading.

COPYING FORMULAS

When you copy a formula from one location to another in a worksheet, the result depends significantly upon the types of references included in the original formula:

- An absolute reference is copied verbatim from the original formula to the copy; each copy refers to a fixed location on the worksheet.
- A relative reference is adjusted according to the location of the copy, so that the row and/or column portions of the reference may be different for each copy of the formula.
- A mixed reference contains a combination of absolute and relative elements.

You can use copy-and-paste, AutoFill, or drag-and-drop operations to copy formulas from one location to another. In addition, you can use the Copy and Paste Special commands to copy a range of formulas to itself, converting all the formulas to fixed values.

To Create and Copy a Formula

1. While you enter the first copy of a formula, decide whether each reference should be absolute, relative, or mixed—depending on how you want the reference to be copied across rows and/or down columns. Enter a reference into the formula bar by pointing with the mouse or by typing the reference directly from the keyboard, and then press F4 repeatedly to step through the possible reference types: relative, absolute, or mixed. In each reference type, Excel inserts a dollar sign ($) before the absolute portions of the reference.

2. After you complete the original formula, use any of the techniques available in Excel for copying an entry from one location to another. (See AutoFill and Copying Data to learn about these various techniques.)

e.g. **EXAMPLE** The following formula contains two mixed references and one absolute reference:

=(C$4+$B5)*$B$1

Suppose you enter this formula into cell C5 of a worksheet. If you then copy the formula down column C to cells C6 and C7, the first mixed reference (C$4) is copied unchanged, but the row portion of the second mixed reference ($B5) is adjusted in each copy:

C6 =(C$4+$B6)*$B$1
C7 =(C$4+$B7)*$B$1

Conversely, if you copy the formula across row 5 to cells D5 and E5, the first reference is adjusted but the second reference remains unchanged in each copy:

D5	E5
=(D$4+$B5)*$B$1	=(E$4+$B5)*$B$1

Notice that the absolute reference, $B$1, remains unchanged in all copies of the formula.

To Convert Formulas to Fixed Values in a Worksheet Range

1. Select the range of cells containing the formulas you want to convert, and choose Edit ➤ Copy.
2. Without changing the range selection, choose Edit ➤ Paste Special.
3. In the Paste Special dialog box, select the Values option and click OK. Excel converts each formula entry in the range to its current value. In other words, the range now contains only constant entries and the background formulas are lost.

NOTES To restore the background formulas, choose Edit ➤ Undo Paste Special or press Ctrl-Z immediately after this operation. To convert a formula in the formula bar to its current value, press the F9 function key while the formula bar is active.

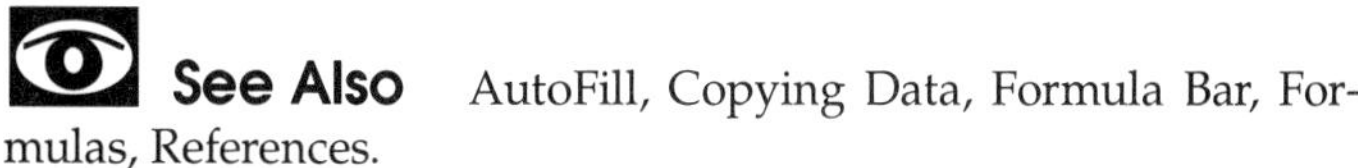

See Also AutoFill, Copying Data, Formula Bar, Formulas, References.

CUSTOM NUMBER FORMATS

The Number tab of the Format ➤ Cells command provides over three dozen built-in numeric display formats in these categories: Number, Accounting, Date, Time, Percentage, Fraction, Text, Scientific, and Currency. You can add your own custom formats to these built-in ones by editing an existing format or by devising an entirely new format.

To Create a Custom Number Format

1. Select the cell or range of cells to which you want to apply the custom format, and choose Format ➤ Cells. Click the Number tab. The resulting dialog box contains a Category list, a Format Codes list, and a Code box, where you can create and edit custom formats.
2. Optionally, select a starting format from the Format Codes list. This format appears in the Code text box.
3. Activate the Code text box. Edit or enter the code for the custom format you want to create. Use new combinations of the same formatting symbols that are used in the built-in format codes.
4. Click OK. Excel applies the new format to the current selection of worksheet cells, and adds the custom format to the Format Codes list in the Number Format dialog box.

You can reuse this custom format anywhere in the active worksheet.

Shortcuts Point to the selection where you want to apply a custom format, hold down the right mouse button, and choose the Format Cells command from the resulting shortcut menu. Then click the Number tab.

EXAMPLE The following custom code is designed to format cells for phone-number entries:

(000) 000-0000" ext. "0000

For example, if you apply this custom format to a cell and then enter the number 41555598761234, the entry will be displayed as follows in the cell:

(415) 555-9876 ext. 1234

This custom code produces a complete date-and-time format:

dddd, mmmm d, yyyy "at" h:mm AM/PM

If you apply this format to a cell and then enter 34257.75, the number appears as:

Friday, October 15, 1993 at 6:00 PM

NOTES You can divide a custom format into four different sections of formatting code, each section separated from the next by a semicolon (;). The resulting format depends upon the kind of data entered in the cell.

- The first section of formatting code applies to positive numeric entries.
- The second section applies to negative numeric entries.
- The third section applies to entries of zero.
- The fourth section applies to text entries.

To Delete a Custom Number Format

1. Choose Format ➤ Cells, and then click the Number tab.
2. In the Categories list, choose Custom. In the Format Codes list, select the custom format that you want to delete.
3. Click the Delete button.
4. Click OK.

NOTES When you delete a custom format, any cells to which the format was applied revert to the general format.

See Also Copying Formats, Date Entries, Formatting Worksheet Cells, Number Formats, Time Entries.

CUSTOMIZING EXCEL

Several important techniques are available for adding features to Excel or for changing its operation. You can use these techniques to make Excel conform to your own work requirements.

To Customize Excel

- Create and install an add-in macro sheet. (See Add-in Macros.)
- Create a custom list of AutoFill labels. (See AutoFill.)
- Create a custom AutoFormat for charts. (See AutoFormat for Charts.)
- Create a custom color palette. (See Colors.)
- Enter the code for a custom number format. (See Custom Number Formats.)
- Create dialog boxes and custom data forms. (See Dialog Sheets.)

- Write or record your own macro commands and macro functions. (See Macro and Macro Recording.)
- Assign a macro to a button. (See Macro.)
- Change the tools on a toolbar, or create a new toolbar. (See Toolbars.)

DATA FORM

data form is a dialog box designed to simplify your work with lists and databases in Excel. A list is a collection of data arranged in rows and columns, where the top row contains a label for each column of data. You can think of a list as a *database,* where each row is a record, each column a field, and the top row contains field names. See Database and Lists for more information.

You use a data form to examine and edit the fields of individual records, to scroll through the list one record at a time, to add new records to the list, to delete records from the list, and to search for records that match specific criteria.

To Open a Data Form for Viewing Records

1. Activate a worksheet that contains a list. Select any cell within the range of the list.
2. Choose Data ➤ Form. The data form for the list appears on the screen. At the left side of the form are labels identifying the fields of the list, and text boxes showing the field entries for the first record. At the right side is a column of command buttons you can use to perform specific operations on your list.
3. Use the vertical scroll bar in the middle of the data form to scroll one record at a time through the list, or to move quickly from one position to another in the list. (Alternatively, press ↓ to move to the next record in the list, or ↑ to move to the previous record.) At the upper-right corner of

the data form, Excel displays the current record number and the total number of records; for example, **5 of 40**.

4. Click the Close button to close the data form when you are finished viewing the records of the list.

NOTES A data form can display as many as 32 fields, in two vertical columns of 16 fields each. If a list has more than 32 fields, Excel will not open a data form.

To Edit a Record in the Data Form

1. Choose Data ➤ Form to open the data form for the current list.
2. Scroll to the record that you want to edit, and make changes in any of the text boxes displaying the fields of the record.
3. Scroll to a different record. Excel copies the changes in the edited record to the list itself.

NOTES To select a field in the current record, you can click the field with the mouse, or you can hold down the Alt key and press the underlined character in the field name. Alternatively, press Tab to move forward from one field to the next, or Shift-Tab to move backward through the fields.

Before scrolling to a different record, you can click the Restore button to bring back the original unedited version of the current record. Once you scroll to a different record, however, any changes you have made are copied to the list.

Calculated fields cannot be edited in the data form. The data form displays the current value of each calculated field, but not in a text box.

To Add New Records to the List in the Data Form

1. Choose Data ➤ Form to open the data form for the current list.
2. Click the New button. The data form displays blank text boxes for all of the fields that can be edited. The words "New Record" appear at the upper-right corner of the data form.
3. Enter a data item for each of the fields of the new record.
4. Press ↵ to add the new record to the list. The data form displays blank fields for the next new record.
5. Repeat steps 3 and 4 for each new record you want to add to the list.
6. Click the Close button to close the data form.

NOTES The data form always appends new records to the end of the list, regardless of the current order of other records. Choose Data ➤ Sort or click one of the two Sort buttons on the Standard toolbar to rearrange the list after you have added one or more records.

If your list contains one or more computed fields, Excel automatically copies the field formulas into each new record that you add into the data form.

To Delete a Record in the Data Form

1. Choose Data ➤ Form to open the data form for the current list.
2. Scroll to the record that you want to delete.
3. Click the Delete button. A message box appears on the screen asking you to confirm the deletion.
4. Click OK to delete the record from the list, or click Cancel to back out of the deletion.

NOTES You cannot undo a record deletion that you complete in the data form. In contrast, if you delete a record by deleting its row directly from the worksheet (select the row and choose Edit ➤ Delete), you can use the Edit ➤ Undo Delete command to bring back the record.

To Search for Records in the Data Form

1. Choose Data ➤ Form to open the data form for the current list.
2. Click the Criteria button. The data form displays a blank text box for each of the fields in the list, including calculated fields. The word "Criteria" appears in the upper-right corner of the data form, and the scroll bar is temporarily removed.
3. Enter a comparison criterion into a field box. The criterion can be any text or numeric entry that you want to search for. Alternatively, you can begin the criterion expression with one of Excel's six comparison operators (=, <, >, <=, >=, <>), or you can include wildcard characters (* or ?) to search for variations of matching text. (See Database Criteria for more information about criteria expressions.)
4. Repeat step 3 for each field in which you want to include a criterion. If you enter multiple criteria into the data form, Excel reads them as "and" conditions—that is, a record must meet all of the criteria to be selected as a match.
5. Click the Find Next button to find the first record that matches your criteria, and then click the same button repeatedly to find subsequent matching records. Optionally, click the Find Prev button to scroll backward through the matching records. Excel beeps in response to either button when there are no more matching records in the specified direction.

6. Click Close to close the data form when you have finished examining the matching records.

NOTES Excel does not retain the criteria when you close the data form. The next time you open the data form and click the Criteria button, all of the field boxes will be blank.

You can revise the search criteria at any time while the data form is open. Click the Criteria button to view the current criteria, and edit the entry in any of the field boxes. Click Clear to erase all the current criteria, or click Restore to bring back the previous criteria.

See Also Database, Database Criteria, Filters, Lists, Query, Sorting.

DATA TABLES

In a data table, Excel calculates multiple results from a formula that contains one or two variables. A one-input data table includes a column or a row of values to be substituted into a single variable. A two-input table has both a column and a row of values to be substituted into two variables. In either case, you choose the Data ➤ Table command to fill in the table when you set up a worksheet for this operation.

To Create a One-Input Data Table with One Formula

1. Enter a single column of values, and then enter a target formula in the cell one row above and one column to the right of the values. Or, enter a single row of values and a target formula just below and to the left. The formula includes a reference to an input cell elsewhere on the worksheet; this is the formula's *variable*.

2. Select the two-column or two-row range that includes the values and the formula.
3. Choose Data ➤ Table. In the resulting dialog box, enter a reference to the input cell into the Column Input Cell box for a column-oriented table, or the Row Input Cell box for a row-oriented table. Click OK, and Excel immediately fills in the table.

e.g. **EXAMPLE** In the column-oriented data table in Figure D.1, cell B7 contains a formula for calculating the break-even point in the unit sales of a manufactured product:

=B3/(B4–B2)

DATATABL.XLS

	A	B	C
1	**Product X**		
2	Manufacturing cost per unit	$1.25	
3	Fixed costs	$28,000	
4	Wholesale price per unit	$8.25	
5			
6	**Break-even point analysis**		column input cell
7		4000	
8	$0.95	3,836	
9	$1.05	3,889	
10	$1.15	3,944	
11	$1.25	4,000	
12	$1.35	4,058	
13	$1.45	4,118	
14	$1.55	4,179	
15	$1.65	4,242	
16	$1.75	4,308	

Break-even / Sheet 2

Figure D.1: A one-input data table

Cell B3 shows the fixed costs associated with the product. B4 is the wholesale price per unit, and B2 is one estimate of the anticipated per-unit manufacturing cost. The column of cells in A8:A16 contains a range of other estimates for the per-unit manufacturing cost. The goal is to find the break-even point corresponding to each of these per-unit cost estimates. To create the table of break-even points, you select the range A7:B16 and choose the Data ➤ Table command. In the Table dialog box, enter a reference to the input cell, B2, in the Column Input Cell box, and click OK. Excel substitutes each of the entries in A8:A16 into the input cell B3, and produces the resulting break-even calculations in B8:B16.

NOTES A one-input data table can contain more than one formula. For example, in the break-even point worksheet, you could enter the following formula into cell C7 to calculate the dollar sales at the break-even point:

```
=B4*B3/(B4–B2)
```

To fill in the two-formula data table, select the range A7:C16 and then choose the Data ➤ Table command.

To Create a Two-Input Data Table

1. Enter the target formula into the upper-left corner cell of the range where you want to create the data table. The formula includes references to two input cells elsewhere on the worksheet; these are the formula's two *variables*.
2. Enter a column of input values beneath the formula, and a row of input values to the right of the formula.
3. Select the two-dimensional range of cells that includes the formula and the row and column of input values.
4. Choose Data ➤ Table. Enter references to the two input cells into the Row Input Cell and Column Input Cell text boxes. Click OK, and Excel fills in the data table.

e.g. EXAMPLE In the break-even point worksheet in Figure D.2, A8:A16 contains a range of per-unit manufacturing cost estimates, and B7:F7 contains a range of fixed cost estimates. The break-even point formula in cell A7 is the same as in the first example:

=B3/(B4–B2)

DATATABL.XLS

	A	B	C	D	E	F
1	Product X					
2	Manufacturing cost per unit	$1.25	← column input cell			
3	Fixed costs	$28,000				
4	Wholesale price per unit	$8.25	← row input cell			
5						
6	Break-even point analysis					
7	4000	$24,000	$26,000	$28,000	$30,000	$32,000
8	$0.95	3,288	3,562	3,836	4,110	4,384
9	$1.05	3,333	3,611	3,889	4,167	4,444
10	$1.15	3,380	3,662	3,944	4,225	4,507
11	$1.25	3,429	3,714	4,000	4,286	4,571
12	$1.35	3,478	3,768	4,058	4,348	4,638
13	$1.45	3,529	3,824	4,118	4,412	4,706
14	$1.55	3,582	3,881	4,179	4,478	4,776
15	$1.65	3,636	3,939	4,242	4,545	4,848
16	$1.75	3,692	4,000	4,308	4,615	4,923

Break-even | Break-even 2 | Sheet3 | She

Figure D.2: A two-input data table

To fill in the data table, select the range A7:F16, and choose Data ➤ Table. Enter a reference to B3 as the Row Input Cell and B2 as the Column Input Cell, and click OK.

NOTES Excel enters an array formula into the worksheet to calculate a one-input or two-input data table. Consequently, you can change any one of the input values in the column at the left side of the table or the row at the top of the table, and the corresponding table results are automatically recalculated.

See Also Array Formulas.

DATABASE

A database is a rectangular arrangement of information stored in a worksheet. The columns in the database range are known as fields, and the rows are records. The top row of the database contains the field names.

In the vocabulary of Excel 5, a database is one kind of *list* you can create to keep records in a worksheet. After you create a list—whether you think of it as a database or not—you can perform a variety of operations, such as searching for records that match specified criteria, copying selected records to a new location, and sorting the database. See Lists for information about these operations. In addition, Excel provides a special data form dialog box that simplifies several basic database operations. See Data Form for details.

To Create a Database

1. In a worksheet, enter a row of field names at the top of the range where you plan to create the database. Enter a unique field name in each cell.
2. Use a formatting option of your choice to give the field names a distinctive appearance from the rest of the database. For example, select the row of field names and click the Bold button on the Formatting toolbar.
3. Enter one record of information in each row after the field names. A field entry may be text, a number, a date, a time value, or even a formula, but the entries in a given field column should all contain the same type of data. Do not leave any rows blank between records.

e.g. **EXAMPLE** The database in Figure D.3 contains records of information about software consultants working in major cities. The database has eight fields that provide the last name, first initial, city, region, specialty area, hourly rate, first contract date, and years

	A	B	C	D	E	F	G	H
1	Last	First	City	Region	Specialty	Rate	Contract	Years
2	Abrams	P.	Atlanta	S	Database	$125	20-Oct-90	3.0
3	Alexander	E.	Los Angeles	W	WP	$150	14-Jun-91	2.4
4	Ballinger	I.	Boston	E	Spreadsheet	$150	12-Feb-87	6.7
5	Cody	L.	Los Angeles	W	Database	$75	20-Jun-90	3.3
6	Davis	G.	San Francisco	W	WP	$150	9-Jul-87	6.3
7	Fitzpatrick	P.	New York	E	Database	$125	7-Nov-86	7.0
8	Garrison	V.	Boston	E	WP	$125	6-May-86	7.5
9	Gill	P.	Los Angeles	W	Spreadsheet	$100	22-Jun-87	6.3
10	Harris	P.	Dallas	S	Spreadsheet	$150	12-Feb-91	2.7
11	Hayes	S.	San Francisco	W	Database	$75	7-Feb-86	7.7
12	Jones	L.	Atlanta	S	Spreadsheet	$125	10-Feb-88	5.7
13	Jordan	E.	Dallas	S	WP	$100	6-Oct-86	7.0
14	Kwan	O.	New York	E	Spreadsheet	$100	21-Jun-86	7.3
15	Lambert	S.	Dallas	S	Database	$150	26-Jun-87	6.3
16	Leung	M.	Chicago	N	WP	$100	26-Mar-91	2.6
17	Manning	P.	Atlanta	S	WP	$75	9-Nov-86	6.9

CONSULT.XLS — Consultant List / Sheet2 / Sheet3 / Sheet

Figure D.3: A sample database

of experience for each consultant. The field names are in row 1, and the records begin in row 2.

NOTES A field name is any text entry. In writing field names, you do not necessarily have to follow the same rules that Excel imposes on range names. (See Names for information about range names.) Some database operations are simplified, however, if field names are written as legal range names.

A computed field is a database column that contains formula entries. To create a computed field, enter a formula for the first record, and then copy the formula down the column to each subsequent record. The Years field in the consultant database is a computed field, calculated as the difference in years between the first contract date (the Contract field) and the current date.

See Also Data Form, Database Criteria, Database Functions, Filters, Lists, Query, Sorting.

DATABASE CRITERIA

One way to perform operations on records in a database or list is to create a criteria range. Excel uses the expressions in this range to determine whether a given record matches your selection criteria. In the criteria range you can write comparison criteria to find records that contain a certain value or a range of values; or computed criteria to find records based on a formula. Once you have created a criteria range, you can use the Advanced Filter command in the Data ➤ Filter submenu to find matching records or to copy matching records to a separate location. (See Filters for details.)

Creating a criteria range is a database technique that has been available in all versions of Excel. In Excel 5, a new technique known as AutoFilter can often simplify your work with lists and databases. (See Filters and List.)

To Create a Criteria Range

1. Select a location in the rows *above* your database. (Insert the rows if necessary, using the Insert ➤ Rows command. Note that a criteria range located in the rows beneath the database range might limit the growth of the database itself. A criteria range next to the database might be hidden when the database is filtered.)
2. Enter a row of field names for the criteria range. The row may contain all of the field names from the database or only a selection of names. (For a computed criterion, enter a name that is not the same as any field name in the database.)
3. In the row or rows beneath the field names, enter the criteria expressions. Multiple criteria in the same row denote an "and" condition—that is, a record must match all of the criteria in the row to be selected. Multiple criteria in different rows denote an "or" condition; a record is selected if it matches all the criteria in any one row.

e.g. EXAMPLE The criteria range in Figure D.4 contains two rows of criteria. To be selected, a record must match the criteria in either row. The criteria range is C1:D3. Each row in the range contains two comparison criteria. The first row searches for records in which the City field contains the entry *Los Angeles and* the Rate field contains a value that is less than or equal to 100. The second row searches for records in which the City field is "New York" *and* the Rate is less than or equal to 100.

CONSULT.X

	A	B	C	D	E
1			City	Rate	
2			Los Angeles	<=100	
3			New York	<=100	
4					
5	Last	First	City	Region	Speci
6	Abrams	P.	Atlanta	S	Databa
7	Alexander	E.	Los Angeles	W	WP

Figure D.4: A criteria range

NOTES A comparison criterion consists of a simple text or numeric entry, or an expression that begins with one of Excel's six comparison operators: =, <, >, ≤, ≥, or <>. In addition, comparison criteria can use the wildcard characters * and ? to search for patterns of text entries.

A computed criterion is a formula that includes a relative reference to at least one of the fields in the database. The reference may appear as a field name, whether or not you have actually defined field names as range names in your worksheet. (See Names for information about defining range names.) For example, in a database of salespeople you might use the computed criterion

=Sales*CommRate>5000

to find all records in which the product of the Sales field and the commission rate is greater than 5000. (The name CommRate could be a field name, or it could be a range name defined elsewhere on the worksheet.) Keep in mind that the name for a computed criterion—that is, the name you enter above the criterion in the criteria range—should not be the same as any of the field names.

See Also Data Form, Database, Database Functions, Filters, Lists, Query.

DATABASE FUNCTIONS

Excel provides a set of statistical and arithmetic functions that operate on selected records in a database. In general, these functions take three arguments: a database range, a target field name enclosed in quotes, and a criteria range. Given a selection of records that match the criteria, each function performs a particular calculation on the data in the target field.

To Perform Calculations on Matching Records in a Database

On a worksheet that contains a database and criteria range, enter any of the following functions at another location in the worksheet:

- DAVERAGE(database,"Field",criteria) finds the average of the target numeric field entries in the records that match the criteria.
- DCOUNT(database,"Field",criteria) counts the numeric entries in the target field of the selected records. (Omit the "Field" argument to count all the records that match the criteria.)
- DCOUNTA(database,"Field",criteria) counts the nonblank entries in the target field of the selected records.

- DGET(database,"Field",criteria) reads a field value from a single record that matches the criteria. (DGET returns the error value #NUM! if there are multiple records that match the criteria, or #VALUE! if no record matches the criteria.)
- DMAX(database,"Field",criteria) returns the largest of the target numeric field values in the selected records.
- DMIN(database,"Field",criteria) returns the smallest of the target numeric field values in the selected records.
- DPRODUCT(database,"Field",criteria) finds the product of the target numeric field values in the selected records.
- DSTDEV(database,"Field",criteria) calculates the standard deviation of the target numeric field values in the selected records. (The DSTDEVP function performs the same statistical calculation based on an entire "population.")
- DSUM(database,"Field",criteria) returns the sum of the target numeric field values in the selected records.
- DVAR(database,"Field",criteria) calculates the variance of the target numeric field values in the selected records. (The DVARP function performs the same statistical calculation based on an entire "population.")
- SQLREQUEST(connection, query) runs a query on an external database.

e.g. **EXAMPLE** The following function returns the average of the Rate field entries in the records that match the current criteria:

=DAVERAGE(Database,"Rate",Criteria)

NOTES The second argument can appear as a field name in quotation marks, or a field number. For example, the following function returns the average of the numeric entries in the sixth field:

=DAVERAGE(Database,6,Criteria)

The database fields, left to right, are numbered consecutively from 1 up to the number of fields.

 **See Also** Database, Database Criteria, Filters, Lists, Query.

DATE AND TIME FUNCTIONS

Excel provides a useful collection of date and time functions that you can use for the following general purposes: entering the current date and time into a cell; converting values between various date and time formats; performing date arithmetic for special business applications; and reading specific calendar or chronological information from a serial number.

To Enter the Current Date and Time into a Cell

Use one of these functions:

- NOW( ) returns a complete serial number representing the current date and time. (The integer portion of the number is the date, and the fractional portion represents the time. For more information about serial numbers, see Date Entries and Time Entries.)
- TODAY( ) returns a serial integer representing the current date.

NOTES Neither NOW nor TODAY takes an argument, but both must be followed by an empty pair of parentheses.

To Convert between Formats

Use these functions:

- DATE(yy,mm,dd) returns a serial number for the specified date.
- DATEVALUE("DateString") returns the serial equivalent of a date string.
- TIME(hh,mm,ss) returns a serial number for the specified time value.
- TIMEVALUE("TimeString") returns the serial equivalent of a time string.

To Perform Date Arithmetic for Business Applications

Use one of these functions:

- DAYS360(date1,date2,method) returns the number of days between the two dates, based on a 360-day business year. The optional *method* argument is 1 (or omitted) for the US method, or 2 for the European method of calculation.
- NETWORKDAYS(date1,date2,holidays) returns the number of business days between the two dates, not including weekends or specified holidays.
- YEARFRAC(date1,date2,basis) returns the fraction of the year represented by the difference between the two dates.
- EDATE(date,months) returns the date that is a specified number of months from the given date.
- EOMONTH(date,months) returns the date at the end of the month, a specified number of months from the given date.
- WORKDAY(date,workdays,{holidays}) returns the date that is a specified number of work days from the given date, not counting the holidays listed in the array.

NOTES Except for DAYS360, all of these functions are supplied by the Analysis Toolpak add-in.

To Get Date or Time Information from a Serial Number

Use these functions:

- YEAR(date) returns the year from a serial date.
- MONTH(date) returns the month, from 1 to 12.
- DAY(date) returns the day of the month, from 1 to 31.
- WEEKDAY(date) returns the day of the week, from 1 to 7, where 1 is Sunday.
- HOUR(date) returns the hour, from 0 to 23, from a serial time value.
- MINUTE(date) returns the minute, from 0 to 59.
- SECOND(date) returns the second, from 0 to 59.

See Also Add-ins, Date Entries, Functions, Time Entries.

DATE ENTRIES

You can enter a date value into a worksheet cell in any of several date formats that Excel recognizes. In response, Excel applies a date format to the cell, but stores the date itself as a special type of numeric value known as a serial number. The serial number format allows you to perform date arithmetic operations in a worksheet.

To Enter a Date into a Worksheet Cell

Select the cell and type the date in a recognizable format.

e.g. EXAMPLE Here are some examples of date-entry formats that Excel recognizes:

3/14/94

3-14-94

March 14, 1994

14 Mar 1994

In response to these entries, Excel applies one of its built-in date formats to the cell and displays the date either as 3/14/94 or 14 -Mar-94. Excel stores the date internally as 34407, which is the serial number for March 14, 1994.

NOTES The starting date of Excel's default serial number system is January 1, 1900; this date has a serial number of 1. The last date in the system is December 31, 2078, which has a serial number of 65380.

A *full* serial number contains digits both before and after the decimal point. In this case, the integer portion before the decimal point represents the date, and the fractional value after the decimal point represents the time. (Specifically, the fraction is the portion of the day that has elapsed at a given time.) For example, 34407.25 represents the date/time value March 14, 1994 6:00 AM.

To provide compatibility with other software, an alternate serial date system is also available in Excel. In this alternate system, January 1, 1904 has the serial value of 0. To switch to the 1904 system, choose Tools ➤ Options, click the Calculation tab, and select the 1904 Date System option. Make this switch cautiously, however; any existing date entries on a worksheet will be reinterpreted according to the new system.

To Find the Difference between Two Dates in a Worksheet

Enter a formula that subtracts one date from the other.

EXAMPLE Suppose you have entered date values in cells B1 and C1. The following formula gives the difference between the two dates:

=C1–B1

Internally, Excel subtracts one date's serial number from the other, resulting in the difference in days between the dates.

NOTES To include a date in a formula, enclose the date in double quotation marks and use a date format that Excel recognizes. For example, the formula

="3/14/93"+90

adds 90 days to the date 3/14/94. The result is the serial number equivalent of the date 6/12/94.

To View the Serial Number for a Date Entry

1. Select the cell that contains the entry displayed in a date format.
2. Choose Format ➤ Cells, and click the Number tab on the resulting dialog box.
3. Select All in the Category box, and then select General in the Format Codes box. Click OK.

Shortcut Select the cell that contains a date entry and press Ctrl- Shift-~ to apply the General format.

See Also Copying Formats, Custom Number Formats, Date and Time Functions, Formatting Worksheet Cells, Number Formats, Time Entries.

DELETING

You can use either the Delete command or a special dragging technique to delete rows, columns, or a selection of cells from a worksheet. When you do so, Excel shifts other cells up or to the left to fill in the deleted area.

To Delete Entire Rows or Columns

1. Select the rows or columns by dragging the mouse along the appropriate row or column headings. (To select a single row or column, click the row or column heading.)
2. Choose Edit ➤ Delete. Or, hold down the Shift key and drag the fill handle up (for rows) or to the left (for columns).

Shortcuts

- Select the rows or columns and press Ctrl-minus sign (–).
- Point to the selected rows or columns, and hold down the right mouse button to view the shortcut menu; then choose the Delete command.
- Select any range of cells within the target rows or columns, and click the Delete Row or Delete Column button. (These buttons are not initially part of any toolbar; see Toolbars for information on installing them.)

NOTES When you select entire rows, the fill handle is located at the lower-left corner of the selection. When you select entire columns, the fill handle is at the upper-right corner of the selection.

The Delete dialog box does not appear when you choose Edit ➤ Delete for a selection of entire rows or columns. If you select a range of cells within the target rows or columns and then choose

Edit ➤ Delete, you can select the Entire Row or Entire Column option on the Delete dialog box.

To undo a deletion, take one of these actions immediately after the deletion: choose Edit ➤ Undo Delete, press Ctrl-Z, or click the Undo button on the Standard toolbar.

To Delete a Range of Cells

1. Select the range you want to delete.
2. Choose Edit ➤ Delete.
3. On the Delete dialog box, select the Shift Cells Left or Shift Cells Up option, depending how you want Excel to fill in the empty area.
4. Click OK.

Shortcuts

- Select the range, hold down the Shift key, and drag the fill handle left to shift cells left, or up to shift cells up. No dialog box appears.
- Select the range and click the Delete button. Excel shifts cells to fill in the space. (This tool is not initially part of any toolbar. See Toolbars.)

See Also Clearing Data, Inserting, Selecting a Range.

DELETING FILES

By using the File ➤ Find File command, you can delete files permanently from disk.

To Delete a File from Disk

1. Choose File ➤ Find File. The resulting Find File dialog box has a list of Excel files stored on disk and a preview window.
2. Select the name of the file you want to delete. A preview of the file's contents appears in the Preview of window.
3. Click the Commands button and choose the Delete command from the resulting menu list. Excel asks you to confirm the file deletion. Click Yes if you are sure you want to delete the file, or click No to cancel the operation.
4. Optionally, repeat steps 2 and 3 to delete additional files. Then click Close to close the Find File dialog box.

See Also Directories, Finding Files, Opening Files, Saving Files.

DIALOG SHEETS

A dialog sheet is one of the tools available to programmers who develop applications in Excel. Like the other types of sheets in Excel—worksheets, charts, macro sheets, and modules—a dialog sheet is stored in a workbook. A workbook can contain any number of dialog sheets.

Each dialog sheet is a work area for developing the appearance and behavior of a custom dialog box. Using the Forms toolbar, you can add a variety of visual *controls* to a dialog—including labels, text boxes, group frames, command buttons, check boxes, option buttons, lists, scroll bars, and spinner controls. Each control may be associated with an *event handler*, a Visual Basic procedure that is called when an action takes place on the control. Event procedures are stored in a workbook's module sheets.

To display a dialog box on the screen and make its features available to the user, you can add a command button to a worksheet, and then assign a procedure to the button. The procedure uses a Visual Basic method named *Show* to display and activate the dialog box.

Developing a custom dialog box generally requires a knowledge of Visual Basic programming, but you can take advantage of some features without writing modules. For example, some controls—including check boxes, option buttons, list boxes, scroll bars, and spinners—can be linked directly to worksheet cells. When the user changes the value of one of these controls in a custom dialog box, the value in the linked cell is also changed.

To Add a Dialog Sheet to a Workbook

Choose Insert ➤ Macro and click the Dialog command in the Macro submenu.

Shortcut Click the tab of the current sheet with the right mouse button. In the resulting shortcut menu, choose the Insert command. Select the Dialog option in the Insert dialog box, and click OK.

NOTES The new dialog sheet contains a dialog box frame with two controls—an OK button and a Cancel button. You can change the name of the dialog box by selecting the text in the title bar, and typing a new entry. You can also resize the frame by selecting it and dragging any of its size handles.

Normally the Forms toolbar is displayed whenever you create or activate a dialog sheet. If it is not, click any toolbar with the right mouse button, and choose Forms on the resulting shortcut menu.

To Add Controls to a Dialog box

1. Click a control button in the Forms toolbar.
2. Move the mouse pointer into the dialog box, and drag the mouse through the area where you want to insert the control. Release the mouse button to complete the process.

The control appears in the dialog box. When a control is selected, size handles appear around its perimeter.

3. To develop an event handler for a selected control, click the Edit Code button in the Forms toolbar. Excel opens a module sheet and enters the *Sub* and *End Sub* statements for the control's event procedure. You can then insert additional Visual Basic statements into the procedure.

To Link a Control to a Worksheet Cell

1. Activate a dialog sheet, and add or select a check box, option button, list box, scroll bar, or spinner control.
2. Choose Format ➤ Object and then click the Control tab in the resulting dialog box.
3. Activate the Cell Link text box. Enter a cell reference, or point to the worksheet cell to which you want to link the control.
4. Click OK.

NOTES When a control is linked to a worksheet cell, the control and the cell always have the same value. Changing the value of one results in a change in the other.

To Create a Button That Opens a Dialog Box

1. In a module sheet, develop a procedure that uses the Visual Basic *Show* method to open the dialog box; for example:

   ```
   Sub ShowDialog
     DialogSheets("DialogSheetName").Show
   End Sub
   ```

   where DialogSheetName is the name of the sheet that contains your custom dialog.
2. Activate the worksheet from which you want the dialog box to be available.

3. If the Drawing toolbar is not yet open, click The Drawing buttton on the Standard toolbar.
4. Click the Create Button button on the Drawing toolbar. Then drag the mouse through the area where you want to insert the button on the worksheet.
5. The Assign Macro dialog box appears on the screen. Select the name of the macro you have developed for opening the dialog box, and click OK.
6. Click elsewhere on the worksheet to deselect the button. (You can also close the Drawing toolbar if you wish.)
7. Click the button once to test it. The custom dialog box you have developed should appear on the screen.

See Also Macro, Macro Recording.

DIRECTORIES

The File ➤ Open command contains a drive list box and a directory list box that you can use to change the path for opening Excel documents.

To Change the Directory for Opening a File

1. Choose File ➤ Open.
2. Optionally, click the down-arrow at the right side of the Drives list and select a drive device.
3. Double-click a directory name in the Directories list to change the current directory.

See Also Deleting Files, Finding Files, Opening Files, Saving Files.

DYNAMIC DATA EXCHANGE (DDE)

Dynamic Data Exchange is one means of sharing and updating data between documents created in different Windows applications. In this context, the origin of the data is known as the source document and the destination is known as the dependent document. DDE creates a link between the two documents. An Excel worksheet can be either a source or a dependent document. For a dependent worksheet, Excel creates a remote formula that includes three items of information: the name of the linked application, the name of the source document, and a reference to the data that is being shared.

To Create a DDE Link from a Source Worksheet

1. Activate the Excel sheet and select the range of cells containing the data that you want to share between documents.
2. Choose Edit ➤ Copy.
3. Switch to the other application and activate the document that will be the destination of the data.
4. In the other application, choose Edit ➤ Paste Link, or Edit ➤ Paste Special. (The exact command sequence for establishing the link depends upon the DDE features of the other application.)

e.g. **EXAMPLE** You can use this technique to create a link between an Excel worksheet and a Word for Windows document. Select the worksheet range, choose Edit ➤ Copy, and then switch to the Word document. In the Word menu, choose Edit ➤ Paste Special and click the Paste Link button in the Paste Special dialog box. A table containing the worksheet data appears in the Word document.

Whenever you change a value in the source Excel worksheet, the table in the linked Word document is automatically updated.

To Create a DDE Link to a Dependent Worksheet

1. Start the other application and select the data that you want to send to Excel.
2. From the other application's menu, choose Edit ➤ Copy.
3. Switch to Excel and select the upper-left corner cell of the location where you want to create the link.
4. From the Excel menu, choose Edit ➤ Paste Special.
5. In the Paste Special dialog box, select the Paste Link option. In the As box, select the type of paste operation you want to perform. (The Result box gives a description of the option you select.)
6. Click OK.

e.g. **EXAMPLE** You can use this technique to create a link between a Word table and an Excel worksheet. Select the table in the Word document and choose Edit ➤ Copy from the Word menu. Then switch to Excel, select the location where you want to paste the data, and choose Edit ➤ Paste Special from the Excel menu. Select Paste Link then select Text in the As box. Click OK. In response, Excel enters the remote reference as an array formula into the range of the linked data:

{=WordDocument|Document1!'!DDE_LINK1'}

Notice the three parts of the remote reference: the application, the document name, and the data reference. Also note the punctuation used in this remote reference. A solid vertical bar (|) separates the application name from the document name, and an exclamation point separates the document name from the data reference. In this example, DDE_LINK1 is a Word bookmark that is automatically inserted into the Word document for the purposes of the DDE link. The bookmark refers to the entire Word table that is shared in the link.

NOTES By default, a dependent worksheet document is automatically updated whenever a change occurs in the data of the source document. This may not be the most convenient way to operate a link if you are planning many changes in the source document. Accordingly, you can use Excel's Edit ➤ Links command to switch to manual updating.

To Switch to Manual Updating in a Dependent Worksheet

1. Activate the worksheet that is the dependent document in a DDE link.
2. Choose Edit ➤ Links from the Excel menu. The Links dialog box appears on the screen.
3. Select and highlight the link that you want to modify.
4. Click the Manual option button at the bottom of the dialog box, and then click OK. The DDE link is now in manual mode, and will be updated only on command.

To Update a Manual Link

1. Activate the dependent worksheet and choose Edit ➤ Links from the Excel menu.
2. Select and highlight the link that you want to modify.
3. Click the Update Now button, then click Close. Any changes that have taken place in the data of the source document are now transferred to the dependent worksheet.

See Also Links and 3-D Formulas, Object Linking and Embedding.

EDITING

In Excel 5 you can edit a worksheet entry directly in the cell where the entry is stored. Alternatively, you can edit in the formula bar above the workbook.

To Edit Directly in a Cell

1. Double-click the cell whose contents you want to edit. A flashing insertion bar appears at the end of the cell's contents. (If the cell contains a formula, it is displayed in the cell.)
2. Use the keyboard to insert, delete, or revise any part of the cell's contents.
3. Press Enter to complete the revision.

NOTES If a cell contains a text entry, Excel 5 allows you to apply different formats to individual characters within the entry. For example, one word in an entry could appear in italics or boldface. To accomplish this, double-click the cell that contains text and highlight the characters to which you want to apply a format. Then choose Format ➤ Cells, click the Font tab, and select the formatting options you want to apply. (Alternatively, click a button in the Formatting toolbar.)

See Also Formatting Worksheet Cells, Formula Bar, Formulas.

ENGINEERING FUNCTIONS

The Analysis ToolPak add-in supplies a library of mathematical and technical functions suitable for engineering applications. If you have installed the add-in, you can enter these functions directly into worksheets, or you can select them from the Function Wizard. (See Functions for details.)

To Select an Engineering Function

1. Select the cell or cells where you want to enter the function and click the Function Wizard button on the Standard toolbar.
2. In the Function Category list, select the Engineering category. In response, Excel lists the engineering functions in the Function Name box.
3. Select a function name and click Next.
4. Use Step 2 of the Function Wizard to enter the arguments for the function you have selected.
5. Click Finish.

NOTES The engineering function category includes the following groups of tools:

- Base conversion functions for converting between binary, octal, decimal, and hexadecimal numbers (BIN2DEC, BIN2HEX, BIN2OCT, DEC2BIN, DEC2HEX, DEC2OCT, HEX2BIN, HEX2DEC, HEX2OCT, OCT2BIN, OCT2DEC, OCT2HEX).
- Bessel functions (BESSELI, BESSELJ, BESSELK, BESSELY).

- Complex number functions (COMPLEX, IMABS, IMAGINARY, IMARGUMENT, IMCONJUGATE, IMCOS, IMDIV, IMEXP, IMLN, IMLOG2, IMLOG10, IMPOWER, IMPRODUCT, IMREAL, IMSIN, IMSQRT, IMSUB, IMSUM).
- Error functions (ERF, ERFC).
- A measurement conversion function (CONVERT).
- Miscellaneous (DELTA, GESTEP).

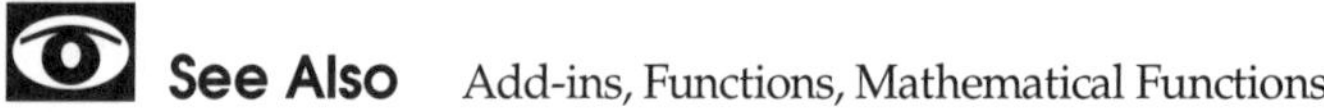

See Also Add-ins, Functions, Mathematical Functions.

EXITING EXCEL

When you close Excel, the program gives you the opportunity to save any documents that have been edited but not updated to disk.

To Exit Excel

Choose File ➤ Exit. For each unsaved document, Excel displays a prompt asking you for instructions: Click Yes to save the document to disk, or click No to abandon the changes in the document. Click Cancel to return to the Excel application window.

Shortcuts Press Alt-F4, or double-click the Control-menu box at the left side of the Excel window's title bar.

See Also Window Operations.

FILE FORMATS

You can use the File ➤ Save As command to save files in the formats used by software other than Excel. Likewise, the File ➤ Open command allows you to open files created in other programs and convert those files into Excel workbooks.

To Save a File in a Selected Format

1. Activate the Excel worksheet that you want to save in a new format, and choose File ➤ Save As. The Save As dialog box appears. Optionally, enter a new name into the File Name text box and select a path in the Drives and Directories list boxes.
2. Click the down-arrow at the right side of the box labeled Save File as Type. A scrollable list of available file formats drops down from the box.
3. Select the format in which you want to save the file. In the File Name text box, Excel supplies the appropriate extension name for the file.
4. Click OK to save the file.

NOTES The Save File as Type list includes the following file formats:

- Microsoft Excel Workbook is the Excel 5 workbook format.
- Template is the format for Excel 5 template files. (See Templates for details.)
- Formatted Text, Text, and CSV save the active sheet in delimited text formats.
- Excel 4.0 Workbook saves worksheets, charts, and Excel 4 macro sheets in a workbook.
- Excel 4.0, 3.0 and 2.1 are formats for previous versions of Excel; they save the active sheet only.

- WKS, WK1, and WK3 are formats for versions of Lotus 1-2-3. (When appropriate, Excel creates an associated format file with an extension name of FMT or FM3.)
- WQ1 is the format for QuattroPro for DOS.
- DBF 2, DBF 3, and DBF 4 are formats for versions of the dBASE II, III, and IV database-management programs.
- Text and CSV (Macintosh, OS/2, or MS-DOS) are text formats for transferring a file to other operating environments.
- DIF (Data Interchange Format) is a data transfer format that many applications can read and write. (It was introduced with VisiCalc, the first popular spreadsheet program for personal computers.)
- SYLK (Symbolic Link) is a data transfer format that many applications can read and write. (It is most commonly associated with Multiplan.)

To Open a File in a Selected Format

1. Choose File ➤ Open. The Open dialog box appears. Optionally, use the Drives and Directories boxes to select the path of the file you want to open.
2. Click the down-arrow next to the List Files of Type box. A drop-down list of readable formats appears.
3. Select the format of the file you want to open. In the File Name text box, Excel enters a pattern for the corresponding extension name or names, and the file list displays only the files that match the pattern.
4. Select a file name, and click OK to open the file.

NOTES Most of the file formats in the Open dialog box match the ones presented by the Save As command.

See Also Lotus 1-2-3 Help, Opening Files, Saving Files, Workbooks.

FILLING RANGES

The Edit ➤ Fill commands are designed to fill a range of cells by copying the contents of a single cell located at the beginning or end of the range. Alternatively, you can fill all the cells of a range by selecting the range before you begin an entry.

To Use the Fill Commands to Copy Entries

1. Enter a number, text entry, or formula into the beginning or ending cell of the range you want to fill. Optionally, apply formats to the entry.
2. Starting from the cell containing the entry, select the row or column range that you want to fill.
3. Choose Edit ➤ Fill. From the Fill submenu, choose Right or Left to fill a row, or Down or Up to fill a column. Excel copies the entry and formats in the first or last cell to all the cells in the range.

Shortcuts Press Ctrl-R to fill a row to the right, or Ctrl-D to fill a column. Or, select the range and click the Fill Right button to fill a row to the right or press Shift and click the Fill Right button to fill to the left. (This button is not initially part of any toolbar. See Toolbars for instructions on adding it.)

Alternatively, the fill handle is often the best tool to use for filling a range of cells. See AutoFill for details.

NOTES You can use the Fill commands to fill multiple rows or columns at once. To fill rows, select a range in which the first or last column contains the data you want to copy, choose Edit ➤ Fill, and click the Right or Left command. To fill columns, select a range in which the first or last row contains the data, choose Edit ➤ Fill, and click the Down or Up command. A fill operation overwrites any existing data in the range of the fill.

To Enter Data or Formulas into an Entire Range at Once

1. Select the range into which you want to enter the data or formulas.
2. Type the entry into the formula bar.
3. Press Ctrl-↵ to complete the entry. Excel copies the entry into each cell of the range.

See Also Array Formulas, AutoFill, Copying Data, Copying Formats, Copying Formulas, Selecting a Range.

FILTERS

Filters allow you to work with selected rows of information in any list, including a list that you have organized as a database. (See the Database and Lists entries for background information.) Excel 5 gives you two effective ways to filter a list or database. The simpler of the two techniques is known as AutoFilter. When you select this feature, Excel provides drop-down lists at the top of every column in your database; you can quickly filter the database by selecting entries in one or more of the drop-down lists.

The second technique, known as Advanced Filter, makes use of a *criteria range* that you create for your database. The criteria range contains values or expressions Excel can use to select records from your database. (See Database Criteria for details.) Using the Advanced Filter command, you can temporarily hide records that do not match your criteria, or you can copy matching records to a new location.

To Filter a List or Database with AutoFilter

1. Activate the worksheet that contains your list or database, and select any cell within the range of data.

2. Choose Data ➤ Filter and then choose AutoFilter from the Filter submenu. In response, Excel displays drop-down arrows in the first row of your database, where the field names are located.
3. Click the drop-down arrow at the top of any column. The resulting list shows all the unique data entries in the column, along with several other options. Select an entry. Excel immediately hides all the records that do not match your selection.
4. Repeat step 3 in other columns to apply additional filters to your database. To be displayed in the filtered database, a record must match *all* of the selections that you make in the drop-down lists.

Shortcuts Click the AutoFilter button to display drop-down arrows at the top of your database and to apply a filter based on the contents of the active cell. (The AutoFilter buttton is not initially part of any toolbar. See Toolbars for instruction on adding it.)

EXAMPLE Figure F.1 shows what a database looks like after you have chosen the AutoFilter command. In the top row of the database, a drop-down arrow appears next to each field name. As shown in the Specialty field, the resulting drop-down list contains all the unique data entries in the field, along with other options.

NOTES In addition to the unique data entries in a given column, each drop-down list contains four additional options that you can use for special purposes:

- Choose (All) to view all the data in the current column. (Filters in other columns remain in effect.)
- Choose (Custom...) to apply complex or compound criteria to your database. (See instructions in the next part of this entry.)
- Choose (Blanks) to display only those records that contain blank cells in the current column.

CONSULT.XLS

	A	B	C	D	E	F	G	H
1	Last	Fi	City	Regio	Specialty	Ra	Contra	Yea
2	Abrams	P.	Atlanta	S		$125	20-Oct-90	3.0
3	Alexander	E.	Los Angeles	W		$150	14-Jun-91	2.4
4	Ballinger	I.	Boston	E		$150	12-Feb-87	6.7
5	Cody	L.	Los Angeles	W		$75	20-Jun-90	3.3
6	Davis	G.	San Francisco	W		$150	9-Jul-87	6.3
7	Fitzpatrick	P.	New York	E	Database	$125	7-Nov-86	7.0
8	Garrison	V.	Boston	E	WP	$125	6-May-86	7.5
9	Gill	P.	Los Angeles	W	Spreadsheet	$100	22-Jun-87	6.3

(All)
(Custom...)
Database
Spreadsheet
WP
(Blanks)
(NonBlanks)

Figure F.1: The effect of the AutoFilter command

- Choose (NonBlanks) to display only those records that contain nonblank entries in the current column.

To Apply Custom Criteria to a Filtered Database

1. Select a cell in the database, choose Data ➤ Filter, and then choose AutoFilter. Drop-down arrows appear at the top of the database.
2. Click any drop-down arrow and choose the (Custom…) entry. The Custom AutoFilter dialog box appears on the screen. It contains four boxes in which you can develop one or two criteria to apply to the current column. Each criterion consists of a *relational operator* selection and a data selection.
3. Click the drop-down arrow next to the first relational operator box. Select one of the six operators in the resulting list:

=	equals (the default for the first criterion)
>	is greater than
<	is less than
≥	is greater than or equal to
≤	is less than or equal to

<> does not equal

4. Click the drop-down arrow for the adjacent box. The list contains all the unique data entries in the current column. Select an entry to complete the criterion. (Alternatively, enter a new value into this box—a value that does not necessarily appear in the database column.)
5. Optionally, repeat steps 3 and 4 to develop another criterion in the second row of text boxes. If you do so, you must select either the And or the Or option button to connect the two criteria. The And option means that a record must match *both* criteria to be selected. The Or option means that a record will be selected if it matches one or both criteria.
6. Click the OK button to apply the custom criteria you have developed. In response, Excel hides all records that do not match your criteria.

NOTES To apply a filter consisting of more than two criteria, create a criteria range and use the Advanced Filter command. (See details below.)

To Display all the Records in a Filtered List or Database

Choose Data ➤ Filter and then choose Show All from the Filter submenu. In response, Excel redisplays all the hidden records in the database.

To Remove a Filter from a List Database

Choose Data ➤ Filter and then choose AutoFilter from the Filter submenu. Excel removes the drop-down arrows from the top of the database, and redisplays any hidden records.

To Use a Criteria Range to Filter a Database

1. Develop a criteria range in the rows above your database, as described in the Database Criteria entry.
2. Select any cell within the database range, and choose Data ➤ Filter. Click the Advanced Filter command in the Filter submenu. In the List Range text box of the Advanced Filter dialog box, Excel automatically enters the range of your database.
3. Activate the Criteria Range text box, and enter a reference to the criteria range you have developed on the worksheet. (Alternatively, use the mouse to point to the range.)
4. Make sure that the default Filter option is selected in the Action group, and click OK. Excel filters the database in place, temporarily hiding all records that do not match the criteria you have expressed in the criteria range.

e.g. **EXAMPLE** Figure F.2 shows a database that has been filtered using a criteria range. The two rows of criteria in C1:D3 instruct Excel to select all records that have a value of "Los Angeles" or "New York" in the City field and a value that is less than or equal to 100 in the Rate field. As you can see, three records are displayed in the filtered database.

CONSULT.XLS

	A	B	C	D	E	F	G	H
1			City	Rate				
2			Los Angeles	<=100				
3			New York	<=100				
4								
5	Last	First	City	Region	Specialty	Rate	Contract	Years
9	Cody	L.	Los Angeles	W	Database	$75	20-Jun-90	3.3
13	Gill	P.	Los Angeles	W	Spreadsheet	$100	22-Jun-87	6.3
18	Kwan	O.	New York	E	Spreadsheet	$100	21-Jun-86	7.3

Consultant List / Sheet2 / Sheet3 / Sheet

Figure F.2: Using a criteria range to filter a database

To Copy Selected Records to a New Location

1. In a database worksheet that contains a criteria range, select a cell in the database range. Then choose Data ➤ Filter and click the Advanced Filter command.
2. In the Action group of the Advanced Filter dialog box, click the Copy to Another Location option.
3. Make sure that the database range is entered correctly into the List Range box. Enter the criteria range into the Criteria Range box.
4. Activate the Copy to box, and enter a reference to the upper-left corner of the range (on the current worksheet) where you want to copy the records that match your criteria. Alternatively, point to the location with the mouse.
5. Click OK. Excel copies the matching records to the location you have specified.

NOTES If you want to copy selected records to a worksheet other than the one that contains the database itself, you must activate the destination sheet before choosing the Advanced Filter command. An attempt to do otherwise results in the following error message: You can only copy filtered data to the active sheet.

SEE ALSO Data Form, Database, Database Criteria, Database Functions, Lists.

FINANCIAL FUNCTIONS

Excel provides a library of financial functions in several categories. Many of these functions are part of the Analysis Toolpak add-in macro.

To Use a Financial Function

1. Select the cell or range where you want to enter the function and click the Function Wizard button on the Standard toolbar.
2. In the Function Category list, select Financial. Excel displays a list of the financial functions in the Function Name box.
3. Select a function name and click Next.
4. In Step 2 of the Function Wizard dialog box, enter arguments for the function. Then click Finish.

NOTES The financial function category includes the following groups of tools:

- Conversion functions (DOLLARDE, DOLLARFR).
- Coupon functions (COUPDAYBS, COUPDAYS, COUPDAYSNC, COUPNCD, COUPNUM, COUPPCD).
- Depreciation functions (DB, AMORDEGRLC, AMORLINC, DDB, SLN, SYD, VDB).
- Internal rate of return functions (IRR, MIRR, XIRR).
- Loan payment calculation functions (CUMIPMT, CUMPRINC, EFFECT, IPMT, NOMINAL, NPER, PMT, PPMT, RATE).
- Net present value, present value, and future value functions (FV, FVSCHEDULE, NPV, PV, XNPV).
- Security functions for calculating interest, discount rate, duration, price, yield, and amount received at maturity (ACCRINT, ACCRINTM, DISC, DURATION, INTRATE, MDURATION, ODDFPRICE, ODDFYIELD, ODDLPRICE, ODDLYIELD, PRICE, PRICEDISC, PRICEMAT, RECEIVED, YIELD, YIELDDISC, YIELDMAT).
- Treasury bill functions (TBILLEQ, TBILLPRICE, TBILLYIELD).

e.g. **EXAMPLE** One of the most frequently used of all these functions is PMT. You can use PMT to calculate the monthly payment on a fixed-rate loan or mortgage. For example, suppose you want to know the monthly mortgage payment on a 30-year home loan of $120,000 at 9.5 percent interest. Enter the PMT formula as follows:

=PMT(9.5%/12,30*12,120000)

Notice that the first and second arguments—giving the interest rate and the term of the loan—are both expressed as monthly amounts. This function calculates the monthly payment as $1,009.03. The return value is a negative amount in this example because it represents money to be paid out.

See Also Formulas, Functions, Mathematical Functions, Statistical Functions.

FINDING FILES

The File ➤ Find File command gives you several ways to search for and preview files stored on disk. You can use the command to find files that meet conditions you specify. For example, you can search for files that contain specific contents or summary information, or files that were saved within a particular range of dates. In the Find File dialog box you can preview a file's contents, examine its summary information, or view a list of file information for a selection of files.

To Find a File

1. Choose File ➤ Find File. The Find File dialog box appears.
2. If the file is listed in the current directory, select its name to view a preview of the file's contents.
3. To change your view of the current file, click the drop-down arrow next to the View box (at the lower-left corner

of the Find File dialog box). The Preview option shows you a preview of the file's contents. The File Info option shows the characteristics of the files in the current directory. The Summary option shows the summary information stored in the current file.

4. To find a different selection of files, click the Search button. The Search dialog box appears on the screen. In the File Name box, use wildcards (* and ?) to indicate the files you want to search for. (The default is *.xl*, for Excel files.) In the Location box, enter the directory path where you want to search.

5. Optionally, click the Advanced Search button. The resulting dialog box contains three tabs—Location, for specifying where you want to search; Summary, for identifying the summary information or file contents you want to search for; and Timestamp, for indicating a range of file dates you want to examine. Fill in any combination of these options, and click OK. Then click OK again on the Search dialog box. Back in the Find File dialog box, the Listed Files box shows the result of your file search.

6. To open a file, select it in the list and click Open. To perform some other file operation, click the Commands button and select an option. For example, you can open a file in read-only mode, or you can print a file. You can also sort the listed files by a variety of characteristics.

7. Click Close to close the Find File dialog box.

NOTES After developing a set of search criteria, you can save it by clicking the Save Search As button on the Search dialog box. Enter a name for the search and click OK. You can then retrieve a given search by selecting its name from the Saved Searches list.

You can select more than one file name in the Listed Files box. Hold down the Ctrl key and click each file name that you want to include in the selection. You can then click the Open button to open all the files in one operation, or click the Commands button to perform other operations on the files.

 **See Also** Opening Files, Printing Worksheets, Saving Files.

FINDING WORKSHEET DATA

The Edit ➤ Find command searches for a sequence of text in the formulas, values, or notes of a worksheet or macro sheet.

To Search for Data in a Worksheet or Macro Sheet

1. Activate the document in which you want to perform the search, and choose Edit ➤ Find. The Find dialog box appears on the screen.
2. In the Find What box, enter the text that you want to search for.
3. In the Search box, select By Rows to search from the top to the bottom of your worksheet, or By Columns to search from left to right.
4. In the Look In box, select the kind of cell contents that you want to search through: Formulas, Values, or Notes.
5. Click the Match Case option, placing an X in its check box, if you want Excel to search for the text in the exact uppercase and lowercase combinations you entered into the Find What box. Leave this option unchecked if you want to perform the search without regard for alphabetic case.

6. Click the Find Entire Cells Only option, placing an X in its check box, if the text you have entered in the Find What box represents an entire cell entry. Leave this option unchecked if you want to search for the text as a portion of a cell entry.
7. Click the Find Next button to begin the search.

Shortcuts Press Shift-F5 to open the Find dialog box.

NOTES If Excel does not find the target text in your worksheet, a dialog box appears on the screen with the message Cannot find matching data. If the search is unsuccessful, but you believe the text does exist in your worksheet, reopen the Find dialog box and make sure you have selected appropriate options in the Search and Look in boxes.

You can use wildcard characters in the search text: ? stands for a single unspecified character, and * stands for a string of unspecified characters.

To restrict the search to a specific range of cells on your worksheet, select the range before choosing the Find command. Otherwise, Excel searches through the entire worksheet for the target text.

See Also Formulas, Notes, Replacing Worksheet Data.

FONTS

You can display and print worksheet data in any of the fonts available in your installation of Windows. You can also select a point size and any combination of styles—including bold, italics, underlining, and others. In addition, Excel 5 allows "rich text" formatting; this means that you can apply different formats to individual characters within a text entry in a cell.

To Change the Font of a Selection

1. Select the target data, choose Format ➤ Cells, and click the Font tab. The resulting dialog box has Font, Font Style, Size, Underline, Color, and Effects options.
2. Select a font name from the Font box, and a numeric setting from the Size box.
3. Select any of the Font Style options: Regular, Italic, Bold, or Bold Italic. Optionally, select an Underline option, and click any of the check boxes in the Effects group.
4. Click OK to apply the font to the current selection of cells.

Shortcuts Press Ctrl-Shift-F to activate the Font list in the Formatting toolbar and then press ↓ to open the list. Press Ctrl-B, Ctrl-I, or Ctrl-U to apply bold, italics, or underlining to the current selection. Alternatively, click the Bold, Italic, or Underline button on the Formatting toolbar.

NOTES As you select options in the Font tab of the Format Cells dialog box, the Preview box shows what the resulting text will look like. To undo all selections and return to the normal font, place an X in the Normal Font check box. The normal font is the default for a given worksheet, as defined by the "Normal" style in the Style list.

The Font tab is also available in Format dialog boxes for text on a chart sheet.

To Apply Fonts and Styles to Individual Characters in a Text Entry

1. Double-click the cell that contains the text entry. A flashing insertion bar appears at the end of the entry in its cell, indicating that you can now edit the text.
2. Use the mouse or the keyboard to highlight the characters whose font or style you want to change.

3. Click buttons in the Formatting toolbar to make changes in the selected text—for example, click the Bold, Italic, or Underline buttons, or make a selection from the Font Color palette. Alternatively, choose Format ➤ Cells, make selections from the Font, Style, Size, Underline, Color, or Effects options, and click OK.
4. Optionally, repeat steps 2 and 3 to change the formatting of other character selections within the text entry.
5. Press Enter to confirm the changes.

NOTES You can also format the characters of a text entry while you are first typing the entry, just as you would in word processed text. One easy way to do this is to use keyboard shortcuts such as Ctrl-B, Ctrl-I, and Ctrl-U to switch into and out of specific formatting effects—in this case, boldface, italics, and underlining.

To Change the Default Font for All the Worksheets in a Workbook

1. Activate the workbook, and choose Format ➤ Style. The Style dialog box appears on the screen.
2. In the Style Name list, choose Normal.
3. Click the Modify button. The Format Cells dialog box appears on the screen. Click the Font tab.
4. Choose a new font and click OK.
5. Click OK on the Style dialog box. The font selection is now the default for the active workbook.

See Also Copying Formats, Formatting Worksheet Cells, Point Size, Styles.

FORMATTING WORKSHEET CELLS

The formatting characteristics of a cell or range in a worksheet include the numeric display format, the alignment, the font selection, borders, patterns, and cell protection.

To Change the Format of a Range of Cells

Select the range, choose Format ➤ Cells, and click one of the following tabs:

Number	Changes the display format of numeric values in the range. (See Number Formats and Custom Number Formats for details.)
Alignment	Determines the horizontal and vertical alignment, and the orientation of individual data entries in their cells. (See Alignment.)
Font	Provides a variety of fonts, sizes, styles, and display colors for the data in a range. (See Fonts.)
Border	Displays borders in several styles along selected sides of cells in a range. (See Borders.)
Patterns	Changes the background pattern and color of a range of cells. (See Patterns and Colors.)
Protection	Creates a protection scheme of locked cells and/or hidden formulas. (See Protecting Cells.)

NOTES Font formatting can be applied to individual characters within a text entry in a cell. See Fonts for details.

To Change the Default Formats for a Worksheet

Choose Format ➤ Style and modify the definition of the worksheet's Normal style. (See Styles for details.)

FORMULA BAR

The formula bar is the line beneath the menu bar (and beneath the default location for the Formatting toolbar), where you enter data. You can use the formula bar to edit an existing entry in a cell, although Excel 5 also allows you to edit an entry directly in the cell where it is stored.

To Enter Text or a Numeric Value into a Worksheet Cell

1. Select the cell and begin typing the entry. Your entry appears on the formula bar. The active formula bar also displays a cancel box (an X icon), an enter box (a check-mark icon), and a Function Wizard button.
2. When you finish typing the entry, press ↵ or click the enter box to complete the entry. If you press ↵, Excel completes the entry and selects the next cell down the current column.

NOTES When you first begin a new entry, the word "Enter" appears on the status bar. In the Enter mode, you can complete your text or numeric entry and control the subsequent cell selection by pressing Tab, ↵, or an arrow key; the cell selection moves in the indicated direction. (If you are entering a formula in the Enter mode, you can press arrow keys to point to a cell or range. See Formulas for details.)

Press Alt-↵ to enter a carriage-return into a text entry in the formula bar. This results in a multiple-line entry in the current cell. Press Ctrl-Tab to enter a tab character into a cell.

To cancel an entry without changing the contents of the current cell, click the cancel box, or press Esc.

To Edit the Current Entry in a Cell

Press F2 to toggle into the Edit mode for the active cell; you can edit the contents either in the formula bar or in the cell itself. (See Editing for details.) In the Edit mode, pressing an arrow key moves the insertion point within the entry.

NOTES In the Edit mode, press Home to move the insertion point to the beginning of the entry, or the beginning of the current line in a multiline entry. Press End to move to the end of the current entry or line. Press ← or → to move the insertion point left or right by one character.

You can use cut-and-paste or copy-and-paste operations to move or copy information within the current entry. Drag the mouse to select text in the formula bar, and then press Ctrl-X to cut the text or Ctrl-C to copy it to the Clipboard. Move the insertion point and press Ctrl-V to paste the text to a new position in the formula bar.

See Also Alignment, Clipboard, Date Entries, Editing, Filling Ranges, Formulas, Time Entries.

FORMULAS

A formula in Excel is an entry that performs a calculation or other operation on one or more operands. A formula begins with an equal sign (=) and may include values, references, names, functions, and operations. In a worksheet, the formula's result is displayed in the cell where you enter the formula; the formula itself appears in the formula bar when you select the cell.

To Enter a Formula into a Cell

1. Type = to begin the formula.
2. Enter an operand. To enter a reference as the operand, type the reference directly from the keyboard, or point to the cell or range with the mouse or the keyboard. Alternatively, enter a name you have defined to represent a range, or choose Insert ➤ Name, click the Paste command, and select a name from the Paste Name list.
3. Optionally, enter an arithmetic operator (+, –, *, /, ^, or %), a comparison operator (<, >, <=, >=, <>, or =), or a text operator (&).
4. Optionally, enter a function by typing the function name and arguments directly from the keyboard, or by clicking the Function Wizard button.
5. Repeat any combination of steps 2, 3, and 4 to complete the formula, and then press ↵.

NOTES To insert a cell reference into the active formula bar, you can click the cell with the mouse or select the cell by using the arrow keys. To insert a range reference, drag the mouse over the range or select the range by holding down the Shift key and pressing any combination of arrow keys. The word "Point" appears on the status bar and Excel displays a moving border around the range you have pointed to.

To step through the possible reference types—relative, absolute, and mixed—press F4 repeatedly while the insertion point is positioned next to a reference in the formula bar. (See Copying Formulas and References for more information.)

To replace a formula with its current value while the formula bar is active, press F9.

You can enter formulas into each cell of a selected range in a single entry operation. See Array Formulas and Filling Ranges for details.

To Find Formulas that Refer to a Selected Worksheet Cell

1. Select a precedent cell—that is, a cell that appears as a reference in one or more formulas elsewhere on the worksheet.
2. Choose Edit ➤ Go To. In the Go To dialog box, click the Special option. Then click the Dependents option.
3. If you want to find only those formulas that contain an explicit reference to the selected cell, select the Direct Only option. If you want to find all formulas that are dependent on the cell, directly or indirectly, select the All Levels option.
4. Click OK. In response, Excel selects cells containing formulas that are dependent on the original cell.

Shortcuts Select the precedent cell and press Ctrl-] to find direct dependents, or Ctrl-Shift-} to find all dependents.

NOTES The Tools ➤ Auditing command gives quick ways to find *precedents* (cells that a formula refers to) and *dependents* (cells containing formulas that refer to the current cell). See Auditing for details.

See Also Arithmetic Operations, Array Formulas, Auditing, Copying Formulas, Filling Ranges, Formula Bar, Functions, Names, References, Text Operations.

FUNCTIONS

A function is a tool that performs a predefined calculation or operation in Excel. Each function has a name and may require one or more arguments as the operands of the calculation. Excel has many built-in functions for specific categories of applications (for example, statistics, engineering, date and time operations, and so on). You can add to this large collection of built-in functions by writing your own custom functions in the form of macros.

Excel 5 provides a Function Wizard to help you enter functions and their arguments correctly into a worksheet.

To Enter a Function into a Worksheet Cell

1. Select the cell where you want to enter the function, and click the Function Wizard button on the Standard toolbar (or choose Insert ➤ Function). The resulting dialog box—Step 1 of the Function Wizard—has a list of function categories and a box that lists all the functions in a selected category.
2. Select a function category. Then, from the Function Name box, select the function that you want to enter into the active cell. (Use the vertical scroll bar to move up or down the Paste Function box, or activate the box and type the first letter of the function you are looking for.) At the bottom of the Function Wizard dialog box you can read a brief description of the function you have selected.
3. Click Next to move to the next step of the Function Wizard.
4. The dialog box for Step 2 contains text boxes for each of the arguments required by the function you've selected. As you select each argument text box, the Function Wizard supplies a brief description of the information required in the argument. Type a value or an expression for each required argument; the value is displayed just to the right of the text box.

5. When you complete all the required arguments, the resulting value of the function is displayed at the upper-right corner of the Step 2 dialog box. Click Finish to enter the function and arguments into the current cell.

Shortcuts To display Step 1 of the Function Wizard dialog box, press Shift-F3.

Alternatively, select a cell and type = to begin the formula; then type the name of the function you want to use. Press Ctrl-A, and Excel opens Step 2 of the Function Wizard.

NOTES You can express the arguments of a function in any suitable form that meets the requirements of your worksheet. For example, an argument can appear as a value, a reference, a name, an expression, another function, or some combination of these elements.

See Also Add-Ins , Array Formulas, Charting, Copying Formulas, Database Functions, Date and Time Functions, Engineering Functions, Financial Functions, Formulas, Information Functions, Logical Functions, Lookup and Reference Functions, Mathematical Functions, Statistical Functions, Text Functions.

GOAL SEEK

The Goal Seek command adjusts a numeric entry that a formula depends on, to achieve a target result from the formula itself.

To Change the Result of a Formula with Goal Seek

1. Select the cell containing a formula whose result you want to change, and choose Tools ➤ Goal Seek. The Goal Seek

dialog box appears. It has three text boxes labeled Set cell, To value, and By changing cell. The Set cell box shows a reference to the cell containing the formula.

2. In the To value text box, enter the result that you want from the selected formula.
3. In the By changing cell box, enter a reference to a cell that the formula depends on. The cell must contain a numeric entry.
4. Click OK. The Goal Seek Status dialog box appears on the screen, and Excel finds the target solution.
5. Click OK to accept the solution. Excel records the new data value in the worksheet.

e.g. **EXAMPLE** Imagine a profit analysis worksheet in which the calculated profit from the sales of a manufactured product depend upon four values:

- the one-time development costs (stored in a cell named DevCost)
- the per-unit production costs (ProdCost)
- the anticipated number of sales (UnitsSold)
- the wholesale price per unit (UnitPrice).

The profit formula is:

=(UnitPrice–ProdCost)*UnitsSold–DevCost

Suppose the initial calculation results in a profit of $133,000. You want to know what the price per unit should be changed to in order to arrive at a target profit amount of $150,000. Select the cell containing the profit formula and choose Tools ➤ Goal Seek. Enter 150000 in the To value box, and a reference to the Unit-Price cell in the By changing cell box. Click OK. To arrive at the target profit, Excel calculates a new per-unit price.

 **NOTES** To revert to the worksheet's original data, click the Cancel button on the Goal Seek Status dialog box. To keep the Goal Seek result on the worksheet, click OK. To return to the original values, immediately choose Edit ➤ Undo Goal Seek or click the Undo button on the Standard toolbar.

See Also Iteration, Scenarios, Solver.

GRAPHIC OBJECTS

Using buttons on the Drawing toolbar, you can add a variety of graphic objects to a worksheet. Drawing objects include lines, arrows, freehand drawings, and geometric shapes—rectangles, ovals, arcs, and freeform polygons. (Geometric shapes can be drawn as opaque or filled objects.) You can also use the Drawing toolbar to add command buttons and text boxes to a sheet. All of these objects can be moved, resized, and formatted in a variety of ways. In addition, you can attach a macro to an object so that the macro runs whenever the object is clicked.

To Add a Graphic Object to a Worksheet

1. Click the Drawing button on the Standard toolbar. In response, Excel displays the Drawing toolbar. (Alternatively, point to any open toolbar and click the right mouse button; then choose Drawing from the toolbar shortcut menu.)
2. Activate the worksheet in which you want to display graphic objects.
3. Click the button representing the object you want to add, and then drag the mouse over the worksheet area where you want the object to be displayed. When you release the mouse button, Excel displays selection handles around the object.

4. Click elsewhere on the worksheet to deselect the object.

Shortcuts To draw more than one object of the same type, double-click the appropriate drawing button, and then drag the mouse over each area where you want to draw the object. To quit drawing objects, select a cell or click another button.

e.g. **EXAMPLES** In the Data Tables entry in this book, Figures D.1 and D.2 both illustrate the use of ovals, arrows, and text boxes to draw attention to features on a worksheet. (See Text Box for more information.)

NOTES To select an object, click its border; the selection handles reappear around the object. Move a selected object by dragging it with the mouse. Change its size and shape by dragging individual selection handles. For freeform polygons, you can also click the Reshape button on the Drawing toolbar, and then drag any of the handles that appear around the shape.

To delete an object, select it and press the Delete key. To copy a selected object, choose Edit ➤ Copy (or press Ctrl-C), then select a location for the copy and choose Edit ➤ Paste (or press Ctrl-V).

The process of drawing a polygon is different than that of drawing other objects. Click the Freeform button on the Drawing toolbar, and then click the mouse at each position in turn where you want to place the corners of the polygon. Excel draws a line between one corner and the next. Complete the drawing by clicking a final time at the object's starting point (creating an enclosed polygon), or double-clicking the mouse at any position (creating an open shape).

The graphic objects represented by buttons on the Drawing toolbar are available for chart sheets as well as worksheets.

To Select Multiple Graphic Objects

Click the border of one object to select it, and then hold down the Shift key while you click the borders of other objects.

NOTES By selecting multiple objects, you can change the patterns or properties of all the objects at once.

You can create a single object out of multiple drawings by selecting the objects and choosing Format ➤ Group. Restore the drawings as individual objects by choosing Format ➤ Ungroup. (Alternatively, click the Group or Ungroup button on the Drawing toolbar.)

To Change the Patterns and Colors of an Object

1. Select the object, and choose Format ➤ Object and click the Patterns tab. The resulting dialog box contains options for changing the appearance of the object's border and fill pattern.
2. Select a style, color, and weight for the object's border, and optionally click the Shadow check box to display a shadow behind the object.
3. Select a pattern style and colors for filling the interior of the object. The Sample box shows what your object will look like after these changes.
4. Click OK to confirm the pattern selections.

Shortcuts Double-click an object's border to view the Format Object dialog box. Or, point to the object's border and click the right mouse button, and then choose the Format Object command from the shortcut menu. To change only the fill color inside an object, click the drop-down arrow next to the Color button in the Standard toolbar. Select a color from the resulting palette.

NOTES To apply patterns to several objects at once, select all the objects before choosing the Format Object command.

To Change Other Properties of an Object

1. Select the object, choose Format ➤ Object, and click the Properties tab. The resulting dialog box includes options for the placement of the object in relation to worksheet cells, and for inclusion of the object in printed output.
2. Select one of the three Object Placement options. (See Notes for an explanation of these options.)
3. Optionally, change the Print Object setting. When this option is checked the object is printed with the worksheet; when it is unchecked, the object is displayed on the screen but not printed.
4. Click OK.

Shortcuts Select the Format Object command from the object's shortcut menu.

NOTES By default, a graphic object is *attached* to its underlying cells—that is, the object changes its size and shape when you change the height and width of rows and columns where the object is located. To detach an object completely from its underlying cells, select the Don't Move or Size with Cells option in the Object Properties dialog box. Alternatively, if you want the object to be moved but not resized, select Move but Don't Size with Cells.

To Assign a Macro to a Graphic Object

1. Open the workbook that contains the macro you want to assign to the object. (This is not necessary if the macro is stored in the Personal Macro Workbook. See Macro Recording for details.)
2. Select the object and choose Tools ➤ Assign Macro. The Assign Macro dialog box contains a list of all available macros.
3. Select a macro from the list and click OK.

4. Click elsewhere on the worksheet to deselect the object.

NOTES When you point to an object that has an assigned macro, the mouse pointer changes to a pointing hand. Click the object to run the macro. To select the object without running the macro, hold down the Ctrl key and click the object.

A button object is designed to represent a macro. To create a button object, click the Create Button tool on the Drawing toolbar, and drag the mouse over the worksheet area where you want to display the button. When you release the mouse button, Excel automatically displays the Assign Macro dialog box. Select a macro and click OK. To change the label displayed on a button, hold down the Ctrl key and select the button, and then type the new label from the keyboard.

See Also Macro, Macro Recording, Text Box.

GROUP EDITING

Group editing allows you to enter and format data on multiple worksheets at once within a given workbook.

To Edit Documents in a Group

1. Open the workbook in which you want to conduct the group editing session. Click the tab of the worksheet from which you want to control the group operations.
2. Hold down the Ctrl key and click the tabs for the other worksheets that you want to include in the group. (To select several worksheets in a row, hold down the Shift key and click the last worksheet in the group.) The notation [Group] appears in the title bar of the workbook.

3. On the active worksheet, perform the operations that you want to complete on all the documents of the group: Enter new data, edit existing data, format the worksheet, print the worksheet, and so on. During the group session, Excel treats each document in the group identically.

4. To end the group session, click the tab of a worksheet that is not in the group, or hold down the Shift key while you click the tab of a worksheet in the group. (Alternatively, choose Ungroup Sheets from the worksheet's shortcut menu.)

NOTES If you print the active document during a group session, Excel prints each document in the group, one after another. Before printing, you can choose File ➤ Print Preview to preview each document before printing it.

To Copy Data to Worksheets in a Group

1. Activate the worksheet that contains the data you want to copy to other worksheets.

2. Hold down the Ctrl key and click the tabs of other worksheets that you want to include in the group.

3. On the active worksheet, select the range of data that you want to copy to the other worksheets in the group.

4. Choose Edit ➤ Fill and then choose Across Worksheets from the Fill submenu. In the Fill Across Worksheets dialog box, select one of the three option buttons—All to copy data and formats, Contents to copy data alone, or Formats to copy formats alone.

5. Click OK. Excel copies the selection to the other worksheets in the group.

NOTE The copied data overwrites any data in the same range on the other worksheets in the group.

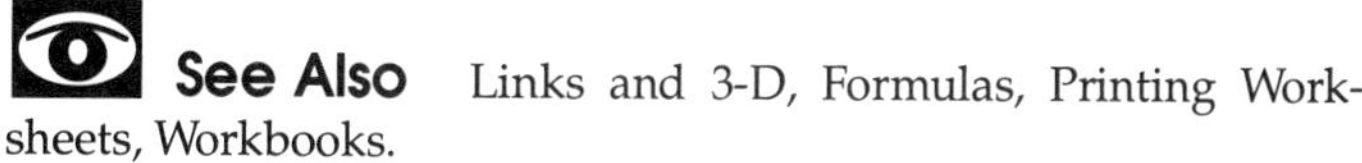

See Also Links and 3-D, Formulas, Printing Worksheets, Workbooks.

HEADERS AND FOOTERS

A header consists of one or more lines of text that appear at the top of each page of a printed document. A footer appears at the bottom of each page. Headers and footers are typically used for information such as the date, the title of the document, and the page number.

To Create a Header and/or a Footer

1. Activate the worksheet for which you want to create the header or footer. Choose File ➤ Page Setup, and click the Header/Footer tab on the resulting dialog box.
2. The Header and Footer lists provide a selection of built-in header and footer suggestions, combining information such as the sheet name, the workbook name, the page number, the date, the registered user and company, and the title from the Summary Info window. To select one of these suggestions, click the arrow next to the Header or Footer box and click the text that you want to use. The corresponding sample box shows what the header or footer will look like. Notice that the built-in entries are divided by commas—for the left, center, and right sections of the header or footer.
3. To create a custom header or footer, click the Custom Header or Custom Footer button. The resulting dialog box divides the header or footer into three side-by-side sections labeled Left Section, Center Section, and Right Section.

4. Enter text into any or all of the three text boxes. To change the font or style, select the text and click the Font button (labeled A) on the Header or Footer dialog box. Make selections on the resulting Font dialog box, and click OK.
5. To include special information in a text box, type one of the following codes, or click the corresponding button on the dialog box:
   - &[Page] for the page number,
   - &[Pages] for the number of pages,
   - &[Date] for the date,
   - &[Time] for the time,
   - &[File] for the file name.
   - &[Tab] for the sheet name.
6. Click OK to record your entries for the header or footer, and then click OK on the Page Setup dialog box.

NOTES You can enter multiple lines into any of the sections in the Header or the Footer dialog box. To start a new line, simply press ↵.

When you save a worksheet, the header and footer text is saved in the file, along with other settings in the Page Setup dialog box.

See Also Page Setup, Previewing, Printer Setup, Printing Worksheets.

HELP

The Excel Help window provides complete information about all aspects of the Excel application. There are several ways to open the Help window and locate the topic you need. For example, you can select a command from the Help menu, click the Help button on the Standard toolbar, click the Help button that appears on Excel dialog boxes, or simply press F1 at any point in your work.

To Get Help

Try any of the following techniques:

- Choose Help ➤ Contents and select one of the major topics in the Contents list. (To go to an underlined topic in the Help window, click the topic with the mouse.)
- Choose Help ➤ Search for Help on, and type a topic name into the Search text box. Click the Show Topics button, and Excel displays a list of topics related to your entry. Select a topic and click the Go To button to view the topic.
- Click the Help button on the Standard toolbar. The mouse pointer turns into an arrow with a bold question mark. Click a button, menu command, or other element in the Excel window to go directly to a relevant help topic.
- Click the Help button on any dialog box to view instructions for carrying out the current command.

NOTES The menu bar at the top of the Help window provides several useful commands for using and customizing the Help facility:

- Choose File ➤ Print Topic to print the current help topic.
- Choose Edit ➤ Annotate to attach your own notes to a help topic.
- Choose Bookmark ➤ Define to define a marker for quick access of a particular help topic.

The TipWizard is a special new feature that provides suggestions for working more efficiently in Excel. See the TipWizard entry for details.

To find out the name and purpose of a button in any toolbar, simply position the mouse pointer over the button. A small box tells you the name of the button, and the status bar provides a brief description. See Toolbars for more information.

 **See Also** Lotus 1-2-3 Help, TipWizard, Toolbars.

HIDING

Use the Window ➤ Hide command when you want to keep a workbook open but out of view. Within a worksheet, you can hide individual rows or columns when you want to keep specific ranges of data out of view.

To Hide an Open Workbook

Activate the workbook that you want to hide, and choose Window ➤ Hide.

NOTES The Personal Macro Workbook is hidden by default. (See Macro Recording for more information.)

To Unhide a Workbook

Choose Window ➤ Unhide (or File ➤ Unhide if no workbooks are displayed), select the name of the workbook you want to unhide, and click OK.

To Hide Columns or Rows on a Worksheet

1. Select the columns or rows that you want to hide, and choose Format ➤ Column or Format ➤ Row.
2. In the resulting submenu, click the Hide command.

Shortcuts To hide a single column, drag the right border to the left border in the column heading. To hide a single row, drag the bottom border up to the top border in the row heading.

To Unhide Columns or Rows

1. Select the columns on both sides of the hidden columns or select the rows above and below the hidden rows.
2. Choose Format ➤ Column or Format ➤ Row.
3. On the resulting submenu, click the Unhide command.

Shortcuts To unhide a column, drag the thick border (representing the hidden column heading) to the right. While you drag, the mouse pointer appears as two parallel vertical lines with attached arrows. To unhide a row, drag the thick border (representing the hidden row heading) down. While you drag, the mouse pointer appears as two parallel horizontal lines with attached arrows.

See Also Macro Recording, Protecting Cells in a Worksheet, Protecting Workbooks.

IMPORTING FILES

Excel can read files that originate from a variety of other software environments, and convert them into workbook format. The file formats include files from Lotus 1-2-3, QuattroPro, Microsoft Works, dBase, and previous versions of Excel. (For more information, see File Formats.)

To Import a File from another Program

Choose File ➤ Open and select a file format from the List Files of Type box. Select a directory and a file name, and click OK.

See Also File Formats, Opening Files, Saving Files.

INFO WINDOW

The Info window gives you complete information about a selected cell on the active worksheet—including the cell's formula, value, format, protection status, name, precedents and dependents, and any note that is recorded in the cell. You can open the Info window temporarily to examine the properties of a particular cell, or you can keep the window open while you develop a worksheet.

To Open the Info Window and Select Information Categories

1. Select the worksheet cell about which you want to view information.
2. Choose the Tools ➤ Options command and select the View tab.
3. In the Show group, click the Info Window option. An X appears in the corresponding check box.
4. Click OK. The Info window appears on the screen, and supplies information about the selected cell. While the window is active, the Excel menu bar displays menus and commands that relate to the Info window.
5. Pull down the Info menu and select an information category that you want Excel to include in the Info window. Repeat this step for all the categories you want to include in the Info window.
6. To view the Info window alongside the worksheet window, choose Window ➤ Arrange, click the Tiled option, and click OK. In this arrangement, you can select any cell on the worksheet and view the cell's properties in the Info window.

NOTES To print the Info window, make sure the window is active and choose File ➤ Print, or simply click the Print button on the Standard toolbar. To close the Info window, choose File ➤ Close while the window is active, or double-click the window's control menu box.

See Also Formatting Cells in a Worksheet, Formulas, Names, Notes, Protecting Cells, Window Operations.

INFORMATION FUNCTIONS

The information functions are designed to identify cell properties and data types in a worksheet. In addition, one function, INFO, provides information about the current operating system and memory environment. These functions can prove valuable for checking data in worksheets.

To Use an Information Function

1. Select the worksheet cell where you want to enter the function, and click the Function Wizard button on the Standard toolbar.
2. Select the Information category, and select a function from the Function Name box.
3. Click Next. In Step 2 of the Function Wizard dialog box, Excel provides help for entering the function's arguments. Complete the required entries, and click Finish. The function appears in the active cell.

 **NOTES** The information functions include the following:

- Cell information function (CELL).
- Data-type functions, or functions that identify the type of entry in a cell (ISBLANK, ISEVEN, ISLOGICAL, ISNONTEXT, ISNUMBER, ISODD, ISREF, ISTEXT, TYPE).
- Error functions (ERROR.TYPE, ISERR, ISERROR, ISNA, NA).
- Numeric conversion function (N).
- Operating system function (INFO).

The functions whose names begin with IS all return logical values of TRUE or FALSE.

e.g. EXAMPLE The following formula uses the ISNUMBER function to test the contents of a cell before performing a numeric calculation:

=IF(ISNUMBER(B1),B1*5,"")

The expression ISNUMBER(B1) is TRUE if cell B1 contains a numeric entry; in this case, the IF function returns the value of the expression B1*5. But if B1 is blank or contains a text entry, the ISNUMBER function returns a value of FALSE, and the IF function returns a blank text value. The cell containing this formula therefore remains blank until B1 contains a number.

 **See Also** Functions, Logical Functions.

INSERTING

You can use either the Insert command or a special dragging technique to insert rows, columns, or a selection of cells into a worksheet. When you do so, Excel shifts other cells down or to the right to make room for the insertion.

To Insert Entire Rows or Columns with the Insert Command

1. Select the rows or columns at the position where you want to perform the insert operation. (To select more than one row or column, drag the mouse along the appropriate row or column headings. To select a single row or column, click the row or column heading.)
2. Choose Insert ➤ Rows or Insert ➤ Columns.

Shortcuts Select the rows or columns and press Ctrl-Shift-plus sign (+).

- Point to the selected rows or columns, and click the right mouse button to view the shortcut menu; then choose the Insert command.
- Select any range of cells within the target rows or columns, and click the Insert Row or Insert Column button. (These buttons are not initially part of any toolbar. You'll find them in the Edit category of the Customize dialog box. See Toolbars for information on installing them.)

NOTES You can also select a range of cells within the target rows or columns and then choose Insert ➤ Rows or Insert ➤ Columns.

To undo an insertion, take one of these actions immediately after the insertion: choose Edit ➤ Undo Insert, press Ctrl-Z, or click the Undo button on the Standard toolbar.

To Insert a Range of Cells Using the Insert Command

1. Select the range at the position where you want to insert cells.
2. Choose Insert ➤ Cells.
3. On the Insert dialog box, select Shift Cells Right or Shift Cells Down, depending on how you want Excel to make room for the new blank cells.
4. Click OK.

Shortcuts Select the range and click the Insert button. Excel shifts cells to make room for the new blank cells. (This button is not initially part of any toolbar. See Toolbars.)

To Insert Cells by Dragging the Fill Handle

1. Select the cell, range, row, or column located *before* the position where you want to perform the insert operation.
2. Hold down the Shift key and drag the fill handle down (to insert rows) or to the right (to insert columns). The number of rows or columns you insert depends on how far you drag the fill handle.

NOTES When you select an entire row, the fill handle is located at the lower-left corner of the selection. When you select an entire column, the fill handle is at the upper-right corner of the selection. You cannot use this dragging technique to insert a column before column A, or a row before row 1; use Insert ➤ Rows or Insert ➤ Columns instead.

See Also Deleting, Selecting a Range.

ITERATION

Iteration is the process of resolving a circular reference by recalculating a worksheet multiple times. A formula that depends directly or indirectly on its own result contains a circular reference. In its default calculation mode, Excel cannot resolve circular references. To find a result from a circular reference, you must activate the Iteration option.

To Resolve a Circular Reference by Iteration

1. Develop a worksheet that contains a circular reference.
2. Choose Tools ➤ Options and click the Calculation tab.
3. Click the Iteration option. An X appears in the corresponding check box.
4. Optionally, enter new values for the maximum number of iterations and for the maximum change.
5. Click OK. Excel begins the iterative calculation in an attempt to find a solution to the circular reference on your worksheet.

NOTES The iterations continue until one of the following conditions is met:

- The number of iterations reaches the value entered in the Maximum Iterations box.
- The difference in the result of the circular formula from one iteration to the next is less than the Maximum Change value.

e.g. **EXAMPLE** Suppose you want to calculate the amount you must earn in annual gross income to achieve a specific after-tax income. You develop a worksheet to solve this problem, with individual cells named GrossIncome, Expenses, NetIncome, TaxRate, Tax, and AfterTax. Three of the cells, Expenses, TaxRate, and AfterTax contain numeric entries that you supply. (AfterTax is the desired after-tax income.) The other three cells contain formulas, as follows:

GrossIncome	=Expenses + Tax + AfterTax
NetIncome	=GrossIncome – Expenses
Tax	=NetIncome * TaxRate

GrossIncome—the calculated gross income—is the sum of the expenses, the tax amount, and the after-tax income. This formula is circular because the tax calculation (Tax) depends indirectly on the gross income itself. When you first enter this sequence of formulas into a worksheet, Excel displays the message "Cannot resolve circular references." But as soon as you activate the Iteration option, Excel successfully calculates the gross income.

See Also Goal Seek.

LINKS AND 3-D REFERENCES

A link between two worksheets is a means of sharing data and updating it when changes occur. Several kinds of links are possible in Excel 5:

- You can create a link between worksheets stored in different workbooks. In this case, the link is created by an *external reference* that identifies the source workbook and the location of the information within the workbook. The workbook that contains the external reference is known as a *dependent workbook*.

- You can also link worksheets that are stored within the same workbook. In this case, a reference identifies the source worksheet and the range of data.
- You can use *3-D references* to combine data from multiple adjacent worksheets within a workbook. This kind of link is a convenient way to summarize large amounts of data stored in related worksheets.

To create a link, you can enter a reference directly from the keyboard or you can use the mouse to point to the source location. Or, if you want to let Excel create the link formula for you, simply click the Paste Link button in the Edit ➤ Paste Special command.

To Create a Link between Two Workbooks

1. Open the workbooks that are to become the source and the destination in the link and activate the relevant worksheets on both workbooks. So that you can view both workbooks at the same time, choose Window ➤ Arrange, select the Tiled option, and click OK.
2. On the source worksheet, select the data that will become the object of the link, and choose Edit ➤ Copy.
3. Activate the destination worksheet and select the cell where you want to establish the link.
4. Choose Edit ➤ Paste Special. On the Paste Special dialog box, click the Paste Link button. Excel enters an external reference into the destination worksheet.

NOTES If both the source worksheet and the destination worksheet are open, the external reference appears in the following form:

=[workbook]worksheet!source

where workbook is the name of the source workbook, worksheet is the name of the source sheet, and source is the location of the data in the worksheet. Notice the punctuation: the workbook name is enclosed in square brackets, and the worksheet name and source location are separated by an exclamation point. (If the worksheet name contains one or more spaces, the workbook name and worksheet name are enclosed in single quotation marks.) When you save the source worksheet to disk and then close it, Excel expands the external reference in the dependent workbook to include the directory path of the source workbook. In this case, the workbook name, its path, and the worksheet name are all enclosed in single quotation marks:

='path\[workbook]worksheet'!source

For example, an external reference might appear as:

'C:\EXCEL\[EXPENSES.XLS]NewProj'!$F$7

The exclamation point appears after the second single-quote character.

You can establish a link by entering an external formula directly into the dependent worksheet. The end result is the same as that of the Paste Link button. You can also create a link by entering a more complex external reference formula—that is, a formula that contains an external reference as one of several operands.

If the source data is in a range consisting of more than one cell, the Paste Link button enters the external formula as an array:

{=[workbook]worksheet!source}

To achieve the same effect directly from the keyboard, you can press Ctrl-Shift-↵ to enter an external array formula into the dependent worksheet. (See Array Formulas for further information.)

The Paste Link button creates an absolute reference to the source range of data. Excel also permits external references consisting of relative or mixed references. When you copy such a formula within the dependent workbook, the relative reference is adjusted in the usual way, according to the position of the copy in relation to the original formula. (See Copying Formulas.)

If you open a dependent workbook at a time when the source workbook or workbooks are not open, Excel displays a dialog box asking you if you want to "re-establish links." Click Yes, and Excel checks the sources for any changes in data, and updates the destination accordingly.

To Create a Link between Worksheets on the Same Workbook

Select the source data on one worksheet, and choose Edit ➤ Copy. Then activate the destination worksheet, choose Edit ➤ Paste Special, and click the Paste Link button.

NOTES In this case, the reference in the dependent worksheet has a simpler form:

=worksheet!source

where *worksheet* is the name of the source worksheet and *source* is the location of the data. If the worksheet name contains one or more spaces, it is enclosed in single quotation marks.

Another simple way to share data between worksheets in a workbook is to create book-level names for data in each source worksheet, and to use those names as references in the destination workbook. (See the Names entry for information about book-level versus sheet-level names.)

When you create a chart from a range of worksheet data in the same workbook, Excel enters SERIES formulas into the chart sheet. The arguments of the SERIES function are references to the source worksheet data, in the form *worksheet!source*. (See Charting for more information.)

e.g. **EXAMPLE** One common use for worksheet links is to create a master worksheet that consolidates data from other worksheets and summarizes their results. For example, suppose you have developed a set of detailed annual sales worksheets—all stored in the same workbook—and you want to combine the total sales from three years in a single worksheet, also in the same workbook. To do so, you could use the Paste Link button to create references to the three source worksheets in a single dependent worksheet. If the three sales worksheets are named Sales91, Sales92, and Sales93, and the total on each sales worksheet is in cell F7, the references will look like this:

```
=Sales91!$F$7
=Sales92!$F$7
=Sales93!$F$7
```

Alternatively, if you assign book-level names to the cells containing the total sales figures in the three worksheets, you can develop the summary worksheet using references to these names. For example, suppose you assign names of Tot91, Tot92, and Tot93 to cells F7 in the three annual sales worksheets. In a column of the summary worksheet you can enter the following three formulas:

```
=Tot91
=Tot92
=Tot93
```

The effect is the same. If you change a value on any of the three source worksheets, the change is automatically carried forward to the summary worksheet.

Creating a 3-D Formula

1. Within a workbook, develop two or more adjacent worksheets that contain related data. These worksheets will be the source of the data in the 3-D formula; they must be organized identically, with data entered into the same range on each sheet.
2. Activate the worksheet where you want to summarize the data in the source worksheets. Select the cell where you'll enter the 3-D formula.
3. Type an equal sign (=) and any other elements you want to include at the beginning of the formula. For example, enter the name of a function such as SUM, AVERAGE, MIN, or MAX; then enter the opening parenthesis for the function. (In this case, the 3-D reference will become the argument of the function.)

4. Click the tab of the first source worksheet. Then hold down the Shift key and click the tab of the last worksheet in the group. In the formula bar, Excel enters a sheet range such as 'Sheet2:Sheet4'. The range is followed by an exclamation point (!).
5. On the first source worksheet, click the cell or range that contains the data you want the 3-D formula to operate on. After the exclamation point in the formula bar, Excel enters a reference to the cell or range you've selected.
6. Complete the formula (for example, by entering the closing parenthesis to complete a function) and press ↵ to enter the formula into the cell of the destination worksheet. Your 3-D formula is complete.

e.g. **EXAMPLE** Suppose you have developed three adjacent worksheets named Sales91, Sales92, and Sales93. On each sheet, cell F7 contains the total sales for a particular year. To calculate the total sales for the three years, create the following 3-D formula:

=SUM(Sales91:Sales93!F7)

This formula finds the sum of the values stored in cell F7 on the three worksheets.

NOTE If you prefer, you can create a 3-D formula by entering it directly from the keyboard. But the pointing technique is generally easier and quicker.

See Also Array Formulas, Charting, Consolidating Data, Copying Formulas, Dynamic Data Exchange, Formulas, Names, Object Linking and Embedding, References, Window Operations, Workbooks.

LISTS

A list is a table of data stored in a worksheet. The top row of a list contains labels identifying the contents of each column. Subsequent rows contain records of information, all arranged in the same way. In previous versions of Excel, lists were known as *databases*; this term is still a valid alternative for describing a table of data.

Whether you think of a table as a list or a database, Excel 5 provides a variety of convenient and powerful operations that you can perform on the data:

- You can open a special *data form* dialog box that is designed to simplify several basic database operations, such as examining the data one record at a time, searching for records that match criteria, deleting records from the list, and adding new records to the list. (See the Data Form entry for more information.)
- You can use a *filter* to isolate rows of data that match specific criteria. With Excel's AutoFilter feature, you can apply a filter and view its result by making selections from drop-down lists of criteria. Alternatively, you can create a range of more complex criteria expressions and then choose the Advanced Filter command from the Data ➤ Filter submenu to find the matching records of information. (See the Filters and Database Criteria entries.)
- You can quickly rearrange the rows in a list—sorting the information alphabetically, numerically, or chronologically—by clicking one of the two Sort buttons on the Standard toolbar or by choosing the Data ➤ Sort command. (See Sorting for details.)
- You can employ a special set of worksheet tools known as *database functions* to calculate statistical values on records that match certain criteria. For example, the DSUM function finds the sum of values in a particular field for selected records. (See Database Functions for a list of the tools available in this category.)

NOTES To perform these operations, begin by activating a worksheet that contains an appropriately formatted list, and in some cases selecting a cell inside the list. (See the Database entry for an example.) Unlike previous versions of the application, Excel 5 does not require additional steps for defining the range of a list or database.

See Also Data Form, Database, Database Criteria, Database Functions, Filters, Query, Sorting.

LOGICAL FUNCTIONS

Using Excel's six logical functions, you can introduce varieties of decision-making formulas into a worksheet. Several of these functions take logical arguments—that is, expressions that result in values of TRUE or FALSE. All but one of the logical functions return logical results.

To Enter a Logical Function into a Worksheet Cell

1. Select the cell, and click the Function Wizard button on the Standard toolbar.
2. Select Logical in the Function Category list. As a result, Excel displays the names of the six logical functions in the Function Name list.
3. Select a logical function and click Next. Step 2 of the Function Wizard helps you complete the function's arguments. Enter a value or an expression for each required argument, and then click Finish. Excel enters the function into the current cell.

NOTES The logical functions include the decision function, IF; functions representing logical operations, AND, OR, and

NOT; and functions that simply return logical values, TRUE and FALSE. The logical arguments of IF, AND, OR, and NOT often appear as comparison expressions, using Excel's comparison operators <, >, <=, >=, <>, and =. Here are brief descriptions of the six functions:

IF	Returns one of two values, depending upon the value of an initial logical argument. The function takes three arguments: =IF(logicalTest,trueReturn,falseReturn). If the value of *logicalTest* is TRUE, the function returns the value of its second argument, *trueReturn*. If *logicalTest* is FALSE, the IF function returns its third argument, *falseReturn*. The arguments *trueReturn* and *falseReturn* can be any type of data, including numeric, text, or logical values.
AND *and* OR	Take as many as 30 logical arguments. AND returns a value of TRUE if all its arguments are true, or FALSE if one or more arguments are false. The OR function returns TRUE if one or more arguments are TRUE, or FALSE if all arguments are false.
NOT	Takes a single logical argument, and returns the reverse of the argument's value. If the argument is true, NOT returns a value of FALSE; if the argument is false, NOT returns TRUE.
TRUE() *and* FALSE()	Return logical values of TRUE and FALSE. These two functions take no argument. Excel also recognizes the logical constants TRUE and FALSE as legal cell entries. TRUE has a numeric value of 1, and FALSE has a value of 0.

e.g. EXAMPLE For worksheets, the IF function is the central tool in the category of logical functions. You can use this tool to decide between two values or computations for the entry in a given cell. For example, the following IF function examines the value in a cell named income. If the value is less than 75000, the function enters the result of one calculation; if not, the function performs another calculation:

```
=IF(income<75000,income*tax1,income*tax2)
```

In writing the first argument of an IF function, you may sometimes want to use the AND, OR, and NOT functions to express complex logical conditions. In the next example, the IF function examines the values in two cells, named status and income:

```
=IF(AND(status=1,income<35000),income*tax1,
  income*tax2)
```

Finally, by nesting one IF function within another, you can write formulas that perform multiple levels of decision making. Consider this example:

```
=IF(income<35000,income*tax1,IF(income<60000,
  income*tax2,income* tax3))
```

This formula chooses among three different formulas:

- income*tax1 if income is less than 35000;
- income*tax2 if income is greater than or equal to 35000, but less than 60000; or
- income*tax3 if income is greater than or equal to 60000.

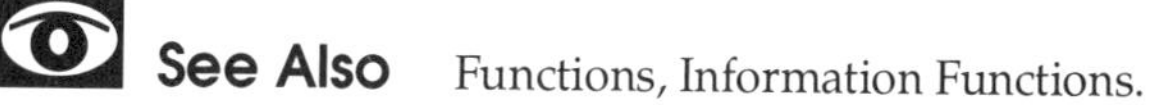

See Also Functions, Information Functions.

LOOKUP AND REFERENCE FUNCTIONS

Excel's lookup functions provide a variety of techniques for reading individual data values from lookup tables. The reference functions are designed to return range references from specific arguments, or, conversely, to provide information about ranges.

To Enter a Lookup or Reference Function into a Worksheet

1. For a lookup function, begin by creating a lookup table on a worksheet. Then select the cell or range where you want to enter the function and click the Function Wizard button in the Standard toolbar.
2. Select Lookup & Reference in the Function Category box, and then select a function name from the Function Name box.
3. Click Next. In Step 2 of the Function Wizard, enter the function's required arguments, and click Finish. Excel enters the argument into the current cell.

NOTES The lookup and reference functions can be grouped into the following three categories:

- Lookup functions that read a value from a worksheet table, a list, or an array (CHOOSE, HLOOKUP, INDEX, LOOKUP, MATCH, VLOOKUP).
- Functions that return information about a reference or an array (AREAS, COLUMN, COLUMNS, ROW, ROWS).

- Functions that return a reference or an array (ADDRESS, INDIRECT, OFFSET, TRANSPOSE).

e.g. **EXAMPLE** The classic example of a lookup table is a tax table, where the columns represent taxpayer status, and the rows represent income levels. The worksheet in Figure L.1 shows a sample from an imaginary tax table; the range B2:E9 is named taxTable. The VLOOKUP function is ideal for reading individual tax amounts from this table. The function takes three arguments:

=VLOOKUP(lookupAmount,table,resultColumn)

VLOOKUP searches down the first column of *table* for the largest value that is less than or equal to *lookupAmount*, and returns the amount from *resultColumn* in the same row.

TAXLOOK.XLS

	A	B	C	D	E
1			Taxpayer Status		
2			1	2	3
3	Income	$28,750	5,051	4,140	4,140
4	Levels	$28,850	5,077	4,154	4,166
5		$28,950	5,104	4,169	4,193
6		$29,050	5,131	4,183	4,220
7		$29,150	5,158	4,196	4,247
8		$29,250	5,185	4,212	4,274
9		$29,350	5,212	4,226	4,301
10					
11					
12					
13		Income	$29,083		
14		Status	2		
15		Tax	$4,183		
16					

Sheet1 / Sheet2 / Sheet

Figure L.1: A lookup table

At the bottom of the worksheet table, cell C13 has the name Income and cell C14 has the name Status. Here is the formula in cell C15:

=VLOOKUP(Income,taxTable,Status+1)

As you can see, this formula reads the value $4,183 from the tax table. (Notice that the formula adds 1 to the Status value; this is because the columns of the table—B, C, D, and E—are numbered from 1 to 4 for the purposes of the VLOOKUP function.)

See Also Array Formulas, Data Tables, Functions, References.

LOTUS 1-2-3 HELP

Excel has an elaborate feature called Help for Lotus 1-2-3 Users that is designed to ease the transition between 1-2-3 and Excel. This feature provides either instructions for accomplishing 1-2-3 tasks in Excel, or actual demonstrations of the tasks.

To Use the Help for Lotus 1-2-3 Users Feature

1. Choose Help ➤ Lotus 1-2-3. The Help for Lotus 1-2-3 Users dialog box appears on the screen.
2. In the Help Options group, select Instructions if you want to see a list of steps for a task, or Demo if you want Excel to demonstrate a task. (If you select Demo, you may also adjust the pace of the demonstration by clicking the Faster or Slower button.)
3. Choose a sequence of 1-2-3 commands from the Menu box. To go through a command sequence, you can double-click the command names in the list, or you can type letters at the keyboard just as you would do in Lotus 1-2-3.
4. As you go through the command sequence, the Help dialog box shows you the steps for accomplishing the same procedure in Excel.

5. When you reach the end of the sequence, press ↵ or click OK. If you have requested instructions, Excel displays a text box with numbered steps. You can keep this box on the screen while you perform the steps of the procedure. If you have requested a demo, Excel elicits any required information from you and then begins the demonstration.

Shortcuts Choose Tools ➤ Options and click the Transition tab. Select the Lotus 1-2-3 Help option, and then click OK. Under this setting, you can simply press the slash key (/) to open the Help for Lotus 1-2-3 Users dialog box at any time during your work.

See Also File Formats, Help.

MACRO

A macro is a program that automates the steps of a procedure in Excel. There are two languages for developing macros in Excel 5:

- The traditional macro language that has been available in all previous versions of Excel. A macro in this language is stored on a macro sheet in a workbook.
- The new Visual Basic language. A macro in this language is stored in a module sheet in a workbook.

The old macro language is supported for compatibility with previous versions of Excel. When you develop new macros in Excel 5, you should use Visual Basic instead.

A macro sheet or module sheet can contain any number of macros, all of which are available for use whenever the workbook is open that contains the sheet. In either one of the languages, you can create two kinds of macros:

- Macros that perform tasks or actions, much like a command in an Excel menu. The easiest and most convenient way to create this kind of macro is with Excel's Macro Recorder. The Recorder even allows you to create a menu command and a shortcut key for performing your macro.

- Macros designed to return a value to a cell in a worksheet, just as Excel's built-in functions do. This kind of macro is known as a *user-defined function.*

To Create a Macro that Performs an Action

Choose Tools ➤ Record Macro, and click the Record New Macro command in the resulting submenu. In the Record New Macro dialog box, enter information about the macro you're planning to create, and click OK. Then perform the actions you want to store in the macro. When you're finished recording, click the Stop Recording Macro button. Depending upon the language you've chosen, Excel records your macro either in a macro sheet or a module sheet. You can examine the macro by activating the sheet in the workbook where you've chosen to store the macro. (See the Macro Recorder entry for more information and detailed instructions.)

To Create a User-Defined Function in Visual Basic

1. Open or activate the workbook where you want to store the macro.
2. Choose Insert ➤ Macro and then choose Module from the resulting submenu. Excel inserts and activates a new module sheet in your workbook. (Module sheets have default names like Module1, Module2, and so on.) The Visual Basic toolbar appears on the screen.
3. In the Module sheet, type the lines of the user-defined function. (If you're not a programmer, you can type a function that someone else has given you to use.) In its simplest appearance, a user-defined function has the following general form:

```
Function FunctionName (arguments)
  FunctionName = expression
End Function
```

where *FunctionName* is the name you give your function, *arguments* is a list of names representing arguments that the function will require, and *expression* is a definition of the function's return value.

4. When you've finished typing the function, save your workbook, and switch to the sheet where you plan to use the function.

NOTES You can develop user-defined functions to expand Excel's already large library of built-in functions. For example, you might want to write functions to modify or simplify the use of existing functions, to add new general-purpose functions that are not already available, or to create functions that return specific information that is relevant to your own work in Excel.

Although a function can be as short as three lines (as shown in the general form above), functions are often long and complex. The Excel on-line help system contains many examples of user-defined functions that you can copy into module sheets as you explore Visual Basic.

To Use a Function in a Worksheet

1. Open the workbook that contains the custom function, and then activate the worksheet where you want to use the function. The worksheet need not be in the same workbook as the function.
2. Select the cell where you want to use the function, and click the Function Wizard button on the Standard toolbar.
3. In Step 1 of the Function Wizard dialog box, select User Defined in the Function Category list. Then select the name of your user-defined function in the Function Name list.
4. Click Next to view Step 2 of the Function Wizard dialog box. Use Step 2 to enter any arguments that your function requires.
5. Click Finish to enter the function into the current worksheet cell.

EXAMPLE The following function is designed to return the serial number for a date that is a specified number of days in the future:

```
Function DatePlus(days)
  DatePlus = Int(Now) + days
End Function
```

The function is named DatePlus. It takes one argument—the number of days that you want to add to the current date to calculate a new date in the future. (See Date Entries for information about serial numbers.) In a worksheet contained in the same workbook as the function itself, a call to DatePlus might appear as:

```
=DatePlus(365)
```

This call provides the date that is 365 days from the current date.

NOTES Excel provides several ways to make macros more conveniently available to your work:

- You can save a workbook in the add-in format, and then choose Tools ➤ Add-Ins to add the workbook's macros to the list of installed add-ins. As a result, all of the macros in the workbook are available each time you start Excel. (See Add-Ins for details.)
- You can save a macro in the Personal Macro Workbook. This book is opened as a hidden document whenever you start Excel, and all of its macros are available for use. (See Macro Recording for more information.)
- Given a macro that performs an action, you can assign the macro to a graphic object (see Graphic Objects) or to a custom button on a toolbar (see Toolbars). After this assignment, you can perform the macro simply by clicking the graphic or the button with the mouse. This feature is available only for macros that perform actions, not for user-defined functions.

See Also Add-Ins, Customizing Excel, Dialog Sheets Graphic Objects, Macro Recording, Toolbars.

MACRO RECORDING

The macro recorder creates a macro from the actions you perform in Excel while the recorder is on. You can record a macro in the active workbook, in a new workbook, or in the Excel's special Personal Macro Workbook (PERSONAL.XLS).You also have a choice of languages for your macro—Visual Basic or the macro language supported in earlier versions of Excel.

To Record a Macro

1. Activate the sheet on which you plan to work while you are recording the macro, and choose Tools ➤ Record Macro. Click the Record New Macro command in the resulting submenu.
2. In the Record New Macro dialog box, enter a name for the macro you are about to create. (The default is a name like Macro1, Macro2, and so on.) Optionally, make changes in the contents of the Description box; Excel will copy this description to your macro as a comment.
3. Click the Options button to expand the options shown on the Record New Macro dialog box.
4. Optionally, click the check box labeled Menu Item on Tools Menu and enter a command name. If you complete this option, Excel places a custom command in the Tools menu to represent your macro.
5. Make sure the Shortcut Key option is checked, and enter a letter in the box labeled Ctrl+. This letter will serve as the shortcut key for running the macro.
6. In the Store In group, select a location for your macro: the Personal Macro Workbook (described later in this entry), the current workbook, or a new workbook.

7. In the Language group, select Visual Basic or the Excel 4 macro language. (Unless you have a specific reason for doing otherwise, you should record new Excel 5 macros in Visual Basic.)
8. Click OK. The Record New Macro dialog box disappears, and the word "Recording" appears in the status bar at the bottom of the Excel window. In addition, a toolbar containing the Stop Recording Macro button appears on the screen.
9. Perform the actions that you want to record. For example, select cells or ranges, enter data and formulas, choose menu commands, click tools. Excel records your actions in the location you selected.
10. When you are finished recording, click the Stop Recording Macro button.

NOTES At any time during the recording session, you can choose Tools ➤ Record Macro and then click Use Relative Reference in the resulting submenu to change the way Excel creates references during the recording. Specifically, this command determines how Excel records a new selection on the current worksheet: as a relative reference in relation to the previous selection, or as an absolute address. If this menu command is unchecked, you are currently recording absolute references; if checked, you are currently recording relative references.

If no document is open (or all are hidden), choose the Record Macro command from the File menu to begin recording a macro.

If you want a macro to be available automatically during every Excel session, you should store the macro in the Personal Macro Workbook, PERSONAL.XLS. Excel initially creates this workbook the first time you select the Personal Macro Workbook option in the Record New Macro dialog box. To display the workbook and examine its contents, select Window ➤ Unhide and select PERSONAL.XLS. You can add new macros to the workbook either by entering them directly or by recording them with the Macro Recorder. Choose Window ➤ Hide to hide the workbook again.

To Run a Command Macro

1. Choose File ➤ Open to open the workbook that contains the macro, if it is not already open. (This step is not necessary if you have recorded the macro in the Personal Macro Workbook.)
2. If necessary, activate the type of sheet that the macro is designed to work on. For example, if the macro performs an operation on a worksheet, make sure that a worksheet is active before you select the macro.
3. Choose Tools ➤ Macro. The Macro dialog box shows a list of all the macros that are currently available for use.
4. Select a macro by name and click OK.

Shortcuts Press the Ctrl-*key* combination that you originally assigned the macro in the Record New Macro dialog box. Excel begins running the macro as soon as you press the shortcut key. Alternatively, pull down the Tools menu and choose the command name that you assigned to the macro in the Record New Macro dialog box.

EXAMPLE One common use for a command macro is to automate the selection of options in a complex Excel dialog box. For example, you might record a macro to save a particular combination of options from the File ➤ Page Setup command. You can then apply these settings to any workbook by pressing the shortcut key for your macro.

 **See Also** Hiding, Macro.

MATHEMATICAL FUNCTIONS

Excel's library of mathematical functions includes several categories of tools, including trigonometric, logarithmic, exponential, integer and rounding, random-number, summation, matrix, and calculation functions.

To Enter a Mathematical Function into a Worksheet

1. Select the cell or range where you want to enter the function.
2. Click the Function Wizard button on the Standard toolbar, and select the Math & Trig category. The Function Name box shows the entire list of mathematical functions.
3. Select the name of a function and click Next.
4. In Step 2 of the Function Wizard, enter arguments for the function and then click Finish. Excel enters the function into the current cell or range.

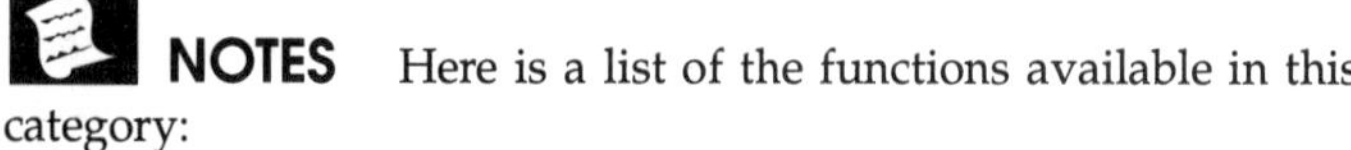

NOTES Here is a list of the functions available in this category:

- Absolute value and sign (ABS, SIGN).
- Algebraic (MULTINOMIAL).
- Common divisor and multiple (GCD, LCM).
- Counting and combinations (COMBIN, COUNTBLANK, COUNTIF).
- Factorial (FACT, FACTDOUBLE).
- Integer and rounding (CEILING, EVEN, FLOOR, INT, MROUND, ODD, ROUND, ROUNDDOWN, ROUNDUP, TRUNC).

- Inverse trigonometric (ACOS, ACOSH, ASIN, ASINH, ATAN, ATAN2, ATANH).
- Logarithmic, exponential, and powers (EXP, LN, LOG, LOG10, POWER).
- Matrix (MDETERM, MINVERSE, MMULT).
- Products, quotients, and remainders (MOD, PRODUCT, QUOTIENT).
- Random number (RAND, RANDBETWEEN).
- Arabic numeral to Roman numeral conversion (ROMAN).
- Square roots (SQRT, SQRTPI).
- Summation (SERIESSUM, SUM, SUMIF, SUMPRODUCT, SUMSQ, SUMX2MY2, SUMX2PY2, SUMXMY2).
- Trigonometric and degree/radian conversion (COS, COSH, DEGREES, PI, RADIANS, SIN, SINH, TAN, TANH).

See Also Engineering Functions.

MOVING DATA

You can move data from one range of worksheet cells to another by using the familiar Cut and Paste commands, or by dragging the range with the mouse.

To Move Data Using Cut and Paste

1. Select the range of data you want to move.
2. Choose Edit ➤ Cut. A moving border appears around the selection.
3. Select the upper-left corner of the location to which you want to move the data.

4. Choose Edit ➤ Paste.

Shortcuts Press Ctrl-X for the Cut command, and Ctrl-V for Paste, or use the Cut and Paste buttons on the Standard toolbar.

NOTES If you move a formula alone—without moving the range of data that it refers to—references in the formula remain fixed, and the result of the formula does not change. If you move a formula along with the entire range it refers to, Excel adjusts the references accordingly, but again the result of the formula remains the same. However, you should generally avoid moving a formula along with only part of the range of data it refers to.

To Move a Range by Dragging

1. Select the range that you want to move.
2. Position the mouse pointer along the border of the selection. The pointer becomes a white arrow.
3. Drag the selection to its new position in the worksheet. While you drag, an empty frame represents the selection that you are moving.
4. Release the mouse button. The entire selection moves to its new location.

NOTES To insert the selection between existing blocks of data, hold down the Shift key while you drag. A horizontal or vertical line represents the position to which the data will be moved and inserted. Release the mouse button to complete the move.

See Also Copying Data, Inserting, Selecting a Range.

NAMES

A name is an identifier that you define to represent a cell or range on a worksheet or macro sheet. You can use commands from the Insert ➤ Name submenu to assign names to cells and ranges, or you can enter a new name directly into the name box on the formula bar. Once you have defined one or more names, you can use them to clarify the meaning of formulas you write: a name takes the place of a cell or range reference, resulting in formulas that people can understand more readily. You can also define names to represent values or formulas that are not actually entered into worksheet cells.

Names in Excel 5 can have book-level or sheet-level *scope*. A book-level name is available anywhere within a workbook, and is therefore a convenient way to create references between worksheets. A sheet-level name is explicitly available only in the worksheet where it is defined, and is a means of avoiding ambiguity when you want to use the same name for ranges in several different worksheets.

To Define a Name

1. Select the cell or range to which you want to assign a name, and choose Insert ➤ Name. Then choose the Define command in the Name submenu. The Define Name dialog box appears on the screen.
2. Enter a name into the Names in Workbook box, and click OK.

Shortcut Press Ctrl-F3 to display the Define Name dialog box.

NOTES A name must begin with a letter or an underscore character, and may contain letters, digits, backslashes, underscores, question marks, and periods. Spaces are not allowed.

Instead of a space, you can use an underscore character or capitalization to clarify the meaning of a name; for example:

Base_Usage
BaseUsage

Although you might choose to make use of capitalization in this way, alphabetic case in names is not significant to Excel. For example, Excel considers the names BaseUsage, BASEUSAGE, and baseusage to be the same. A name can be as long as 255 characters, although names are typically short enough to be entered easily into a formula.

If you select a cell or range that contains a text entry—or is located below or to the right of a cell that contains a text entry—the Define Name dialog box suggests the text for the name.

In the Refers To box of the Define Name dialog box, you can enter any cell or range reference, beginning with an equal sign, =. (The default entry is a reference to the selected cell or range.) In practice, names usually represent absolute references, though Excel allows you to define a name for a relative or mixed reference. You can also enter a numeric or text value or an entire formula into the Refers To box; in this case, the name you define represents a value or formula that is not present on the worksheet itself.

The Names in Workbook box contains a list of all the names that are already defined for the current workbook. You can delete a name's definition by highlighting the name in the list and clicking the Delete button. When you do so, any formula that uses the deleted name results in a #NAME? error value.

e.g. **EXAMPLE** Suppose you are developing a worksheet to calculate a monthly billing charge for electricity usage. Your worksheet includes two different rates charged for usage. In cell B3, the rate of $0.11 per kwh (kilowatt-hour) is for usage up to a given base monthly usage; in cell B4 the second rate of $0.14 per kwh is for usage beyond the base. Cell B5 contains the base usage amount, 700 kwh; and cell B7 contains the current month's usage.

An IF function in cell B8 chooses between two possible formulas—one for usage that exceeds the monthly base, and another for usage that is within the base:

=IF(B7>B5, B5*B3+(B7–B5)*B4, B7*B3)

If the usage is greater than the base, the formula adds the charge for the base usage to the charge for the usage beyond the base. If the usage is within the base, the formula just multiplies the usage by the base rate. (See Logical Functions for information about the IF function.)

You can simplify and clarify the presentation of this formula by defining names for the cells that contain the rates, the base, and the month's usage: Assign the names Rate1 to B3, Rate2 to B4, Base to B5, and Usage to B7. When these names are applied to the formula, here is the result:

=IF(Usage>Base, Base*Rate1+(Usage–Base)*Rate2, Usage*Rate1)

(The last section of this entry describes the steps for applying names to a formula.) As you can see, the range names make this detailed formula easier to decipher.

To Create a Name in the Name Box

1. Select the cell or range to which you want to assign a name.
2. Click the name box, located at the left side of the formula bar.
3. Enter a name for the selected range, and press ↵.

To Create Names from Text Entries

1. Select a range that includes text entries that you want to assign as names to corresponding cells, rows, or columns in the range selection. The text entries can appear on the top or bottom row and/or the left or right column of the selection.

2. Choose Insert ➤ Name and then choose Create from the Names submenu.
3. In the Create Names dialog box, select any combination of the four check box options: Top Row, Left Column, Bottom Row, and Right Column. Then click OK. Excel assigns names from the indicated rows and columns to the corresponding adjacent cells in the range.

Shortcut Press Ctrl-Shift-F3 to display the Create Names dialog box.

e.g. **EXAMPLE** Imagine a business expense table that compares expenses incurred in three different offices of the same company. A column of text entries in A4:A7 represents the expense categories (Rent, Utilities, Supplies, Repairs), and a row of entries in B3:D3 represents the offices (identified simply as Office1, Office2, and Office3). The actual expense amounts are entered into the range B4:D7. You can use the Create Names dialog box to assign names from column A and row 3 to the ranges inside the expense table. In response, Excel assigns the names Rent, Utilities, Supplies, and Repairs to the four row ranges B4:D4, B5:D5, B6:D6, and B7:D7. Likewise, the names Office1, Office2, and Office3 are assigned to the column ranges B4:B7, C4:C7, and D4:D7. You can then use these names in SUM formulas that calculate the totals in row 8 and column E. For example, here is the formula to find the total expenses in Office1:

```
=SUM(Office1)
```

This is the formula for the total rent expense for all three offices:

```
=SUM(Rent)
```

To Go to a Named Cell or Range

Choose Edit ➤ Go To, select a name from the list of defined names, and click OK.

Shortcuts Press F5 to display the Go To dialog box. Alternatively, click the down-arrow button located just to the right of the name box on the formula bar. In the resulting drop-down list, click the name of the cell or range that you want to select.

NOTES When you select a named cell or all of a named range—for example, as a result of the Go To command—Excel displays the name itself in the name box at the left side of the formula bar.

To Paste a Name into a Formula

Choose Insert ➤ Name, and then choose Paste from the Name submenu. In the Paste Name dialog box, select a name from the list of defined names, and click OK. Excel activates the formula bar (if you have not already begun a formula) and enters the name as an operand in the formula.

Shortcut Press F3 to view the Paste Name dialog box—either while you are entering a formula into the formula bar, or before you begin the formula.

NOTES To create a two-column list of all the names defined on the current worksheet along with their corresponding ranges, select an empty location on the worksheet and choose Insert ➤ Name. Choose Paste from the Name submenu, and click the Paste List button on the Paste Name dialog box. Excel enters the list onto the worksheet.

To Apply Names to an Existing Formula

1. Select a cell or range containing one or more formulas. The references in the formulas should be ones for which you have defined names.
2. Choose Insert ➤ Names and then choose Apply from the Names submenu. In the Apply Names list, select all the names that you want to apply to the current formula.
3. Click OK. Excel replaces references with names in the currently selected formulas.

See Also Formulas, Info Window, Links and 3-D Formulas, References, Selecting a Range.

NOTES

A note is a text annotation that you attach to a cell in a worksheet. On a computer that has the appropriate hardware and software, a note can also include a voice recording or other sound effect.

To Annotate a Cell

1. Select the cell and choose Insert ➤ Note. The Cell Note dialog box contains a scrollable text box, labeled Text Note, in which you can enter a note for the current cell.
2. Type a note for the current cell in the Text Note box. (When the Text Note box is active, a flashing vertical insertion point indicates the current position in the text box.)
3. Click OK to attach the note to the current cell.

NOTES Word wrap takes place automatically as you type a note into the Text Note box. You can use standard Windows editing features—including cut-and-paste and copy-and-paste—inside the Text Note box.

While the Cell Note dialog box is open, you can also attach notes to other cells in the active sheet: First click the Add button to attach the contents of the Text Note box to the current cell. Then activate the Cell box and click a different cell on the sheet or type a reference directly into the Cell box. Activate the Text Note box and type a new note or edit the current note. Finally, click the Add button to attach the note to the new cell. Repeat this process for each cell that you want to annotate.

A cell that contains a note has a special marker that is displayed at the upper-right corner of the cell. On a color monitor, the cell note indicator appears as a small red bullet.

To View or Edit the Notes Attached to Cells in the Active Sheet

1. Select any cell that displays a cell note indicator, and choose Insert ➤ Note. The Text Note box displays the note for the current cell.
2. Optionally, enter changes in the note, or append text to the end of the note displayed in the box. Then click the Add button to attach the edited note to the cell.
3. To view the note for another cell, select any one of the cells listed in the Notes in Sheet box. Excel displays the selected note in the Text Note box.
4. Repeat steps 2 and 3 for as many notes as you want to view and/or edit.
5. Click the Close button to close the Cell Notes dialog box.

Shortcuts To open the Cell Note dialog box and view the note for a cell, select a cell that contains a note and press Shift+F2 or click the Attach Note button on the Auditing toolbar.

NOTES While the Cell Note dialog box is open, you can delete the note from any individual cell: Select the cell in the Notes in Sheet list and click the Delete button. Excel displays a warning box with the message "Note will be permanently deleted." Click OK to delete the note. (Using the Edit ➤ Clear command, you can delete an entire range of cell notes all at once. See the last section of this entry for details.)

To Copy Notes

1. Select the cell or range containing the notes you want to copy, and choose Edit ➤ Copy. A moving border appears around the selection.
2. Select the cell or the upper-left corner of the range to which you want to copy the notes.

3. Choose Edit ➤ Paste Special. In the Paste Special dialog box, select the Notes option, and click OK. Excel copies the note or notes from the source range to the destination.

NOTES To copy notes along with the other contents of a cell or range, you can use any of the techniques available for copying data in a worksheet. (See Copying Data for details.)

To Print Notes

1. Choose File ➤ Page Setup and click the Sheet tab on the Page Setup dialog box.
2. In the Print group, select the Notes option and the Row & Column Headings option. An *X* appears in each of the corresponding check boxes. Click OK.
3. Choose File ➤ Print.
4. Click Print Preview for a preview of the printed worksheet and notes, or click OK to begin printing.

To Attach a Sound Note to a Cell

1. Select the cell and choose Insert ➤ Note.
2. In the Cell Note dialog box, click the Record button. (If this button is dimmed, your computer does not have the necessary hardware and software resources to record sound.)
3. Click the Record button in the resulting dialog box, and use the microphone attached to your system to record the sound. Click Stop to end the recording.
4. Back on the Cell Note dialog box, click Add to attach the recording to the cell. Then click OK to close the Cell Note dialog box.

NOTE To listen to the sound note attached to a cell, select the cell and press Shift-F2. The Cell Note dialog box appears. Click the Play button to play the note.

To Delete Notes from a Range of Cells

1. Select the range from which you want to delete notes.
2. Choose Edit ➤ Clear.
3. In the Clear submenu, choose the Notes command.

NOTES You can choose Edit ➤ Undo Clear (or press Ctrl-Z) immediately after a deletion if you decide you want to restore the notes to the range of cells. Alternatively, click the Undo button on the Standard toolbar.

See Also Info Window, Previewing, Printer Setup, Printing Worksheets.

NUMBER FORMATS

You can use the Number tab in the Format Cells dialog box to display numeric entries in any of a large variety of built-in formats. The format categories include Number, Accounting, Date, Time, Percentage, Fraction, Scientific, Text, and Currency.

To Format Numeric Values in a Worksheet

1. Select the cell or range of values that you want to format.
2. Choose Format ➤ Cells, and click the Number tab on the resulting dialog box.

3. Select the name of a format category. The Format Codes box lists all the built-in codes available in the selected category.
4. Select a format code and click OK.

Shortcuts Point to the selected range, click the right mouse button, and choose the Format Cells command from the resulting shortcut menu. Alternatively, hold down the Ctrl-Shift combination and press one of the following keys to apply a selected format:

$	For currency with two decimal places.
!	For numeric with two decimal places.
%	For percentage with no decimal places.
^	For scientific notation.
~	For the General format.
@	For the *h:mm* time format.
#	For the *d-mmm-yy* date format.

In addition, the Formatting toolbar has five tools that apply numeric formats: the Currency, Percent, and Comma Style tools, which apply three of the most commonly used built-in styles; and the Increase Decimal and Decrease Decimal tools, which change the number of decimal places displayed for numeric values.

NOTES If you use one of the built-in date or time formats when you enter a date or time value in a cell, Excel recognizes the value as a chronological entry and automatically applies the appropriate format to the cell. The numeric value stored in the cell is a serial date or serial time value. (See Date Entries and Time Entries for details.)

You can use Excel's standard format codes to create custom formats for use in a worksheet. (See Custom Number Formats.)

See Also Autoformat for Worksheet Data, Copying Formats, Custom Number Formats, Date Entries, Formatting Worksheet Cells, Time Entries.

OBJECT LINKING AND EMBEDDING (OLE)

Object linking and embedding is a technique for sharing information and features between Excel and other Windows applications that support OLE. Using OLE, you can *embed* or *link* documents:

- When you embed a document from another application into an Excel worksheet, the embedded document appears as an object that you can move and resize in any way that suits your presentation. Likewise, you can embed an Excel chart or worksheet range into a document created in a different Windows application.
- When you link two documents, you create a *remote reference formula* that identifies the source application and document, and the location of the data. As a result of this reference, data in the destination document is updated whenever a change occurs in the source document.

Excel 5 supports both OLE and DDE. To embed an object, the other application must also support OLE. To establish a link, the second application must support OLE or DDE. (See Dynamic Data Exchange for more information.)

To Embed an Object in a Worksheet

1. Activate the worksheet and select the cell where you want to embed the object.
2. Choose Insert ➤ Object. In the Object dialog box, click the Create New tab.

3. Select an application from the Object Type list, and click OK. Excel starts the selected application.
4. Develop the document that you want to embed into your worksheet. When your work is complete, choose the command that exits from the application—for example, File ➤ Exit and Return. (If a message box displays a question such as "Save changes in Sheet1?" click Yes.) Excel reappears, and the embedded object is now part of your worksheet.

NOTES Another way to embed an object is to open the source application and develop the graphics or data that you want to embed. Then select the information and press Ctrl-C to copy it to the Clipboard. Return to Excel and choose Edit ➤ Paste Special. In the As list of the Paste Special dialog box, select the format in which you want to paste the object, and click OK.

To select an embedded object, click it with the mouse; Excel displays selection handles around the perimeter of the object. You can resize the object by dragging a selection handle. Reposition the object by dragging its border. To deselect the object, click elsewhere on your worksheet.

Most of the features described in the Graphic Objects entry also apply to embedded objects. In particular, you can perform the following operations on embedded objects:

- Change the color, style, and pattern of the object's border and interior. (Select the object, and choose Format ➤ Object, and click the Patterns tab.)
- Specify the object's relation to its underlying cells. (Select the object, and choose Format ➤ Object, and click the Properties tab.)
- Attach a macro to the object. (Select the object, and choose Tools ➤ Assign Macro. If a macro is attached to an object, you can click the object to run the macro. To select the object, press the Ctrl key while you click it.)

See the Graphic Objects entry for more information about all these operations. Also, note that a shortcut menu is available for an embedded object. To view this menu, point to the object and click the right mouse button.

To Insert or Link a Document File

1. Activate the sheet on which you want to view the object or the linked document.
2. Choose Insert ➤ Object, and then click the Create from File tab on the Object dialog box.
3. Use the Directories box to locate the path of the document file you want to insert or link. Then select the file's name from the File Name list.
4. If you want to establish a link to the source file, click the Link to File option, placing an X in the corresponding check box. Alternatively, if you want to insert the source document as an embedded object, leave this option unchecked.
5. Click OK.

To Edit an Embedded Object

1. Double-click the object. In response, Excel reopens the source application and displays the object as a document in the application.
2. Use the features of the source application to complete any changes you want to make.
3. Close the document again. The edited document appears once again as an embedded object in your worksheet.

NOTES If an embedded object has an attached macro, select the object first (press Ctrl and click the object), and then double-click the object to open its source application.

To Embed an Excel Object in Another Application

1. Select the worksheet range or the chart that you want to embed, and choose Edit ➤ Copy.
2. Start the other application, and open the document in which you want to embed the Excel object.
3. Choose Edit ➤ Paste Special and paste the object (or choose the command required by the host application to complete the OLE operation).

NOTES To complete these steps successfully, you must select an application that supports OLE operations. You can double-click the Excel object to switch back to Excel and edit the original sheet or chart.

See Also Dynamic Data Exchange, Graphic Objects, Macro.

OPENING FILES

Use the File ➤ Open command to open Excel workbooks from disk. Use File ➤ New to create a new workbook.

To Open One or More Excel Workbooks from Disk

1. Choose File ➤ Open.
2. If necessary, use the Directories and Drives list boxes to change to the correct path location for the file you want to open.
3. Select a document's name from the File Name list.

4. To open two or more documents in one operation, hold down the Ctrl key while you click the names of other documents that you want to open.
5. Click OK.

Shortcuts If the file you want to open is among the four most recently opened files (listed at the bottom of the File menu), select the name directly from this list. Alternatively, click the Open tool in the Standard toolbar. This tool displays the Open dialog box.

NOTES If you want to examine a document but not change its contents, click the Read Only option on the Open dialog box. If you make changes in the file, Excel will allow you to save the file under a new name, but not update the file under its existing name.

To Open a New Workbook

Choose File ➤ New. (If the New dialog box appears, select Workbook from the New list, and click OK.)

Shortcuts Click the New Workbook button in the Standard toolbar.

See Also Directories, File Formats, Finding Files, Passwords, Saving Files, Template, Workbooks.

OUTLINES

You can create an outline in any worksheet that is organized in sections with subtotals and totals. To simplify your work with the outline, Excel displays *row and column level symbols, show detail symbols,* and *hide detail symbols* just to the left and/or just above the outlined worksheet. Using these symbols, you can select levels of the outline to view and hide—that is, you can focus on the whole worksheet or on selected levels of subtotals and totals.

To Create an Outlined Worksheet

1. Develop a worksheet in which numeric data is divided into sections, with levels of subtotals and totals at the end of each section. The subtotals can be in rows, columns, or both.
2. Select the range of data that you want to outline, if less than the entire worksheet. Otherwise, Excel will automatically determine the data to be outlined.
3. Choose Data ➤ Group and Outline, and then choose Auto Outline from the resulting submenu. Excel creates the outline and displays level symbols and hide detail symbols along the left and upper borders of the worksheet.

NOTES Excel determines the levels of the outline from the way you have organized subtotals and totals (or other summary-type formulas) at the end of each section of your worksheet. If the Auto Outline command does not produce the results you want, you can regroup the outline using the Group and Ungroup commands in the Group and Outline submenu. Select the rows or columns that you want to regroup, choose Data ➤ Group and Outline, and choose the Group or Ungroup command. Alternatively, hold down the Alt and Shift keys and press ← to ungroup or → to group; or click the Ungroup or Group button on the Query and Pivot toolbar.

Another way to plan or modify an outline is to choose Data ➤ Group and Outline and click the Settings command in the submenu. The resulting Outline dialog box contains check boxes for selecting row or column outline organization and for automatic styles.

An outline does not change the content of your worksheet in any way; rather, it gives you tools for temporarily hiding detail sections of your worksheet so you can focus on the subtotals and totals.

To Focus on Selected Levels of the Outlined Worksheet

Click one of the numbered outline level symbols that Excel displays for the row levels or the column levels. Excel temporarily hides all levels of the worksheet *after* the level that you click.

e.g. **EXAMPLE** The worksheet in Figure O.1 shows an outlined sales worksheet—the quarterly retail sales for a group of products carried in three different stores. Given this outline, you can simply click row and column level symbols to view different levels of the outline. For example, you can click row level symbol 2 to hide the sales data and view only the store totals, and column level symbol 1 to hide the quarterly data and view only the annual totals. The result appears in Figure O.2.

	A	B	C	D	E	F	G	H
1		Sales of Three Computer Models						
2		(in thousands of $)						
3			Q1	Q2	Q3	Q4	Totals	
4	L.A. Store	Home Model	$54	$83	$53	$95	$285	
5		Business Model	$86	$74	$93	$66	$319	
6		SuperTech Model	$61	$88	$50	$60	$259	
7		L.A. Total	$201	$245	$196	$221	$863	
8	S.F. Store	Home Model	$62	$65	$50	$53	$230	
9		Business Model	$89	$58	$81	$99	$327	
10		SuperTech Model	$87	$67	$55	$84	$293	
11		S.F. Total	$238	$190	$186	$236	$850	
12	N.Y. Store	Home Model	$61	$82	$75	$53	$271	
13		Business Model	$82	$86	$67	$67	$302	
14		SuperTech Model	$83	$83	$57	$80	$303	
15		N.Y. Total	$226	$251	$199	$200	$876	
16	*** Grand Total ***		$665	$686	$581	$657	$2,589	

Computer Sales / Sheet2 / Sheet3 / Sheet4 / Sheet5

Figure O.1: A worksheet organized for outlining

NOTES You can also collapse or expand individual sections of the outline by clicking the hide detail symbols (minus signs) or the show detail symbols (plus signs).

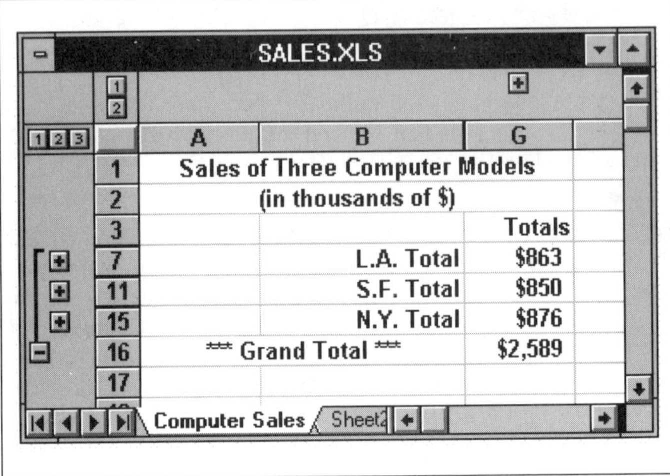

Figure O.2: Viewing levels of the outline

You can hide the outline level and detail symbols if you wish. Choose Tools ➤ Options, click the View tab, and clear the Outline Symbols check box. Then click OK.

To select a range of visible rows or columns in an outline, collapse the outline to the level you want to select, select the range, and press Alt-; (the Alt key and the semicolon). Alternatively, choose Edit ➤ Goto, click the Special button, select Visible Cells Only, and click OK. You might want to do this in order to create a chart from subtotals in your outline.

To Clear an Outline

Choose Data ➤ Group and Outline, and click the Clear Outline command from the resulting submenu. Excel removes the outline symbols and displays the entire worksheet.

 **See Also** Hiding, Subtotals, Summation.

PAGE SETUP

The options of the File ➤ Page Setup command give you control over the layout of sheets that you print from a workbook.

To Select Options for Printing a Worksheet

Activate a worksheet, choose File ➤ Page Setup, and select options from any of the tabs that appear on the Page Setup dialog box:

- Click the Page tab. Select Portrait to print the document from the top to the bottom of the paper, or Landscape to print the document sideways. In the Scaling box, enter a value less than 100% to reduce the size of a printed document, or a value greater than 100% to enlarge the printed document. Alternatively, click the Fit To option button if you want Excel to scale the document automatically to fit the number of pages you specify. Select an option from the Paper Size list. The sizes include standard paper dimensions such as letter, legal, and executive, along with standard envelope sizes. Select a Print Quality option of High, Medium, Low, or Draft. Finally, if you want the page numbering to start at some point other than 1, enter a value in the First Page Number box. (By default, page numbers are printed in the footer. See Headers and Footers for details.)
- Click the Margins tab. Enter measurements for the top, bottom, left, and right margins, and for the position of the header and footer. To center the document on the page, click one or both of the Center on Page check boxes, labeled Horizontally and Vertically.
- Click the Header/Footer tab, and enter information about the header and footer you want printed on each page. (See Headers and Footers for details.)
- Click the Sheet tab. Optionally, enter a reference in the Print Area box. (Alternatively, you can select a Print What option in the Print dialog box. See Printing Worksheets for

details.) If you want to print certain rows or columns of information as "titles" on each page, select the Rows to Repeat at Top and/or Columns to Repeat at Left box and point to the rows or columns that contain the titles. Select any combination of options in the Print group: keep the X in the Cell Gridlines check box if you want to print the gridlines; select the Notes option if you want the printout to include notes you have stored in worksheet cells; select Draft Quality for faster printing; select the Black and White check box for black and white printing; and select the Row & Column Headings check box if you want to print the sheet's row numbers and column letters. In the Page Order box, select one of the two options—Down, then Across; or Across, then Down—to specify how the pagination should be organized in a multipage document.

NOTES If the active document is a chart, the Sheet tab is replaced by the Chart tab on the Page Setup dialog box. Select one of the three options in the Printed Chart Size box: Use Full Page, Scale to Fit Page, or Custom. You can also select Printing Quality options. (See Printing Charts for details.)

A column of command buttons appears on the right side of the Page Setup dialog box. Click the Print button to open the Print dialog box and print the document. Click Print Preview to preview your document before printing it. Click Options to open the Setup dialog box for your printer.

See Also Headers and Footers, Previewing, Printer Setup, Printing Charts, Printing Worksheets.

PANES

By dividing a worksheet or macro sheet into panes, you can view two or four different parts of the sheet at once.

To Divide a Sheet into Panes

Select the row, column, or cell at which you want to divide the sheet, and choose Window ➤ Split.

Shortcuts Drag the vertical split bar to the left, across the horizontal scroll bar; or drag the horizontal split bar down the vertical scroll bar. (The split bars are small, solid, black rectangles, initially located at the right end of the horizontal scroll bar and at the top of the vertical scroll bar.) Alternatively, double-click a split bar to create two panes that are approximately the same size.

NOTES The Window ➤ Split command creates two or four panes, depending on the range or cell selection at the time you choose the command:

- To create two panes that are split vertically, select an entire column or a single cell in row 1 (other than cell A1).
- To create two panes split horizontally, select an entire row or a single cell in column A (other than cell A1).
- To create four panes, select any cell except in row 1 or column A.
- To create four panes of approximately equal size, select cell A1.

Scrolling is synchronized in the panes of a split sheet. With a horizontal split, the two panes stay together during horizontal scrolling; and with a vertical split, the two panes stay together during vertical scrolling.

To Freeze the Panes

Choose Window ➤ Freeze Panes.

NOTES This command prevents the top pane from scrolling vertically, or the left pane from scrolling horizontally. It may be useful if the left or top pane contains labels or other data that you want to keep in view, even while you scroll in the other panes.

Choose Window ➤ Unfreeze Panes to return the panes to their original scrolling capabilities.

To Remove Panes from a Sheet

Activate the sheet and choose Window ➤ Remove Split.

 **Shortcut** Double-click a split bar to send it back to its initial position.

 **See Also** Window Operations.

PARSING

Parsing is the process of separating long lines of text into individual data items, and entering each item into a separate cell on a worksheet. You may need to parse data that you have copied into Excel from another application.

To Parse Lines of Text in a Worksheet

1. Select a column range (one column wide) in which each cell contains a similarly formatted line of text.
2. Choose Data ➤ Text to Columns. A dialog box named Convert Text to Columns Wizard appears on the screen. The Text Wizard is designed to guide you through the steps required for a successful parse.
3. In Step 1, the Text Wizard determines whether the selected data is *delimited*—that is, individual data items are separated by special characters like commas or semicolons; or *fixed width*—that is, arranged in columns. Click the Next button to move to the next step of the process.

4. The next step depends on whether the data is delimited or fixed width:

    - For delimited data, select the relevant character in the Delimiters box (Tab, Semicolon, Comma, Space, or Other), and select the single-quote, double-quote, or {none} option in the Text Quantifier box. When you do so, the Data Preview box shows how your selection will be parsed into columns.
    - For fixed width data, drag the column break lines to their correct positions in the Data Preview box.

    Click Next when the columns of data are arranged the way you want them.

5. In the final step of the Text Wizard, you define the data type of each column of parsed data. Select a column in the Data Preview box, and then select the correct data type in the Column Data Format group. Repeat this for each column of data.
6. Click the Finish button. Excel copies the parsed data into the appropriate number of columns on your worksheet.

 **See Also** Formatting Worksheet Cells, Text Operations.

PASSWORDS

You can use passwords to restrict access to an Excel workbook that is saved on disk. Two kinds of passwords are available. If you create a *protection password,* a user must supply the password correctly in order to open the workbook file. If you create a *write reservation password,* it must be supplied in order to make changes to the workbook; without this password, a user is allowed to open the file in a read-only mode. (In addition, passwords are an optional part of the schemes for protecting the contents of a worksheet and the structure of a workbook. See the Protecting Cells in a Worksheet and Protecting Workbooks entries for details.)

To Save a File with Passwords

1. Activate the file you want to save, and choose File ➤ Save As.
2. In the Save As dialog box, enter a name for the file and then click the Options button.
3. In the Save Options dialog box, enter a password in the text box labeled Protection Password. Excel displays an asterisk for each character you type. (You can press the Backspace key to erase any character that you want to retype.)
4. Optionally, enter a second password in the text box labeled Write Reservation Password.
5. Click OK when you complete the password entries. A Confirm Password dialog box appears.
6. Type the protection password again, and click OK.
7. If you created a write protection password, another Confirm Password dialog box appears. Retype the password and click OK.
8. Finally, click OK on the Save As dialog box to save the file to disk.

NOTES A password may be up to 15 characters long. Alphabetic case is significant. If the passwords you reenter into the Confirm Password dialog boxes are not the same as those in the Save Options dialog box, Excel displays a warning box with the message Confirmation password is not identical. You are then returned to the Save Options box to try again.

To Open a Password-Protected Document

1. Choose File ➤ Open and select the name of the file you want to open. When you click OK, Excel displays the Password dialog box on the screen.

2. Enter the password and click OK.
3. If the workbook has a write protection password, a second Password dialog box appears. Enter the password properly and click OK.
4. If your password is correct, Excel opens the file.

NOTES If the password you enter is not correct, Excel displays a warning box with the message Incorrect password. You cannot open the file without the correct password.

To Save a File without its Password

1. Open a password-protected file, and then choose File ➤ Save As to save it again.
2. On the Save As dialog box, click the Options button. In the Save Options dialog box, delete the asterisks that represent the password or passwords, and then click OK.
3. Complete the save operation. The file can now be opened without a password.

See Also Opening Files, Protecting Cells in a Worksheet, Protecting Workbooks, Saving Files.

PATTERNS

You can use options on the Patterns tab to apply shading to a range of cells on a worksheet, or select a border style and a fill color for a graphic object. (When a chart is active, you can use the Patterns options to change the color and appearance of individual elements of the chart, including the series, the individual data markers, the legend, the chart area, the plot area, and the axes. See the Charting and Printing Charts entries for details.) The options available on the Patterns tab depend on the type of selection you have made.

To Apply Shading to a Range of Cells

1. Select the range, choose Format ➤ Cells, and click the Patterns tab. The resulting dialog box contains a Color palette, a Pattern box, and a Sample box.
2. Click the drop-down arrow at the right side of the Pattern box, and select a shading pattern from the top three rows of the resulting palette. Optionally, click the drop-down arrow a second time, and select a color for the pattern.
3. In the Color palette, select a color for the background of the pattern.
4. Examine the result of your selections in the Sample box. If the pattern appears the way you want it, click OK.

Shortcut Point to the selected range, click the right mouse button, and choose the Format Cells command from the shortcut menu.

To Change the Fill Pattern and Border of a Graphic Object

1. Select the object, and choose Format ➤ Object. Click the Patterns tab on the resulting dialog box.
2. Make selections from the Pattern and Color palettes in the Fill group.
3. In the Border group, select a border style (solid, broken, dotted, or patterned) from the Style list. Then make selections from the Color and Weight lists.
4. Click the Shadow check box if you want a black shadow to appear behind the object.
5. Click the Rounded Corner check box if you want round rather than square corners. (This option is available only for objects that start out with square corners.)
6. Click OK to apply the patterns.

Shortcut Choose the Format Object command from the object's shortcut menu.

See Also Borders, Charting, Colors, Formatting Worksheet Cells, Graphic Objects, Shading.

PIVOT TABLE

A pivot table is a dynamic, customizable tool designed to help you rearrange, summarize, and explore information from a database or list. The PivotTable Wizard provides a simple four-step graphical approach to creating the initial version of a new pivot table; subsequently you can use efficient drag-and-drop actions to revise and customize the table in a variety of useful ways.

The pivot table is one of the innovations of Excel 5; it replaces and significantly improves upon the crosstab report feature available in Excel 4. The more you experiment with this new feature, the better you'll appreciate its versatility and power.

To Create a Pivot Table from an Excel List or Database

1. Activate a worksheet that contains a list or a database. (See the Database and Lists entries for background information.)
2. Choose Data ➤ PivotTable. The PivotTable Wizard —Step 1 of 4 dialog box appears on the screen.
3. In the Create PivotTable options, make sure that the Microsoft Excel List or Database button is selected. Then click the Next button.
4. The next step of the PivotTable Wizard (Step 2) gives you the opportunity to define the worksheet range of the source data. Excel automatically supplies a reference to

the list or database on the active worksheet. If this is correct, click Next again.

5. The next dialog box (Step 3) is where you define the pivot table. At the right side of the dialog box you see a list of field buttons, identifying the fields of your database. In the center of the dialog box is a graphical representation of the pivot table's structure. To create a table, you drag any selection of field buttons to the four areas of the pivot table:

   - Drag fields to the ROW area to create rows of summary data in the pivot table.
   - Drag fields to the COLUMN area to create columns of data.
   - Drag fields to the DATA area to define the actual numeric content of the table. Excel initially identifies each item in this area as a Sum operation, but you can select other summary functions for each field if you wish, as you'll see in the next step.
   - Drag fields to the PAGE area to create drop-down lists of data categories that you can view one at a time in the pivot table.

6. To customize a field in the DATA area, double-click any of the field buttons you've dragged to the area. In the resulting PivotTable Field dialog box, you can select from a list of functions (Sum, Count, Average, Max, Min, and so on) that define how your pivot table will summarize information from your database. You can also define the numeric format of a field; click the Number button, select a format from the resulting Format Cells dialog box, and click OK. (To develop a more complex summarization formula, click the Options button.) When you have finished defining the field, click OK on the PivotTable Field dialog box. Repeat this step for any fields that you want to customize in the DATA area.

7. Click Next to move to the final step of the PivotTable Wizard (Step 4). In the resulting dialog box you can indicate where you want the pivot table to appear. To do so, enter a reference into the PivotTable Starting Cell text box, or

point to a starting cell on any worksheet while the box is active. Alternatively, leave the box empty and Excel will create a new worksheet for your pivot table, just to the left of the active worksheet.

8. Select or deselect any of the check boxes in the PivotTable Options group. These options determine whether the table will contain grand totals, whether a hidden copy of the source data will be saved with the table, and whether Excel will apply an AutoFormat to the table.

9. Click the Finish button to complete the process of defining your pivot table. The table appears in the location you selected on the final dialog box.

Shortcut Click the PivotTable Wizard button on the Query and Pivot toolbar to start the process of developing a pivot table. By default, the Query and Pivot toolbar appears automatically on the screen when you create a new pivot table or activate a worksheet that contains one.

NOTES You can also create a pivot table from other sources of data—including a database created in a different application, a selection of similarly organized worksheet ranges, or another pivot table. These options are presented in Step 1 of the PivotTable Wizard.

e.g. **EXAMPLE** Figure P.1 shows the layout of a sample pivot table, as developed in Step 3 of the PivotTable Wizard dialog box. The source of the data in this example is a database of computer consultants who work in major cities in four different regions. The database contains fields for each consultant's name, region, city, specialty area, hourly rate, and number of years in business. (Turn to the Database entry to examine the database itself.)

In this pivot table, City is the ROW field and Specialty is the COLUMN field. The two DATA fields are Years and Rate, and the summary operation selected for these fields is Average. Finally, the PAGE field is Region.

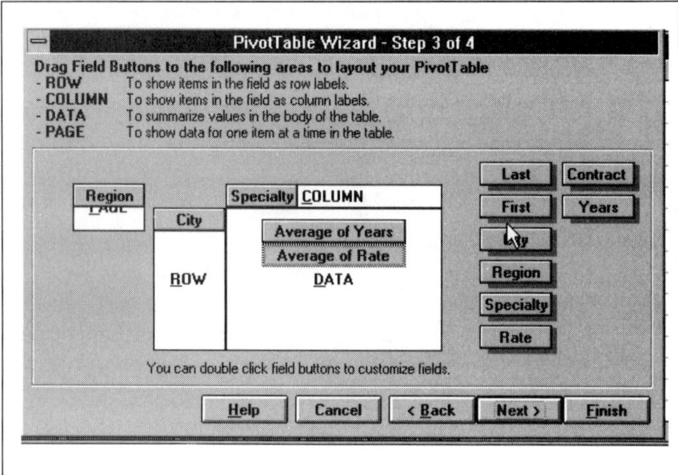

Figure P.1: Developing a pivot table

As shown in Figure P.2, the resulting pivot table contains rows for the average years in business and the average hourly rate for the consultants in a given city. Columns C, D, and E provide the averages for the three specialty areas, and column F gives the city-wide and region-wide averages. Notice that the field names are displayed in gray, button-like cells on the pivot table; as you'll soon see, you can drag these fields to new locations in the worksheet to reorganize the layout of the pivot table.

In cell B1, the Region field is displayed with an accompanying drop-down arrow, indicating that this is a PAGE field. You can click this arrow to view a list of all the regions in the database; when you make a selection from the list, the pivot table immediately displays the summary data for the region you've selected.

To Change the Layout of a Pivot Table

On the worksheet that contains the pivot table, use the mouse to drag a field from one area of the layout to another. This is a quick visual way to transform a PAGE, ROW, COLUMN, or DATA field to another role in the table's layout.

CONSULT.XLS

	A	B	C	D	E	F
1	Region	S				
2						
3			Specialty			
4	City	Data	Database	Spreadsheet	WP	Grand Total
5	Atlanta	Average of Years	3.0	5.7	7.0	5.2
6		Average of Rate	125.00	125.00	75.00	108.33
7	Dallas	Average of Years	6.3	2.7	7.1	5.4
8		Average of Rate	150.00	150.00	100.00	133.33
9	Total Average of Years		4.7	4.2	7.0	5.3
10	Total Average of Rate		137.50	137.50	87.50	120.83
11						

Pivot Table / Consultant List / Sheet2 / S

Figure P.2: A pivot table with a PAGE field

NOTES Another way to change a field in a pivot table is to click the field with the right mouse pointer, and choose the PivotTable Field command in the shortcut menu. In the resulting dialog box you can select a new option in the Orientation group (Row, Column, or Page). You can also select a summary function for the field and select a category of data to be hidden in the field.

For other changes in the layout of a pivot table, activate the worksheet containing the table, and click the PivotTable Wizard button on the Query and Pivot toolbar. Step 3 of the PivotTable Wizard appears on the screen, and you can use this dialog box to reorganize your table in any way you wish.

e.g. **EXAMPLE** Figure P.3 shows what happens to the Consultant pivot table when you drag the region field from its original position in the PAGE area down to the beginning of the ROW area. Instead of showing one region's summary data at a time, the table now shows all four regions in one worksheet.

To Update a Pivot Table

1. Activate the list or database that the pivot table is based on, and make any changes that you wish to make in the

	A	B	C	D	E	F	G
3				Specialty			
4	Region	City	Data	Database	Spreadsheet	WP	Grand Total
5	E	Boston	Average of Years	7.0	6.7	7.5	7.1
6			Average of Rate	100.00	150.00	125.00	125.00
7		New York	Average of Years	7.0	7.4	6.5	6.9
8			Average of Rate	125.00	100.00	150.00	125.00
9	E Average of Years			7.0	7.0	7.0	7.0
10	E Average of Rate			112.50	125.00	137.50	125.00
11	N	Chicago	Average of Years	6.1	2.2	2.6	3.6
12			Average of Rate	150.00	100.00	100.00	116.67
13	N Average of Years			6.1	2.2	2.6	3.6
14	N Average of Rate			150.00	100.00	100.00	116.67
15	S	Atlanta	Average of Years	3.0	5.7	7.0	5.2
16			Average of Rate	125.00	125.00	75.00	108.33
17		Dallas	Average of Years	6.3	2.7	7.1	5.4
18			Average of Rate	150.00	150.00	100.00	133.33
19	S Average of Years			4.7	4.2	7.0	5.3
20	S Average of Rate			137.50	137.50	87.50	120.83

Pivot Table / Consultant List / Sheet2 / Sheet3 / She

Figure P.3: Reorganizing the pivot table

source data—specifically, in the fields that are part of the DATA area in the pivot table.

2. Activate the worksheet that contains the pivot table.

3. Choose Data ➤ Refresh Data. Excel updates the information in the table.

Shortcut Activate the worksheet that contains the pivot table and click the Refresh Data button on the Query and Pivot toolbar.

NOTES Although you can reorganize a pivot table interactively—by dragging its fields to new areas, as described earlier in this entry—you cannot directly edit information in the DATA area of the table. An attempt to do so results in an error message.

To Copy All the Pages of a Pivot Table

1. Point to any part of the table and click the right mouse button to view the pivot table shortcut menu.

2. Choose the Show Pages command from the menu. The Show Pages dialog box displays a list of all the PAGE fields on the current pivot table.
3. Select the field whose pages you want to copy, and click OK. Excel copies each page of the pivot table to its own new worksheet in the current workbook.

Shortcut Click the Show Pages button on the Query and Pivot toolbar to open the Show Pages dialog box.

To View the Source Data for Any Item in the DATA Area

Double-click an item in the DATA area. In response, Excel creates a new worksheet, and copies to it all the database records that are the source data for the item you've clicked.

See Also Data Form, Database, Filters, Lists.

POINT SIZE

The size of the type in a given font is measured in points, where one inch is equivalent to 72 points. You can choose from a range of point sizes in a selected font.

To Change the Font Size in a Range of Cells

1. Select the range, choose Format ➤ Cells, and click the Font tab.
2. Select a size in the scrollable Size list, or enter a size value directly into the Size text box. Then click OK.

Shortcuts Select a size from the Font Size list in the Formatting toolbar, or enter a size into the box. Legal sizes range from 1 to 409 points.

Click the Increase Font Size button or the Decrease Font Size button. Each time you click one of these tools, the size changes to the next higher or lower available measurement. These buttons are not initially part of any toolbar; to use them, you have to add them to a new or existing toolbar. (See Toolbars for details.)

NOTES When you change the point size in a range of cells on a worksheet, Excel automatically adjusts the row height to accommodate the new size.

You can also change the font of any text displayed in a chart, including titles, legend text, and labels displayed along axes. (See Charting.)

See Also Fonts, Formatting Worksheet Cells, Row Height.

PREVIEWING

The File ➤ Print Preview command displays a preview window in which you can see how each page of the active sheet will look on the printed page. This window gives you the opportunity to examine the document's page layout, formatting, and content before you actually print it.

To Preview a Document Before You Print It

Activate the sheet that you want to preview, and choose File ➤ Print Preview. The preview window displays a full-page picture of the sheet. Across the top of the window you'll find a variety of tools you can use to study or modify the printed sheet:

- Click the Next or Previous tool to scroll to the next or previous page in the sheet.

- Click the Zoom button (or point to the sheet itself and click the mouse button when you see the magnifying glass pointer) to enlarge the view of the printed document. In the Zoom mode, use the scroll bars to move up, down, or across the document. To return to the regular page preview display, click the mouse anywhere on the zoomed document.
- Click the Print button to open the Print dialog box, or the Setup button to open the Page Setup dialog box.
- Click the Margins button if you want to adjust margins in your document. Excel displays margin lines and handles that you can drag to make visual adjustments in the top, bottom, left, or right margins. For a worksheet, Excel also displays handles to represent the current column widths; you can drag any of these handles to increase or decrease the width of a column. Click the Margins button again to remove the margin handles from the window.
- Click Close to return to your document in the Excel application window.

Shortcuts Click the Print Preview button on the Standard toolbar to open the preview window. Alternatively, hold down the Shift key and click the Print tool on the Standard toolbar.

See Also Page Setup, Printing Charts, Printing Worksheets.

PRINTER SETUP

To select a printer on a system that includes more than one, you can click the Printer Setup button on the File ➤ Print dialog box. To change a printer's operational settings, you then click the Setup button on the Printer Setup dialog box. Printer settings for a given driver are used by all the applications you run in Windows.

To Change the Printer Settings

1. Choose File ➤ Print, and then click the Printer Setup button on the Print dialog box.
2. Select a printer driver from the list. If you have no changes to make in the settings of this driver, click OK to return to the Print dialog box.
3. If you want to change the settings of the driver you've selected, click the Setup button on the Printer Setup dialog box. The options displayed in the resulting Setup dialog box vary according to the characteristics and capabilities of a given printer.
4. After you change the printer settings, click OK on the Setup and Printer Setup dialog boxes. This returns you to the Print dialog box.

NOTES You can also get to the Setup dialog box by choosing File ➤ Page Setup and then clicking the Options button.

See Also Page Setup, Printing Charts, Printing Worksheets.

PRINTING CHARTS

To print a chart without its source worksheet, you must create the chart in a sheet of its own, not as an embedded object in a worksheet. Using the Page Setup command, you can specify how you want the chart sheet to appear on the printed page.

To Print a Chart Sheet

1. Activate the chart sheet that you want to print.
2. Choose File ➤ Page Setup. In the Page Setup dialog box, click the Chart tab, and then select one of the three option buttons in the Printed Chart Size group:

   - Use Full Page stretches the chart over the length and width of the page, ignoring the chart's height-to-width ratio.
   - Scale to Fit Page fills as much of the printed page as possible, while maintaining the height-to-width ratio that you have established in the chart's plot area.
   - Custom prints the chart in the same size as the actual chart window you have produced.
3. Click OK. Then choose File ➤ Print to open the Print dialog box. Enter a new value in the Copies text box if you want to print more than one copy of the chart. Click OK to begin printing.

Shortcuts Click the Print button on the Standard toolbar to print the chart. This tool bypasses the Print dialog box, and begins printing immediately.

NOTES When you print a full-color screen chart on a black-and-white printer, Excel selects shades of gray, black, white to substitute for the colors. The effect may be clearer and visually more effective if you select the Print in Black and White option in the Chart tab of the Page Setup dialog box. Experiment with this option and decide which effect you prefer.

See Also Charting, Colors, Patterns, Previewing, Printer Setup, Printing Worksheets.

PRINTING WORKSHEETS

The File ➤ Print command gives you the options of printing a selection of worksheet data, the active sheet, a selection of sheets, or an entire workbook.

To Print Information from a Workbook

1. Open and activate the workbook that contains the information you want to print.
2. Make one of the following selections:
   - Select a range if you want to print a selection of data.
   - Activate a worksheet if you want to print that sheet alone.
   - Select two or more sheets if you want to print multiple sheets in one operation. (To select a range of contiguous sheets, click the tab of the first sheet, hold down the shift key, and then click the tab of the last sheet. To select noncontiguous sheets, hold down the Ctrl key while you click the tabs of the sheets you want to include in the selection. See Workbooks for more information.)
   - Activate any sheet if you want to print the entire workbook.
3. Choose File ➤ Print. The Print dialog box appears.
4. Select an option in the Print What group:
   - Click the Selection option to print a range you have selected. (If you select this option, Excel ignores any Print Area specified in the Page Setup dialog box.)
   - Click the Selected Sheets option to print the active sheet or the multiple sheets you have selected.

- Click Entire Workbook to print sheets or designated print areas on all the sheets of the workbook.

5. If you want to change any aspect of the page layout, click the Page Setup button and select options in the various tabs of the resulting dialog box. (See Page Setup for details.) Click OK to return to the Print dialog box.
6. In the Copies box, enter the number of copies if you want more than one.
7. In the Print Range group, click Pages and enter a range of page numbers in the From and To boxes if you want to print less than the entire document.
8. Click OK to begin printing.

Shortcuts Click the Print button on the Standard toolbar to print the document immediately without viewing the Print dialog box.

To Set a Manual Page Break

1. Activate the worksheet on which you want to define a page break.
2. Select a column for a vertical page break, a row for a horizontal page break, or a single cell for both.
3. Choose Insert ➤ Page Break.

NOTES Manual page breaks appear just above a selected row, just to the left of a selected column, or just above and to the left of a selected cell. Excel marks manual page breaks with a line of dashes. If you do not set manual page breaks, Excel calculates automatic page breaks appropriate for the page size and the margin settings.

To remove a manual page break, select the row, column, or cell where the page break is located, and choose Insert ➤ Remove Page Break.

See Also Page Setup, Previewing, Printer Setup, Printing Charts.

PROTECTING CELLS IN A WORKSHEET

By applying cell protection to a worksheet, you can prevent any changes to the entries in the cells, and you can hide the formulas in the cells. Cell protection is a two-step process: First you select a combination of protection options from the Protection tab of the Format ➤ Cells command, and then you activate the protection by choosing the Protect Sheet command in the Tools ➤ Protection submenu. You can create a password to prevent others from removing the protection.

To Protect a Range of Cells on a Worksheet

1. Select a range in which you want to change the protection options.
2. Choose Format ➤ Cells, and click the Protection tab. The resulting dialog box has two check box options: Locked prevents changes to entries in the cells, and Hidden hides the formulas in the cells. (By default, the Locked option is checked for all cells in a worksheet.)
3. Check the combination of options that you want to apply to the current range, and click OK.
4. If you want to select different protection options for different ranges on the worksheet, repeat steps 1 through 3 for each range you want to change.
5. Choose Tools ➤ Protection and click the Protect Sheet command in the resulting submenu. The Protect Sheet dialog box has three check box options: Contents, Objects, and

Scenarios. (All three are checked by default; the Contents box must remain checked to activate cell protection.)

6. If you want to use a password to enforce protection, enter a word into the Password text box. Excel displays an asterisk for each character you type.
7. Click OK. If you are using a password, the Confirm Password dialog box appears. Enter the password again and click OK to confirm. Cell protection is now active in the selected range.

Shortcuts You can use the Lock Cell button to change the Locked status of a range of cells or an object. This button is a toggle: click it once to remove the Locked status—because Locked is checked by default for all cells and objects—and click it again to reapply the status. To use this button, you first have to add it to a toolbar. (See Toolbars for instructions.)

NOTES To lock the cells only in a selected range of a worksheet, begin by selecting the entire worksheet (click the Select All button) and unchecking the Locked option on the Protection tab of the Format ➤ Cells command. Then select the range you want to lock, and reset the Locked option for this range. Finally, choose the Protect Sheet command from the Tools ➤ Protection submenu to activate the selected protection options.

Once you activate protection, no changes are allowed in the contents of locked cells. If you try to enter a new value or formula into a locked cell, a warning box appears with the message "Locked cells cannot be changed." Excel also dims menu commands that would result in changes to the protected worksheet. If you have selected the Hidden option as well, no formula or other entry appears in the formula bar when you select a cell in the protected range.

Formulas in locked cells can still be recalculated. For example, if you change a value in an unlocked cell that affects a formula in a locked cell, Excel recalculates the formula and displays the new result.

You can copy a protected range of cells. Select the range and choose Edit ➤ Copy; then choose an unlocked range on the current worksheet—or activate an unprotected worksheet—and choose Edit ➤ Paste. If the Hidden option is checked for the source worksheet range, Excel copies only values—not formulas—to the destination worksheet. (Any formulas in the source are converted to their current values in the destination.)

To Remove Cell Protection

1. Select the sheet where you want to remove protection.
2. Choose the Tools ➤ Protection, and click the Unprotect Sheet command.
3. If you used a password to protect the cells, you must now reenter the password to remove protection. If there is no password, Excel removes protection immediately.

See Also Copying Data, Formatting Worksheet Cells, Formula Bar, Formulas, Hiding, Passwords, Protecting Workbooks.

PROTECTING WORKBOOKS

The Protect Workbook command in the Tools ➤ Protection submenu prevents changes in the structure of a workbook and the appearance of its window.

To Protect a Workbook

1. Open and activate the workbook.
2. Choose Tools ➤ Protection and click the Protect Workbook command.

3. Select any combination of the two check boxes in the resulting dialog box:

   - The Structure option (checked by default) prevents changes in the sheet structure of the workbook. When this option is activated, you cannot add, remove, rename, hide, unhide, or rearrange the sheets on a workbook.
   - The Windows option (unchecked by default) prevents changes in the appearance of the workbook window. When this option is activated, you cannot move, resize, minimize, maximize or hide the window. The control-menu box is removed from the window, as are the minimize, maximize, and restore buttons.

4. Optionally, enter a password into the Password text box.
5. Click OK.
6. If you entered a password, the Confirm Password dialog box appears. Reenter the password to confirm. Then click OK.

NOTES To unprotect a workbook, choose Tools ➤ Protection and click the Unprotect Workbook command. If the workbook is protected with a password, you'll have to enter the password correctly to remove protection.

See Also Passwords, Protecting Cells in a Worksheet.

QUERY

Microsoft Query is a Windows database application that comes with Excel. You can run Query on its own in Windows to gain access to databases created in a variety of programs, including Access, FoxPro, dBASE, and Excel itself. Or, with Query and an add-in macro named XLQUERY.XLA, you can extract data from external database files and then transfer the data to Excel for further work.

To Load the XLQUERY.XLA Add-In Macro

1. Choose Tools ➤ Add-Ins from Excel's menu bar. The Add-Ins dialog box appears.
2. In the Add-Ins Available list, scroll to the Xlquery entry.
3. If the option is not checked, click it. An X appears in the corresponding check box.
4. Click OK.

NOTES If Xlquery does not appear in the Add-Ins Available list, click the Browse button, and search for the add-in file in the EXCEL\LIBRARY\MSQUERY directory. If you don't find it, you'll have to rerun Microsoft Excel Setup to install Microsoft Query on your hard disk. Double-click the Setup icon in the Microsoft Office group. In the first Setup dialog box, click the Add/Remove icon. Next select the Data Access option and click the Change Option button. In the Data Access dialog box, check the options that you want to install—including Microsoft Query and the database drivers that correspond to the data formats you'll be working with. Complete the setup process by following the instructions that appear on the screen.

When you load XLQUERY.XLA, the Get External Data command appears in Excel's Data menu.

To Work with Data from an External Database

1. In Excel, activate the worksheet you'll use to work with the data. Then choose Data ➤ Get External Data. The Microsoft Query application window opens onto the desktop.
2. The Select Data Source dialog box appears on the screen. To identify a new data source, click the Other button.
3. The ODBC Data Sources dialog box appears. (ODBC stands for *Open Database Connectivity.*) Click New.
4. The Add Data Source dialog box appears. Select the driver that corresponds to the data format that you want to work with, and click OK.

5. Use the next dialog box to identify the path location and file location of the database you want to use, and click OK. Click OK again on the ODBC Data Sources dialog box. Then click Use on the Available Data Sources dialog box.
6. A new Query window opens, and the Add Tables dialog box also appears on the screen. This box contains a list of the tables available in the database you've opened.
7. Select a table to add to your query and click Add. Optionally, repeat this step to add multiple related tables to your query. When you've selected the tables you want, click Close on the Add Tables dialog box.
8. Drag fields, one at a time, from the table (or tables) down to the columns of the data grid in the lower half of the Query window. As you do so, Microsoft Query displays the corresponding database records.
9. When you have completed the query definition, choose File ➤ Return Data to Microsoft Excel, or click the Return Data to Excel button on the Microsoft Query toolbar. Excel reopens onto the screen, and the Get External Data dialog appears.
10. Select any of the available options. In particular, the Keep Query Definition box should be checked if you want to be able to update information when changes occur in the original database.
11. Click OK to continue. Records from the Query you've developed are copied to the active worksheet.

NOTES If you use the Microsoft Access database management program, the process of developing a query will be familiar to you. The graphical interface in Microsoft Query is similar to the query component of Access.

When the result of the query appears in your worksheet, you can work with the data just as you would with any other list or database in Excel. For example, you can activate filters, perform sorts, or open a data form to view the data one record at a time. (See Filters, Sorting, and Data Form for details.)

To Modify a Query

Double-click in any cell of the database table in your worksheet. In response, Excel switches you back to Microsoft Query, where you can make any changes to the query—such as adding or deleting fields or tables. Click the Return Data to Excel button when you've finished making changes in the query.

To Update a Query

Choose Data ➤ Get External Data, and click the Refresh button on the resulting dialog box. Excel replaces the current table with the latest information from the database.

 **See Also** Add-Ins, Database, Database Criteria, Filters, Lists.

RECALCULATION

By default, recalculation is automatic in Excel. This means that Excel recalculates dependent formulas whenever you change an entry on a worksheet. In some circumstances—notably when you are dealing with a detailed worksheet containing complex formulas—you may want to switch to manual recalculation. Under this setting, Excel recalculates open worksheets only on command.

To Switch to Manual Recalculation

1. Choose Tools ➤ Options, and click the Calculation tab on the Options dialog box.
2. In the Calculation group, select the Manual option button, and then click OK.

NOTES Under the Manual recalculation setting, the status bar displays the word Calculate whenever a change takes place that would affect the result of a dependent formula. In other words, when you see the word *Calculate*, you know that one or more formulas need to be recalculated.

To Recalculate Manually

1. Choose Tools ➤ Options and click the Calculation tab.
2. Click the Calc Now button to recalculate worksheets on all open workbooks, or click Calc Sheet to calculate the active worksheet.

Shortcuts

- Press the F9 function key or press Ctrl-= to recalculate all open workbooks.
- Press Shift-F9 to recalculate the active worksheet.

NOTES When you use these techniques to recalculate, the word *Calculate* disappears from the status bar.

To switch back to automatic recalculation, choose Tools ➤ Options, click the Calculation tab, select the Automatic option, and click OK.

See Also Formula Bar, Formulas, Info Window, Iteration.

REFERENCES

A reference identifies a cell or a range of cells by position on a worksheet. In a formula, a reference stands for the value stored in a cell or the values stored in a range. For the purposes of copying a formula, you can write a reference in any of three types—relative, absolute, or mixed—depending on how you want the reference to appear in copies you make of the formula. Excel also has two different reference styles, known as the A1 and R1C1 styles; each style has its own way of denoting relative, absolute, and mixed references.

An *external reference* identifies a cell or range on another workbook, and creates a link between two workbooks. A *3-D Reference* is a reference to a cell or range of cells on two or more contiguous worksheets in a workbook.

To Change a Reference Type in the Formula Bar

Position the insertion point just after the reference in the active formula bar, or highlight the entire reference in the case of a range. Then press the F4 function key one or more times to change the reference from relative to absolute to mixed.

NOTES Press F4 four times to step through the complete cycle of reference types and back to the original reference. In the A1 reference style, Excel uses dollar signs to denote absolute or mixed references. For example:

- $E$9 is an absolute reference. When you copy a formula containing $E$9 as an operand, the reference is copied unchanged and always refers to cell E9.
- E$9 is a mixed reference, where the column reference (E) is relative and the row reference ($9) is absolute. When you copy a formula containing E$9 as an operand, the reference to row 9 remains fixed, but the reference to column E can change relative to the column of the copied formula.
- $E9 is a mixed reference, where the column reference ($E) is absolute and the row reference (9) is relative. When you copy a formula containing $E9 as an operand, the reference to column E remains fixed, but the reference to row 9 can change relative to the row of the copied formula.
- E9 is a relative reference, where both the column and the row are relative. When you copy a formula containing E9 as an operand, both the column and the row can change relative to the position of the copied formula.

See Copying Formulas for more information and examples.

Excel has an alternate reference style, known as R1C1, in which columns and rows are both numbered on the worksheet.

To Change to the R1C1 Reference Style

1. Choose Tools ➤ Options, and click the General tab on the Options dialog box.
2. In the Reference Style group, click the R1C1 option button.
3. Click OK.

NOTES When you make this change, the letter column headings are replaced with numbers on all worksheets in all workbooks. Columns are numbered from 1 to 256. For example, the A1-style reference E9 becomes R9C5 in the R1C1 style.

A relative reference in the R1C1 style is denoted with brackets around the relative portions of the reference. For example:

- R[9]C[5] is a relative reference to the cell that is nine rows down and five columns to the right of the current cell. R[– 9]C[–5] is a reference to the cell that is nine rows up and five columns to the left of the current cell.
- R9C[5] is a mixed reference to the cell in row 9 that is five columns to the right of the current cell.
- R[9]C5 is a mixed reference to the cell in column 5 that is nine rows down from the current cell.
- R9C5 is an absolute reference to the cell at the intersection of row 9 and column 5—in other words, cell E9 in the A1 reference style.

NOTES To switch back to A1-style references, choose Tools ➤ Options, click the General tab, and select the A1 option in the Reference Style group. Then click OK.

To Create an External Reference

1. Open the workbooks that will become the source and the destination of the data, and activate the target worksheets in both workbooks. For convenience, choose Window ➤ Arrange, select Tiled, and click OK, to display the two windows side by side on the screen.
2. Select the cell in the destination workbook where you want to create an external reference.
3. Enter an equal sign (=) to begin a formula.
4. Activate the source worksheet, point to the cell for which you want to create a reference, and click the mouse button. Excel creates an external reference on the destination workbook.
5. Press ↵ to complete the formula.

NOTES An external reference has the following format:

=[BookName]SheetName!Reference

For example, here is an absolute reference to cell B8 on Sheet1 of Book1:

=[Book1]Sheet1!$B$8

You can also use the Edit ➤ Copy and Edit ➤ Paste Special commands to enter an external reference and create a link between worksheets. (See Links and 3-D Formulas for details.)

A reference from one worksheet to another within a workbook takes the following shorter form:

=SheetName!Reference

A 3-D reference identifies the same cell or range on a sequence of contiguous worksheets. For example, the following SUM formula contains a 3-D reference to a particular cell on a range of five worksheets:

=SUM(Sheet1:Sheet5!$B$8)

See Links and 3-D formulas for more information.

See Also Array Formulas, Copying Formulas, Formula Bar, Formulas, Info Window, Links and 3-D Formulas, Names, Summation.

REPEATING COMMANDS

The Edit ➤ Repeat command gives you a quick way to repeat the last operation you performed in Excel.

To Repeat the Previous Command

Pull down the Edit menu and choose the Repeat command.

Shortcuts Click the Repeat button on the Standard toolbar, or press F4 or Alt-↵.

NOTES If the previous command cannot be repeated, Repeat is dimmed in the Edit menu, or the command is displayed as Can't Repeat.

You can perform an operation in one workbook, such as a formatting command or File ➤ Page Setup, and then repeat the same operation in another workbook. After completing the operation in the first workbook, activate the second workbook and then choose Edit ➤ Repeat.

See Also Group Editing, Undo.

REPLACING WORKSHEET DATA

The Edit ➤ Replace command searches for an entry or part of an entry in a worksheet and replaces it with another entry.

To Replace Data in a Worksheet or Macro Sheet

1. Activate the sheet in which you want to replace data, and choose Edit ➤ Replace. The Replace dialog box appears on the screen.
2. In the Find What box, enter the text that you want to replace.
3. In the Replace With box, enter the replacement text.
4. In the Search list, select By Rows to search from the top to the bottom of your worksheet, or By Columns to search from left to right.
5. Click the Match Case option, placing an X in its check box, if you want Excel to search for the text in the exact uppercase and lowercase combinations you entered into the Find What box. Leave this option unchecked if you want to perform the search without regard for alphabetic case.
6. Click the Find Entire Cells Only option, placing an X in its check box, if the text you have entered in the Find What box represents an entire cell entry; leave the option unchecked if you want to search for the text as a portion of a cell entry.
7. To begin the search-and-replace operation, use any sequence of the following command buttons:
   - Click Find Next to find the next occurrence of the Find What text, or hold down the Shift key and click Find Next to find the previous occurrence.

- Click Replace to replace the target text in the current cell and then find the next occurrence.
- Click Replace All to replace all the remaining occurrences of the target text and close the Replace dialog box.
- Click Close to close the Replace dialog box without changing any additional entries.

NOTES If Excel does not find the target text in your worksheet, a dialog box appears on the screen with the message Cannot find matching data to replace. If the search is unsuccessful, but you believe the text does exist in your worksheet, reopen the Replace dialog box and make sure you have selected the appropriate settings for the Match Case and Find Entire Cells Only options.

You can use wildcard characters in the search text: ? stands for a single unspecified character, and * stands for a string of unspecified characters.

To restrict the search-and-replace operation to a specific range of cells on your worksheet, select the range before choosing the Replace command. Otherwise, Excel searches through the entire worksheet for the target text. To perform a search-and-replace over a group of worksheets, select all the worksheets before choosing Edit ➤ Replace.

e.g. **EXAMPLE** You can use Edit ➤ Replace to edit formulas on a worksheet. For example, to change all the SUM functions on a worksheet to AVERAGE functions, follow these steps:

1. Activate the worksheet and choose Edit ➤ Replace.
2. Enter SUM in the Find What box and AVERAGE in the Replace With box.
3. Make sure the Find Entire Cells Only option is *not* checked.
4. Click the Replace All button.

Excel replaces the functions as instructed, and immediately recalculates the edited formulas.

 **See Also** Finding Worksheet Data.

REPORTS

A report is a printed sequence of scenarios and views that you have defined for a workbook. The Report Manager is an add-in that prints reports from the definitions you create using two other Excel features:

- The View Manager (View ➤ View Manager) lets you define different ways of displaying and printing the information in a worksheet.
- The Scenario Manager (Tools ➤ Scenarios) lets you define sets of input values for a variety of different "what-if" scenarios on a worksheet.

Given these two kinds of definitions, the Report Manager combines scenarios and views in any way you choose, and prints the resulting report.

To Create and Print a Report

1. Activate a workbook containing data from which you want to create a report.
2. Choose Tools ➤ Scenarios and create the scenarios you want in your report. (See Scenarios for steps and examples.)
3. Choose View ➤ View Manager and create the views you want to use in your report. (See Views for details.)
4. Choose File ➤ Print Report. The Print Report dialog box appears. If this is the first time you have used the Report Manager for this workbook, the list box labeled Reports is empty. A column of command buttons appears at the right side of the dialog box.

5. Click the Add button to create a report and assign it a name. The Add Report dialog box appears on the screen.
6. In the Report Name box, enter a name to identify the report you are about to create, and then read the instructions displayed beneath the text box. As you can see, a report consists of sections, where each section is characterized by a sheet selection from the active workbook, a view, and/or a scenario that you select.
7. If the Sheet box does not display the sheet you want to include in the current section, pull down the Sheet list and select a name.
8. Pull down the View list and select a view for the current section of the report.
9. Pull down the Scenario list and select a scenario for the current section.
10. Click the Add button. Excel displays a description of the section in the list labeled Sections in this Report.
11. Repeat steps 7 through 10 for each section that you want to include in your report. Then click OK when you have defined all the sections.
12. Back in the Print Report dialog box, select the name of the report you want to print from the Reports list. Then click Print.
13. In the Print dialog box, enter the number of copies you want to print of your report, and click OK. Excel begins printing your report.

NOTES You can define multiple reports in the Report Manager, and assign a name to each one. When you save your workbook, Excel saves the report definitions as well as the scenarios and views. To print another defined report, choose File ➤ Print Report, select the name of the report you want to print, and click Print.

The Report Manager and the View Manager are add-ins; the Scenario Manager is not. As you begin using these three commands, you may begin to think of them as three parts of the same feature, the goal of which is to print multisection reports from detailed worksheet scenarios.

See Also Add-Ins, Scenarios, Views.

ROW HEIGHT

Adjusting the height of a row allows you to display multiple lines of text within a single cell, or to display large or small font sizes within the row.

To Change the Height of a Single Row

1. Select a cell in the row, or click the row heading to select the entire row.
2. Choose Format ➤ Row, and then click Height on the resulting submenu.
3. Enter a new value in the Row Height text box, and then click OK.

Shortcuts Position the mouse pointer over the line located just under the row's heading, and drag the line down (for a greater height) or up (for a smaller height). Double-click the line to adjust the row height to the best fit for the current contents. Alternatively, point to the row heading, press the right mouse button, and choose Row Height from the shortcut menu to view the Row Height dialog box.

To enter a multiline title in a cell, follow these general steps:

1. Select the cell, and type a line of text. Then press Alt-↵ to insert a carriage return into the entry. The height of the formula bar increases to accommodate the next line of the entry.

2. Repeat step 1 for each line of text that you want to include in the entry.
3. Press ↵ to complete the entry. Excel automatically wraps the text in the cell, but not necessarily in the same line arrangement as your original entry.
4. Optionally, adjust the column width and the row height to produce the text arrangement you want.

NOTES To change the heights of a group of rows, select the rows and choose the Format ➤ Row Height command.

The standard row height row is the best fit for the largest font displayed in the row. Excel automatically adjusts the height of a row when you change the font of an entry in the row.

See Also Alignment, Column Width, Fonts, Hiding, Point Size.

SAVING FILES

Use the File ➤ Save As command to save a workbook to disk for the first time. Use File ➤ Save to update a file after you have made changes in a workbook.

To Save an Excel Workbook to Disk for the First Time

1. Choose File ➤ Save As.
2. If necessary, use the Directories and Drives list boxes to select the path for saving the file. (To change from one directory to another, double-click a name in the Directories list.)
3. Enter a name for the workbook in the File Name box.

4. If you want to save the file in a format other than Excel's Workbook format, click the arrow next to the Save File as Type list, and select a format.
5. Click OK to save the file.

Shortcuts Press F12 or Alt-F2 to open the Save As dialog box. Or, click the Save button on the Standard toolbar for a workbook that you have not saved before; Excel recognizes that you are saving the file for the first time, and opens the Save As dialog box.

NOTES Click the Options button on the Save As dialog box if you want to create passwords for restricting access to the current file. (See Passwords for details.) In addition, the Save Options dialog box has a check box labeled Always Create Backup. If you check this option, Excel automatically maintains a backup copy (with a .BAK extension) each time you save the file.

To Update a File after Making Changes in a Workbook

Activate the Workbook and choose File ➤ Save.

Shortcuts Click the Save tool on the Standard toolbar, or press Shift-F12.

See Also Add-Ins, Directories, Exiting Excel, File Formats, Links and 3-D Formulas, Opening Files, Passwords, Protecting Workbooks, Window Operations.

SCENARIOS

Using the Scenario Manager, you can define and save sets of input data for exploring "what-if" scenarios on a worksheet. The Scenario Manager is especially useful on a worksheet that is organized into distinct "input" and "output" areas. In this context, the input area displays the values that serve as parameters for calculations performed in the output area. When you select a scenario, Excel enters the input values into specified cells and recalculates the worksheet accordingly.

To Define and View Scenarios on a Worksheet

1. Develop a worksheet that uses a range of input values to calculate data in an output area.
2. Assign names to the cells containing the input values—see the Names entry for instructions. (These names are optional, but they make the Scenario Manager easier to use, as you'll see shortly.)
3. Choose Tools ➤ Scenarios. The Scenario Manager dialog box contains boxes labeled Changing Cells and Comment, along with a column of command buttons. If this is the first time you've created a scenario in the active worksheet, a list box in the upper-left corner of the dialog box displays the message No Scenarios defined. Choose Add to add scenarios.
4. Click the Add button. The Add Scenario dialog box appears on the screen. In the Scenario Name box, enter a name for the scenario you're creating. Then activate the Changing Cells text box.
5. On the active worksheet, point to the range of cells that contains the input values. If values are displayed in a noncontiguous range, hold down the Ctrl key while you point to multiple ranges. As you do so, Excel enters the appropriate references into the Changing Cells box. (Multiple noncontiguous references are separated by commas.)
6. Optionally, revise the text displayed in the Comment box. This box is for any description you want to save along with the scenario. Then click OK on the Add Scenario dialog box.
7. The Scenario Values dialog box appears on the screen. It contains a column of text boxes labeled with the names

you assigned to the selected input cells on your worksheet. The text boxes themselves contain the current data from those input cells. (If you did not assign names, the boxes are instead labeled with absolute references.) You can enter or edit values in the text boxes to supply the input data for a scenario. Alternatively—for the first scenario you define—you may want to keep the current data, which Excel has copied directly from your worksheet. Click OK when the input data is complete for the current scenario. The Scenario Manager dialog box returns to the screen, and the name of the scenario you've just defined appears in the Scenarios list.

8. Repeat steps 4 through 7 for each scenario you want to define. Each scenario you create can contain a different set of input values to be used in calculating formulas on the worksheet.
9. To view a scenario, highlight its name in the Scenarios list on the Scenario Manager dialog box and then click the Show button. Excel replaces the entries in the input cells with the values of the selected scenario, and recalculates the worksheet accordingly.
10. Repeat step 9 for all the scenarios you want to view, and then click the Close button.

NOTES When you save your worksheet, Excel saves all the scenario definitions along with it. To review a particular scenario, open the worksheet and choose the Tools ➤ Scenarios command. To print a sequence of scenarios, activate the worksheet on which you have defined scenarios and choose the File ➤ Print Report command. (See Reports for complete instructions.)

To Create a Scenario Summary

1. Activate the worksheet on which you have defined the scenarios, and choose Tools ➤ Scenarios.
2. Click the Summary button. The Scenario Summary dialog box appears on the screen.

3. In the Report Type group, click the Scenario Summary option button if it is not already selected. In the Result Cells box, enter a reference to the cell or cells that you want to display as the result of each scenario.

4. Click OK to create the scenario summary. Excel creates a new worksheet in the current workbook to display the summary.

NOTES The summary includes a column of input data for each scenario you have defined, along with the corresponding result cells you chose to include in the summary.

You can also create a pivot table to summarize a set of scenarios. Click the Scenario PivotTable option in the Scenario Summary dialog box. (See the Pivot Tables entry for information about using pivot tables.)

e.g. EXAMPLE Figures S.1 and S.2 illustrate the kind of worksheet organization that is best suited to the features of the Scenario Manager. This example uses a group of six input values to

FirstPmtCalc

	A	B	C	D	E	F	G	H
1				Loan Terms				
2		Price	$200,000					
3		Down	20%		Rate Increment		0.125%	
4		Rate	7.50%		Price Increment		$500	
5		Term	15	years				
6								
7				Monthly Payment Terms				
8		7.500%	7.625%	7.750%	7.875%	8.000%	8.125%	8.250%
9	$160,000	$1,483.22	$1,494.61	$1,506.04	$1,517.52	$1,529.04	$1,540.61	$1,552.22
10	$160,400	$1,486.93	$1,498.34	$1,509.81	$1,521.31	$1,532.87	$1,544.46	$1,556.11
11	$160,800	$1,490.64	$1,502.08	$1,513.57	$1,525.11	$1,536.69	$1,548.31	$1,559.99
12	$161,200	$1,494.34	$1,505.82	$1,517.34	$1,528.90	$1,540.51	$1,552.17	$1,563.87
13	$161,600	$1,498.05	$1,509.55	$1,521.10	$1,532.69	$1,544.33	$1,556.02	$1,567.75
14	$162,000	$1,501.76	$1,513.29	$1,524.87	$1,536.49	$1,548.16	$1,559.87	$1,571.63
15	$162,400	$1,505.47	$1,517.03	$1,528.63	$1,540.28	$1,551.98	$1,563.72	$1,575.51
16	$162,800	$1,509.18	$1,520.76	$1,532.40	$1,544.08	$1,555.80	$1,567.57	$1,579.39
17	$163,200	$1,512.88	$1,524.50	$1,536.16	$1,547.87	$1,559.62	$1,571.42	$1,583.27
18	$163,600	$1,516.59	$1,528.24	$1,539.93	$1,551.66	$1,563.45	$1,575.28	$1,587.15

Scenario Summary / Monthly Payments / Sheet2 / Sh

Figure S.1: Scenario example: "Home1"

FirstPmtCalc

	A	B	C	D	E	F	G	H
1				Loan Terms				
2		Price	$280,000					
3		Down	20%		Rate Increment		0.125%	
4		Rate	6.25%		Price Increment		$1,000	
5		Term	30	years				
6								
7				Monthly Payment Terms				
8		6.250%	6.375%	6.500%	6.625%	6.750%	6.875%	7.000%
9	$224,000	$1,379.21	$1,397.47	$1,415.83	$1,434.30	$1,452.86	$1,471.52	$1,490.28
10	$224,800	$1,384.13	$1,402.46	$1,420.89	$1,439.42	$1,458.05	$1,476.78	$1,495.60
11	$225,600	$1,389.06	$1,407.45	$1,425.95	$1,444.54	$1,463.24	$1,482.03	$1,500.92
12	$226,400	$1,393.98	$1,412.44	$1,431.00	$1,449.66	$1,468.43	$1,487.29	$1,506.24
13	$227,200	$1,398.91	$1,417.43	$1,436.06	$1,454.79	$1,473.61	$1,492.54	$1,511.57
14	$228,000	$1,403.84	$1,422.42	$1,441.12	$1,459.91	$1,478.80	$1,497.80	$1,516.89
15	$228,800	$1,408.76	$1,427.41	$1,446.17	$1,465.03	$1,483.99	$1,503.05	$1,522.21
16	$229,600	$1,413.69	$1,432.41	$1,451.23	$1,470.15	$1,489.18	$1,508.31	$1,527.53
17	$230,400	$1,418.61	$1,437.40	$1,456.28	$1,475.28	$1,494.37	$1,513.56	$1,532.86
18	$231,200	$1,423.54	$1,442.39	$1,461.34	$1,480.40	$1,499.56	$1,518.82	$1,538.18

Scenario Summary | Monthly Payments | Sheet2 | Sh

Figure S.2: Scenario example: "Home2"

generate an output table of monthly home mortgage payment calculations. The input values include.

- The price of a particular home (in cell C2, which is named Price).
- The percent down payment (in C3, named Down).
- The interest rate for the loan (in C4, named Rate).
- The term of the loan in years (in C5, named Term).
- Increment values for the interest rate (in G3, named RateIncr) and the price (in G4, named PriceIncr).

The output (in the range A8:H18) is a lookup table in which you can find the monthly payment corresponding to a particular home price and interest rate. Because each value in the output table is the result of a formula, changing one of the input values results in a completely new table.

To create the scenarios, begin by developing the initial worksheet (as shown in Figure S.1), and then choose Tools ➤ Scenarios. Select the ranges C2:C5 and G3:G4 as the entries in the Changing Cells box, and then define the scenarios (with names like Home1, Home2, and so on). Once you have defined the scenarios, you can quickly view any one of them by selecting a scenario name and clicking the Show button on the Scenario Manager dialog box. Figure S.3 shows a Scenario Summary sheet with input and output values for three such scenarios.

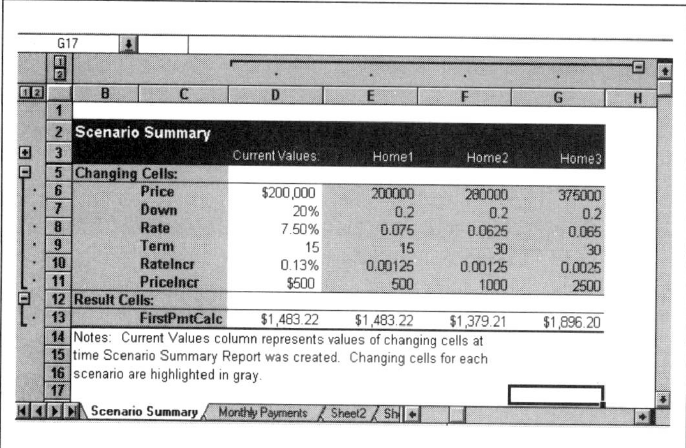

Scenario Summary				
	Current Values:	Home1	Home2	Home3
Changing Cells:				
Price	$200,000	200000	280000	375000
Down	20%	0.2	0.2	0.2
Rate	7.50%	0.075	0.0625	0.065
Term	15	15	30	30
RateIncr	0.13%	0.00125	0.00125	0.0025
PriceIncr	$500	500	1000	2500
Result Cells:				
FirstPmtCalc	$1,483.22	$1,483.22	$1,379.21	$1,896.20

Notes: Current Values column represents values of changing cells at time Scenario Summary Report was created. Changing cells for each scenario are highlighted in gray.

Figure S.3: A scenario summary report

See Also Pivot Tables, Reports, Views.

SELECTING A RANGE

Excel provides a variety of mouse and keyboard techniques for selecting a cell, a range of cells, a group of noncontiguous ranges on a worksheet, or a 3-D range across the sheets of a workbook.

To Select a Cell

Click the cell with the mouse, or move the cell pointer by pressing any combination of arrow keys, →, ←, ↓, or ↑.

NOTES To move quickly to the beginning or end of a block of data in a worksheet, hold down the Ctrl key and press an arrow key in the direction you want to move. Alternatively, press the End key and then press an arrow key. (The notation END appears on the status bar when you press End.)

To Select a Range

Drag the mouse over the range, or hold down the Shift key and press any combination of arrow keys.

NOTES Another keyboard technique for selecting a range is to press the F8 function key to toggle into Extend mode, and then press any combination of arrow keys to select the range. The notation EXT appears on the status bar. Press Esc or F8 again to toggle out of Extend mode.

To Select Noncontiguous Ranges

Select the first range, and then hold down the Ctrl key while you select additional ranges.

NOTES The notation for noncontiguous ranges is a list of range references separated by commas.

To Select a Row or Column

Click the row heading or column heading with the mouse, or press Shift-spacebar for a row or Ctrl-spacebar for a column.

To Select an Entire Worksheet

Click the Select All button located at the intersection of the row and column headings, or press Ctrl-Shift-spacebar.

To Point to a 3-D Range while Entering a Formula

Click the tab of the first worksheet in the 3-D range. Hold down the Shift key while you click the tab of the last worksheet in the range. Then select the cell range. Excel creates a reference such as Sheet1:Sheet5!B2:B7. (See the Links and 3-D Formulas entry for more information.)

See Also Array Formulas, AutoFill, Copying Data, Filling Ranges, Formula Bar, Formulas, Group Editing, Hiding, Links and 3-D Formulas, References, Transposing Ranges.

SERIES

The Series command in the Edit ➤ Fill submenu is a versatile tool for entering series of numeric and date values in the rows or columns of a worksheet. (In this context, a series is a sequence of values in which the entries are calculated from a linear or exponential formula.) In addition to a choice of series types, the Series command gives you control over the step and stop values in a series. The start value is an existing entry in the worksheet range where you create the series. You can also use this command to produce trend series, for which Excel calculates the linear or exponential "best fit" and modifies the data accordingly.

To Create a Series

1. In the first cell of a row or column range on the active worksheet, enter the initial value for the series you want to create. Then select the range for the series.
2. Choose Edit ➤ Fill and then click the Series command in the resulting submenu. The Series dialog box displays

three groups of option buttons, labeled Series In, Type, and Date Unit. For the Series In option, Excel automatically selects Rows or Columns according to the range you have already selected on the worksheet.

3. In the Type group, select the type of data series you want to create. If you select Date, Excel activates the Date Unit group. Select one of the unit options in this group.
4. Optionally, enter a value in the Step Value box. (The default is 1.)
5. Optionally, enter a value in the Stop Value box.
6. Click OK to create the series.

Shortcut You can use Excel's AutoFill feature to create some types of series on a worksheet. See AutoFill for details.

NOTES Excel's use of the Step Value depends on the type of series you select:

- For a linear series, the step value is added to each value to produce the next value in the series.
- For a growth series, each value is multiplied by the step value to produce the next value in the series.
- For a date series, the step value represents the number of days between one entry and the next in the series. (You can further refine the steps of a date series by selecting an option in the Date Unit group.)

The end of a series is determined either by the number you supply as the Stop Value, or by the end of the selected range, whichever comes first.

EXAMPLE Columns A through D in Figure S.4 show examples of date, linear and growth series:

- The date series in column A is a weekday series—that is, a sequence of dates in which Saturdays and Sundays are omitted. To create a series like this one, enter the first date and select the range for the series. Then choose Edit ➤ Fill, click the Series command, and select the Date and Weekday options. (In Figure S.4, the series is formatted by the *ddd, m/d/yy* custom format code; see Custom Number Formats for more information.)

- The date series in column B contains entries that are one month apart. To create this series, select the Date and Month options in the Series dialog box.
- The numeric series in column C is a linear series where the step value from one entry to the next is 0.25. To create this series, select the Linear option in the Series dialog box, and enter 0.25 in the Step Value box.
- The numeric series in column D is a growth series where each value is multiplied by 1.125 to calculate the next value. To create this series, select the Growth option in the Series dialog box, and enter 1.125 in the Step Value box.

SERIES.XLS

	A	B	C	D	E	F	G	H
1		Series Examples						
2								
3	Date	Date	Linear	Growth		Trend		Trend
4	(weekday)	(month)	(step = .25)	(step = 1.125)		(Linear)		(Growth)
5	Mon, 11/1/93	11/1/93	-1	1,000.00	1	1.17	1	1.14
6	Tue, 11/2/93	12/1/93	-0.75	1,125.00	3	2.67	3	2.29
7	Wed, 11/3/93	1/1/94	-0.5	1,265.63	4	4.17	4	4.58
8	Thu, 11/4/93	2/1/94	-0.25	1,423.83		5.67		9.16
9	Fri, 11/5/93	3/1/94	0	1,601.81		7.17		18.32
10	Mon, 11/8/93	4/1/94	0.25	1,802.03		8.67		36.63
11	Tue, 11/9/93	5/1/94	0.5	2,027.29		10.17		73.26
12	Wed, 11/10/93	6/1/94	0.75	2,280.70		11.67		146.52
13	Thu, 11/11/93	7/1/94	1	2,565.78		13.17		293.05
14	Fri, 11/12/93	8/1/94	1.25	2,886.51		14.67		586.09

Sheet1 Sheet2 Sheet3 Sheet4

Figure S.4: Series examples

To Create a Trend Series

1. In a row or column range, enter two or more tentative values for the trend series, and then select the entire range in which you want to create the series.
2. Choose Edit ➤ Fill and then click the Series command. In the Series dialog box, click the Trend option, placing an X in the corresponding check box.
3. Select either Linear or Growth in the Type group, and click OK.

NOTES To create a trend series, Excel determines the "best fit" formula for the series—that is, the linear or exponential equation that best describes the tentative sequence of entries you have already entered into the series range. In the resulting series, Excel supplies new values in the series and also adjusts the existing values to make them fit the formula.

When you create a trend series, make sure that you apply a format with one or more decimal places to the numeric entries in the series. If the series entries are formatted as integers you may not be able to see exactly how the series has been formed.

e.g. EXAMPLE In Figure S.4 (shown earlier in this entry), columns F and H contain examples of trend series. As displayed in columns E and G, the tentative entries for both of these series were 1, 3, and 4. For the linear series in column F, Excel calculates a step value of 1.5. To produce the growth series in column H, Excel uses a step multiplier of 2. Notice that Excel has adjusted the first three tentative values in both series.

See Also AutoFill, Filling Ranges, Formulas.

SHADING

You can use shading to highlight ranges of data on a worksheet.

To Apply Shading to a Worksheet Range

1. Select the range that you want to shade.
2. Choose Format ➤ Cells and click the Patterns tab.
3. In the Cell Shading box, select a color from the palette.
4. Optionally, click the arrow next to the Pattern box, and select a shading pattern from the top three rows of the pattern palette. Click the arrow again and select a color for the pattern.
5. Examine the result of your selections in the Sample box. Click OK if this is the shading effect that you want to apply.

Shortcuts Select a range and click the Light Shading or Dark Shading button. (These buttons are not initially part of any toolbar. See Toolbars for instructions on displaying tools in a toolbar.)

See Also Colors, Patterns.

SHORTCUT MENUS

The shortcut menus are designed to give you quick access to Excel's most commonly used menu commands. Shortcut menus are available for almost any item you work with in the Excel application window.

To Choose a Command from a Shortcut Menu

Point to an item in the Excel window and click the right mouse button to view the shortcut menu. Then choose any available command in the menu.

NOTES Most shortcut menus contain a selection of commands from Excel's Edit and Format menus. In addition, some shortcut menus contain special-purpose commands that apply to the specific item you are pointing to. Here are descriptions of the shortcut menus for items in Excel:

- Cell, range, column, or row selections on a worksheet. The shortcut menu contains commands for cut-and-paste, copy-and-paste, deletions, and insertions, along with the Format Cells command.
- Graphic objects in a worksheet, including buttons, drawn objects, text boxes, embedded charts, and other embedded objects. The shortcut menu for these objects contains commands from the Edit, Format, and Tools menus.
- Selected items or areas in a chart window. The shortcut menus for chart items include commands from the Edit, Insert, and Format commands.
- Toolbars. When you click a toolbar with the right mouse button, Excel displays a list of available toolbars. To open a toolbar, choose a name from this list. In addition, the toolbar shortcut menu contains the Toolbars command from the Options menu, and the Customize command. (See Toolbars for details.)
- Workbooks. When you click any sheet tab with the right mouse button, the resulting shortcut menu contains options for inserting or deleting sheets, renaming a sheet, moving or copying a sheet, and selecting all sheets in the workbook.

See Also TipWizard, Toolbars.

SOLVER

In a worksheet containing a system of interrelated formulas, you can use Solver to find the best solution to a problem by varying the input data. To find an optimum value, Solver adjusts specified data values within specified constraints. Solver is an add-in macro that you open and run by choosing the Tools ➤ Solver command.

To Use the Solver

1. Set up a worksheet that includes:
   - A formula whose result you want to optimize by finding its maximum, minimum, or best value.
   - One or more data entries that can be adjusted in order to find the optimal solution.
2. Select the cell that contains the formula whose value you want to optimize, and then choose the Tools ➤ Solver command. The Solver Parameters dialog box appears on the screen. The Set Target Cell box contains a reference to the selected cell.
3. Click one of the three option buttons in the Equal To group: Max to find the maximum result from the formula, Min to find the minimum result, or Value to find a specified result. If you choose Value, enter the result you want to achieve in the text box labeled Value Of.
4. Activate the By Changing Cells box. On the worksheet, select the cell or cells containing the data values that you want to adjust in order to find the optimum solution. If you want to include more than one cell reference in this box, hold down the Ctrl key while you make multiple selections on the worksheet. (Move the Solver Parameters dialog box to any convenient location on the screen if it is covering a cell that you want to select.)

5. Click the Add button. The Add Constraint dialog box appears on the screen. In the Cell Reference box, enter a reference to a cell for which you want to express a constraint. (You can enter the reference directly from the keyboard, or you can click the cell on the worksheet.)

6. Click the down-arrow next to the operation list box, and select one of the three relational operators (<=. =, >=); or select *int* if you want the constraint cell to remain an integer.

7. In the Constraint box, enter a value or formula (starting with an equal sign) that expresses the constraint you want to impose on the value in the selected cell. Then click OK. Back on the Solver Parameters dialog box, the constraint appears in the list box labeled Subject to the Constraints.

8. Repeat steps 5, 6, and 7 for any additional constraints you want to express. (You can use the Change button to edit an existing constraint, or the Delete button to remove a constraint from the list.)

9. Click the Solve button to attempt a solution. When Solver completes its analysis, the Solver dialog box appears on the screen. If a solution has been found, the result is now shown on your worksheet.

10. Select the Keep Solver Solution option if you want to retain this new version of your worksheet data, or select Restore Original Values to revert to the previous version. If you want to generate reports from the Solver analysis, select any of the report titles listed in the Reports box. (To select more than one report, hold down the Ctrl key while you select the titles.) Then click OK.

e.g. **EXAMPLE** The worksheet in Figure S.5 illustrates a problem for Solver analysis. The situation is as follows: a company specializing in computer installation and training uses a combination of staff consultants who are full-time employees, and freelance consultants who are called upon to work when they are needed. The worksheet shows the expenses related to each group of consultants. In addition, the range F13:F16 shows the total number of consulting hours per year, the number of hours required annually from each

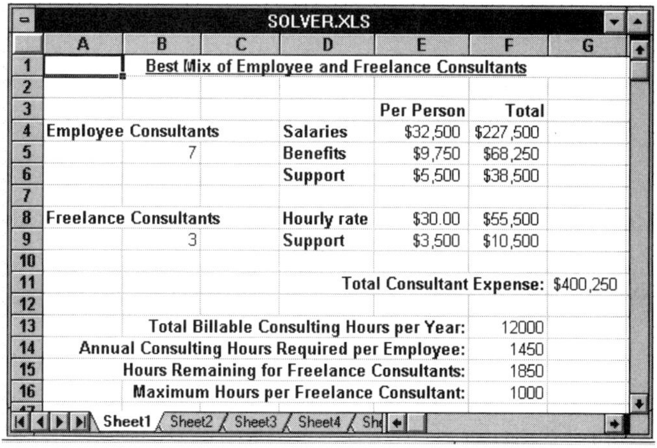

	A	B	C	D	E	F	G
1		Best Mix of Employee and Freelance Consultants					
2							
3					Per Person	Total	
4	Employee Consultants			Salaries	$32,500	$227,500	
5		7		Benefits	$9,750	$68,250	
6				Support	$5,500	$38,500	
7							
8	Freelance Consultants			Hourly rate	$30.00	$55,500	
9		3		Support	$3,500	$10,500	
10							
11						Total Consultant Expense:	$400,250
12							
13				Total Billable Consulting Hours per Year:		12000	
14				Annual Consulting Hours Required per Employee:		1450	
15				Hours Remaining for Freelance Consultants:		1850	
16				Maximum Hours per Freelance Consultant:		1000	

Figure S.5: A Solver illustration

employee consultant, the number of remaining hours that must be covered by contract consultants, and the maximum number of hours that can be assigned to any one freelancer per year.

Because some of the current employees have expressed interest in working instead on a freelance basis, the company wants to analyze the worksheet to find the best mix of employee and contract consultants. Here are the steps for using the Solver to perform this analysis:

1. Select cell G11, which contains the formula for total consultant expense.
2. Choose Tools ➤ Solver. The reference $G$11 appears in the Set Target Cell box.
3. Click the Min option to minimize the result of the expense formula.
4. Activate the By Changing Cells box. Hold down the Ctrl key and click cells B5 and B9. These cells, containing the number of consultants in each category, are the values that will be adjusted during the Solver analysis.

5. Click the Add button. The company wants a minimum of four employee consultants and a maximum of eight. In addition, ten consultants are needed in all to satisfy scheduling requirements. (The number of employees and the number of freelancers must both be integers, of course.) By company policy, each freelancer can be assigned a maximum of 1,000 hours per year, as specified in cell F16. To express these conditions, enter the following constraints:

```
$B$5 <= 8
$B$5 = Integer
$B$5 >= 4
$B$9 = 10 - $B$5
$B$9 = Integer
$F$15 <=$F$16 * $B$9
```

6. Back on the Solver Parameters dialog box, click Solve.

Figure S.6 shows the new mix of employee and contract instructors that Solver suggests as the best solution for this problem.

SOLVER.XLS

	A	B	C	D	E	F	G
1		Best Mix of Employee and Freelance Consultants					
2							
3					Per Person	Total	
4	Employee Consultants			Salaries	$32,500	$162,500	
5		5		Benefits	$9,750	$48,750	
6				Support	$5,500	$27,500	
7							
8	Freelance Consultants			Hourly rate	$30.00	$142,500	
9		5		Support	$3,500	$17,500	
10							
11					Total Consultant Expense:		$398,750
12							
13			Total Billable Consulting Hours per Year:			12000	
14		Annual Consulting Hours Required per Employee:				1450	
15			Hours Remaining for Freelance Consultants:			4750	
16			Maximum Hours per Freelance Consultant:			1000	

Sheet1 / Sheet2 / Sheet3 / Sheet4 / Sh

Figure S.6: The result of the Solver analysis

NOTES Click the Options button on the Solver Parameters dialog box to adjust the way Solver performs its analysis. The Solver Options dialog box includes boxes for the maximum amount of time spent on the analysis, the number of trial solutions (iterations), the precision required for satisfying constraints, and other options.

When Solver completes its solution, the Solver dialog box lists the three reports that can be generated from the analysis:

- The Answer report shows the original data values alongside the new values produced for the Solver solution.
- The Limit report describes the upper and lower limit values of the adjustable cells and the formula result.
- The Sensitivity report gives information about the sensitivity of the solution to adjustments in constraints.

Finally, the Solver dialog box also has a Save Scenario button. By clicking this button, you can supply a name for the solution and save it as a scenario. You can then choose Tools ➤ Scenarios whenever you want to review the solution.

See Also Goal Seek, Scenarios.

SORTING

The Data ➤ Sort command rearranges a range of worksheet data in alphabetical, numeric, or chronological order, or in a customized order that you choose. Although the Sort command is best suited to rearranging the rows of a list or database, you can also use the command to rearrange columns of data. Either way, you can define as many as three keys for each sort operation.

To Sort a List or a Database

1. Activate the worksheet that contains the list and select any cell within the list.
2. Choose Data ➤ Sort. Excel selects all the records of the list and opens the Sort dialog box.
3. Click the down-arrow next to the Sort By box. The resulting drop-down list contains the names of all the fields in your table. Click the name of the field that will be the first key to the sort—that is, the column by which the list will be rearranged first.
4. Click Ascending or Descending for the first key. (See Notes below for an explanation of these two options.)
5. If you want to choose fields for the second and third sorting keys, repeat steps 3 and 4 to select fields in one or both of the Then By list boxes. Excel will use the second key to arrange records that contain identical entries in the first key; likewise, the third key is for sorting records that contain identical entries in the first and second keys.
6. Click OK. Excel carries out the sort that you have specified.

Shortcut Select a cell in the column by which you want to sort the list or database. Then click the Sort Ascending button in the Standard toolbar for an ascending sort, or click the Sort Descending button for a descending sort.

NOTES When you select a cell in your list and choose the Data ➤ Sort command, Excel attempts to determine whether or not your list contains a top row of field names. The outcome of the sort depends on this characteristic:

- If Excel finds a row of field names, it selects the Header Row option in the My List Has group. On the worksheet, the selection includes all the records of your list, but not the top row of field names. As a result, only the records in the list will be sorted, and the field names will remain on top.

- If Excel does not find a row of field names, the No Header Row will be selected in the My List Has group. On the worksheet, the selection will include the entire list, from the first row to the last. The whole range of rows will therefore be sorted.

When you use the Sort command, take a careful look at the My List Has group, and make sure Excel has selected the correct option for your list or database.

To sort by a text key, click Ascending for alphabetical order or Descending for reverse alphabetical order. To sort by a key that contains date or time values, click Ascending for chronological order or Descending for reverse chronological order.

To sort a list or database by more than three keys, sort first by the least significant keys, and then by the most significant keys.

You can undo a sort by choosing Edit ➤ Undo Sort (or pressing Ctrl-Z) immediately after the sort operation. When you design a large database that you intend to work with in a variety of sorted orders, consider including a record number field, where the values represent the original unsorted record order. You can then restore the original order by using this number field as a key.

To Rearrange Columns of Data

1. Choose Data ➤ Sort and click the Options button on the Sort dialog box.
2. In the Orientation group of the Sort Options dialog box, click the Sort Left to Right option.
3. Click OK. Back on the Sort dialog box, define one or more keys for the sort, and click OK.

To Sort in a Custom Order

1. Choose Data ➤ Sort and click the Options button on the Sort dialog box.
2. In the Sort Options dialog box, click the down-arrow next to the First Key Sort Order list. The list displays predefined

custom sort orders, including the days of the week and the names of the months. (If you have defined any additional custom orders, they also appear in the First Key Sort Order list.)

3. Select one of the entries in the list and click OK.
4. Click OK on the Sort dialog box.

NOTES To create new custom orders, choose Tools ➤ Options and click the Custom Lists tab. Type the list entries in the order in which you want them to appear. See the AutoFill entry for more information about using custom lists.

See Also AutoFill, Database, List, Undo.

SPELLING CHECKS

The Tools ➤ Spelling command checks and corrects the spelling of words in one or more worksheets or charts.

To Check the Spelling

1. Activate a sheet and choose Tools ➤ Spelling. If Excel finds a misspelled word in the sheet, the Spelling dialog box appears. The message Not in Dictionary appears at the top of the dialog box, and a suggestion for the correct spelling appears in the Change To box.
2. Click one of the following buttons in the Spelling dialog box:

   - Change replaces the word with the Change To suggestion.
   - Change All replaces all occurrences of the word in the current document.

- Ignore or Ignore All leaves the word as it appears in the document.
- Add inserts the word to the current dictionary file. (You can also enter the name for a new dictionary file in the Add Words To box.)
- Cancel stops the spelling check.

3. Repeat step 2 for each misspelled word that Excel finds.

Shortcut Click the Spelling button on the Standard toolbar, or press the F7 function key.

NOTES To check the spelling in a range of text entries, select the range before you choose Tools ➤ Spelling. Otherwise, if a single cell is selected on the active worksheet, Excel checks the spelling in all text entries, notes, and text boxes on the worksheet. (The Spelling command also checks the spelling of headers and footers if you have added them to your worksheet, and of hidden ranges if any.)

Excel does not check the spelling of cells that contain formulas. Also, you can check the Ignore Words in UPPERCASE option to omit all-uppercase text from the spelling check.

To check the spelling on several worksheets in a workbook, select the sheets before you choose Tools ➤ Spelling.

See Also Text Box, Text Operations.

STATISTICAL FUNCTIONS

Excel's library of statistical functions includes commonly used tools—such as average, count, minimum, and maximum functions—along with a large collection of technical tools used by statisticians.

To Enter a Statistical Function into a Worksheet

1. Select the cell or range where you want to enter the function.
2. Choose Insert ➤ Function. The Function Wizard dialog box appears on the screen.
3. Select Statistical in the Function Category list. The Function Name list shows the names of all the available statistical functions.
4. Select the name of a function and click Next.
5. In Step 2 of the Function Wizard, enter arguments for the function.
6. Click Finish. Excel enters the function with its arguments into the active cell or range.

Shortcuts Click the Function Wizard button on the Standard toolbar. From the keyboard, enter an equal sign followed by the function's name, and then press Ctrl-A to view Step 2 of the Function Wizard. This dialog box serves as a guide for entering appropriate arguments for the function.

NOTES Here is a grouped list of the functions available in this category:

- Average, median, and mode functions (AVERAGE, CONFIDENCE, GEOMEAN, HARMEAN, MEDIAN, MODE, TRIMMEAN).
- Correlation coefficient functions (CORREL, FISHER, FISHERINV, PEARSON).
- Counting functions (COUNT, COUNTA).
- Deviation and variance functions (AVEDEV, COVAR, DEVSQ, STDEV, STDEVP, VAR, VARP).
- Distribution functions (BETADIST, BETAINV, BINOMDIST, CHIDIST, CHIINV, CHITEST, CRITBINOM, EXPONDIST, FDIST, FINV, FREQUENCY, FTEST,

GAMMADIST, GAMMAINV, HYPGEOMDIST, KURT, LOGINV, LOGNORMDIST, NEGBINOMDIST, NORMDIST, NORMINV, NORMSDIST, NORMSINV, POISSON, PROB, SKEW, STANDARDIZE, TDIST, TINV, TTEST, WEIBULL, ZTEST).

- Gamma function (GAMMALN).
- Linear regression functions (INTERCEPT, RSQ, SLOPE, STEYX).
- Maximum and minimum functions (MAX, MIN).
- Percentile, rank, and standing functions (LARGE, PERCENTILE, PERCENTRANK, QUARTILE, RANK, SMALL).
- Permutations (PERMUT).
- Trend functions (FORECAST, GROWTH, LINEST, LOGEST, TREND).

See Also Analysis Tools, Mathematical Functions.

STYLES

A style is a combination of formatting attributes that you define for use in a particular workbook. The categories you can include in a style are represented by the tabs of the Format Cells dialog box: Number, Alignment, Font, Border, Patterns, and Protection. You can create a style by example or by definition. After creating a style and assigning it a name, you can easily apply the style's entire set of format definitions to any range of cells. You can also copy styles from one workbook to another. Excel's Normal style represents the default formatting characteristics for a workbook.

To Create a Style by Example

1. Select a range of cells and apply any combination of formats to the range.
2. While the range is still selected, choose Format ➤ Style.
3. In the Style Name box, enter a name for the style you are creating.
4. Click OK.

Shortcut Install the Style box in a toolbar of your choice. (See Toolbars for instructions.) You can then create a new style by selecting the range that contains the formatting attributes and entering a name for the style directly into the Style box.

To Apply a Style to a Range

1. Select the range where you want to apply a style.
2. Choose Format ➤ Style.
3. In the Style Name list, select the name of the style that you want to apply.
4. Optionally, use the check boxes in the Style Includes group to select or deselect categories of styles that you want to include or omit from the selection.
5. Click OK.

Shortcuts Select a name from the Style box in the toolbar where you have installed it.

To Create a Style by Definition

1. Choose ➤ Style.
2. In the Style Name box, enter a name for the style you are about to define. Then click the Modify button. The Format Cells dialog box appears on the screen.

3. Click a tab representing a formatting category that you want to modify for the new style. Then select specific formatting options for the style.
4. Repeat step 3 for as many formatting categories as you want to modify for the style. Then click OK on the Format Cells dialog box.
5. Click OK on the Style dialog box.

NOTES By selecting or deselecting categories in the Style Includes group, you can define the exact set of formats that the style will affect. Categories that are not checked will not be changed when you apply the style to a range.

To delete a style definition, choose Format ➤ Style, select the style name, and click the Delete button. You cannot delete the Normal style, although you can change the combination of formats that it represents.

To Change the Normal Style for a Workbook

In the Style dialog box, select the Normal style; then follow the steps (outlined earlier in this entry) for defining the format attributes of a style. Click OK. Excel applies the new Normal style to all unformatted cells in all the sheets of the active workbook.

To Copy Style Definitions from One Workbook to Another

1. Open both workbooks, and activate the workbook to which you want to copy styles.
2. Choose Format ➤ Style and then click Merge.
3. In the Merge Styles dialog box, select the name of the workbook from which you want to copy styles. Click OK.
4. Click the Close button on the Style dialog box.

NOTES After the Merge Styles operation, the Styles box for the destination document contains all the style names from the source document.

See Also Alignment, AutoFormat, Borders, Copying Formats, Custom Number Formats, Fonts, Formatting Worksheet Cells, Number Formats, Patterns, Point Size, Protecting Cells, Template.

SUBTOTALS

The Data ➤ Subtotals command is an efficient tool for adding subtotal and total lines to a list or database. To use this command, you select a field column that contains groups of data entries for which you want to find subtotals. You can also select a function to use for the subtotal calculations; Sum is the most common choice, but other functions are also available, such as Average, Max, Min, and so on.

For successful use of the Subtotals command, your list or database must have a top row of field names and must be sorted by the column containing the group entries.

To Insert Subtotal Lines into a List or Database

1. Activate the worksheet containing your list or database.
2. If the database is not sorted already, select a cell in the column containing group entries and click the Sort Ascending button in the Standard toolbar.
3. Choose Data ➤ Subtotals. Excel selects the records of your database and displays the Subtotal dialog box on the screen.
4. If the At Each Change In box does not already display the field by which you want to group the subtotals, pull down the list and select the correct field name.

5. If the Use Function box does not display the function that you want to use for calculating the subtotal lines, pull down the list and select a different function.
6. In the Add Subtotal To box, place an X in the check box for each field that you want to include in the subtotals.
7. Check any combination of the three check boxes at the bottom of the Subtotal dialog box:

    - The Replace Current Subtotals option is for use in a database that already contains subtotals; place an X in this check box if you want to replace previous subtotal lines with new ones, or leave the box unchecked if you want to insert additional subtotal lines.
    - Check the Page Break Between Groups option if you want each group to be on a separate page in the printed database. Leave this option unchecked to omit the page breaks.
    - Check the Summary Below Data option to insert a grand total line at the end of the database. Leave this option unchecked if you want only subtotal lines, with no grand total.

8. Click OK. Excel inserts the new subtotal lines according to your instructions.

NOTES Excel creates an outline on your worksheet when subtotal rows are inserted. You can therefore click a numbered outline level symbol to hide or view detail rows of the database. For example, click 1 to view only the grand totals, 2 to view subtotals and grand totals, and 3 to view one level of detail records.

Excel uses the SUBTOTAL function to perform the calculations in subtotal lines. This function takes two arguments:

=SUBTOTAL(FunctionNum, Range)

The first argument is an integer from 1 to 11 that represents one of the 11 available subtotal functions, and the second argument is a reference to the range of data that will be totaled.

You can create *nested* subtotals by choosing the Data ➤ Subtotal command multiple times for the same database. Each time, select a different field name in the At Each Change In list, and make sure the Replace Current Subtotals option is unchecked.

See Also Database, List, Outlines, Summation.

SUMMATION

Summation is one of the most common arithmetic operations performed in a worksheet. The SUM function calculates the sum of all the values in a range or list of ranges. Because you frequently need to find the total of all the values in a row or column, Excel supplies a special AutoSum tool that automatically enters a SUM function in the cell beneath a column of numbers or to the right of a row of numbers. The AutoSum tool is on the Standard toolbar.

To Use the AutoSum Button

1. Select the cell just beneath a column of numbers, or just to the right of a row of numbers.
2. Click the AutoSum button. Excel enters a SUM function into the formula bar. The function's argument is the numeric range just above or just to the left of the current cell.
3. If necessary, adjust the argument of the SUM function, either by pointing to a new range on the worksheet, or by editing the reference directly in the formula bar.
4. Press ↵ to enter the function into the selected cell.

Shortcuts Select a cell beneath or to the right of a range of numbers, and double-click the AutoSum button. Excel determines an appropriate range argument for the SUM function, and enters the function into the current cell.

NOTES To enter totals for several columns or rows of a table, select the range immediately beneath the table or just to the right of the table, and click the AutoSum button once.

See Also AutoFill, Formula Bar, Formulas, Functions, Mathematical Functions.

TEMPLATE

A template is a model workbook that you design for the convenience of opening other new workbooks. In a template, you can store formats and styles, along with text, numbers, formula entries, and graphic objects on any sheets in the workbook. When you open a new document based on a template, Excel copies all the formats and other contents of the template to the new workbook.

To Create a Template

1. Create a workbook that contains all the formats, styles, and entries that you want to save in the template.
2. Choose File ➤ Save As. In the Save As dialog box, enter a name for the template file, and optionally select a path location for storing the file.
3. In the Save File as Type list, select Template. Excel adds an .XLT extension to the file name.
4. Click OK to save the template. Then choose File ➤ Close to close the template file.

NOTES For maximum convenience, you can save a template file in the subdirectory named XLSTART. When you do so, Excel adds your template's name to the New list in the File ➤ New dialog box.

To Open a New Workbook Based on a Template

If you have stored the template file in the XLSTART directory, choose File ➤ New, select the template name in the New list, and click OK.

If the template file is stored elsewhere, choose File ➤ Open, select or enter the name of the template file, and click OK.

NOTES You can open multiple new workbooks based on the same template. Excel gives each new document a temporary name. For example, suppose your template is named INVOICE.XLT. The workbooks you open from this template will be named Invoice1, Invoice2, Invoice3, and so on. When you save each new workbook, Excel supplies the default .XLS extension.

In the File ➤ Open dialog box, select Templates (*.XLT) from the List Files of Type box if you want to see only template files in the file list.

To open a template file for editing, choose File ➤ Open, select the template file name, and hold down the Shift key while you click OK. In this case, Excel opens the XLT file itself, not a new document based on the template. You can make changes to the template, and then choose File ➤ Save to save the changes.

See Also Directories, Styles, Workbooks.

TEXT BOX

A text box is an object that you can use for displaying a block of text at any location within a worksheet. Like other graphic objects, a text box can be moved and resized to meet the requirements of a particular document. You can apply patterns to the interior and border of a text box, and you can apply fonts, styles, and point sizes selectively to the text within the box. (You can also assign a macro to a text box in a worksheet. See Graphic Objects for details.)

To Add a Text Box to a Worksheet

1. Activate the sheet in which you want to add the text box.
2. Click the Text Box button in the Standard toolbar. When you now point to the active sheet, the mouse pointer appears in a cross-hair shape.
3. Hold down the left mouse button and drag the mouse over the area where you want to display the text box. Release the mouse button to complete the box. Excel activates the box and displays a flashing insertion point at the upper-left corner.
4. Type the text that you want to display inside the box. Then click elsewhere on the active document to deselect the box.

NOTES To move a text box to a new location, drag its border with the mouse. To change the size and shape of the text box, click the object's border, and then drag any one of the sizing handles displayed around the perimeter of the box.

To edit the contents of a text box, click the box once to select the object and then click inside the box to place the insertion point at any location in the text.

To change the border style or fill pattern of a text box, double-click the object's border to view the Format Object dialog box. Click the Patterns tab and select options from the Border and Fill groups. Use other tabs in the Format Object dialog box—Font, Alignment, Protection, and Properties—to change other characteristics of the text box. See Graphic Objects for details.

To assign a macro to a text box, select the object and choose Tools ➤ Assign Macro. If a macro is assigned to a text box, the mouse pointer appears as a pointing hand when positioned over the object. To run the macro, click the object. To select the object without running the macro, hold down the Ctrl key while you click.

You can combine a text box with an arrow object to draw attention to a particular entry in a worksheet. (The Arrow tool appears on the Drawing toolbar. See Figure D.1 in the Data Tables entry for an example of this combination.)

To delete a text box from a document, select the object, then press the Del key.

To Change the Alignment or Orientation of Text in a Text Box

1. Select the box and choose Format ➤ Object. Click the Alignment tab in the Format Object dialog box.
2. Select an option in the Horizontal alignment group. Text can be left-aligned, centered, right-aligned, or justified horizontally.
3. Select an option in the Vertical alignment group. Text can be top-aligned, centered, bottom-aligned, or justified vertically.
4. Select an option in the Orientation group. You can display text horizontally or vertically inside the text box.
5. Click OK to apply the new alignment and orientation options.

Shortcuts Select the text box and click the Align Left, Center, or Align Right button on the Standard toolbar. Alternatively, click the text box with the right mouse button to view the object's shortcut menu; then choose the Format Object command.

NOTES If you select a vertical orientation for the text in a text box, Excel temporarily switches to the default horizontal orientation whenever you edit the contents of the box. The vertical orientation is restored when you deselect the box.

To Change the Font, Style, or Size of Text in a Text Box

1. Select the entire text box, or select only the portion of the text that you want to reformat.
2. Choose Format ➤ Object. On the Font tab, make selections in the Font, Font Style, and Size boxes, and click OK.

Shortcuts Select the text box or a portion of the text, and click any of the formatting tools on the Formatting toolbars. For example, click the Bold, Italic, or Underline tool, or select a font name from the Font box or a point size from the Size box.

NOTES You can apply different text formatting options to selections of text within the text box. For example, you can display more than one font or point size within a box, and you can apply bold, italics, and underlining to selected words within the box.

The Font tab in the Format Object dialog box also has options for special effects (Strikethrough and Underline) and a Color list from which you can select colors for the text. You can display text in multiple colors within a text box.

To Add Text to a Chart

Activate the chart window, and click the Text Box button on the Standard toolbar. Drag the mouse through the area of the chart where you want to place the text, and then type the text into the resulting box. Select elsewhere in the chart to deselect the box. The text appears directly on the chart without a text box border. The entry is known as *unattached text*.

Shortcuts Press Esc to deselect any chart item, and simply begin typing the text into the formula bar. Press Enter to complete the text. Then move the text to any location on the chart.

 **See Also** Charting, Graphic Objects, Macro.

TEXT FUNCTIONS

Excel has a collection of over twenty text functions that perform various operations on text entries in a worksheet.

To Enter a Text Function into a Worksheet

1. Select the cell or range where you want to enter the function.
2. Choose Insert ➤ Function, or click the Function Wizard button on the standard toolbar.
3. Select Text in the Function Category box. The Function Name box shows the entire list of text functions.
4. Select the name of a function and click Next.
5. In Step 2 of the Function Wizard, enter arguments for the function you've chosen.
6. Click Finish. Excel enters the function and its arguments into the active cell.

Shortcuts From the keyboard, enter an equal sign followed by the function's name, and then press Ctrl-A (or click the Function Wizard button on the formula bar) to display Step 2 of the Function Wizard dialog box.

NOTES Here is a grouped list of the functions available in this category:

- Alphabetic-case conversion functions (LOWER, PROPER, UPPER).
- ANSI code conversion functions (CHAR, CODE).
- Character removal functions (CLEAN, TRIM).
- Comparison function (EXACT).
- Concatenation (CONCATENATE).
- Length function (LEN).
- Numeric and text conversion functions (DOLLAR, FIXED, T, TEXT, VALUE).
- Repetition function (REPT).
- Replacement functions (REPLACE, SUBSTITUTE).
- Search functions (FIND, SEARCH).
- Substring functions (LEFT, MID, RIGHT).

See Also Functions, Text Operations.

TEXT OPERATIONS

The process of combining two or more text values is known as concatenation. In Excel, the ampersand character (&) represents this text operation.

To Concatenate Two or More Text Values

Use the & operator in a formula to join the text values and display the result in a cell.

e.g. **EXAMPLE** The following two formulas use concatenation to produce messages giving the date and the time:

```
="Today is"&TEXT(TODAY(),"ddd, mmm dd, yyyy")&"."
="The time is"&TEXT(NOW(),"hh:mm AM/PM")&"."
```

If you enter these formulas into cells in a worksheet, the result will be text entries such as the following:

Today is Mon, Nov 01, 1993.
The time is 06:57 AM.

 **See Also** Macro, Text Functions.

TIME ENTRIES

You can enter time values into worksheet cells in any of several time formats that Excel recognizes. In response, Excel applies a time format to the cell, but stores the time itself as a special value known as a serial number. The serial number format allows you to perform time arithmetic operations in a worksheet.

To Enter a Time into a Worksheet Cell

Select the cell and enter the time in a recognizable format.

e.g. **EXAMPLE** Here are some examples of time entry formats that Excel recognizes:

6:00

6AM

6:00AM

6:00:00AM

- In response to any of these entries, Excel applies one of its built-in time formats to the cell—displaying the time as 6:00 or 6:00AM or 6:00:00AM. Excel stores the time internally as the serial number 0.25, which represents the fraction of the day that is over at 6:00AM.

NOTES A *full* serial number contains digits both before and after the decimal point. The integer portion before the decimal point represents the date, and the fractional value after the decimal point represents the time. For example, 34407.25 represents the date/time value March 14, 1994 6:00AM. (See Date Entries for more information.)

To Find the Difference Between Two Time Entries

Enter a formula that subtracts one time from the other.

e.g. **EXAMPLE** Suppose you have entered the following values in cells B1 and C1:

B1 6:00 AM
C1 8:24 AM

The following formula gives the difference between the two times:

=C1–B1

Internally, Excel subtracts one entry's serial number from the other, resulting in the difference between the two times. In this case, 6:00AM is represented by the serial value 0.25 and 8:24AM is represented by 0.35. The difference between them is therefore 0.1.

NOTES To include a time value in a formula, enclose the time in double quotation marks and use a time format that Excel recognizes. For example, the formula ="6:00 AM"+.5 adds half a day to the time 6:00 AM. The result is 0.75, the serial-number equivalent of 6:00 PM.

To View the Serial Number for a Time Entry

1. Select the cell that contains the entry displayed in a time format.
2. Choose Format ➤ Cells and click the Number tab on the Format Cells dialog box.
3. Select All in the Category box, and then select General in the Format Codes box. Click OK.

Shortcuts Select the cell and press Ctrl-Shift-~ to apply the General format, or Ctrl-Shift-@ to apply a time format.

See Also Custom Number Formats, Date and Time Functions, Date Entries.

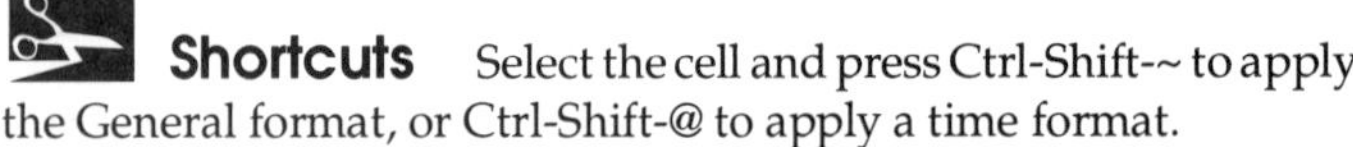

TIPWIZARD

As you work in Excel, the TipWizard provides ongoing suggestions for accomplishing specific tasks more efficiently. You can read the latest suggestion—or review all the suggestions that have been provided during the current session—by clicking the TipWizard button on the Standard toolbar.

To Display and Use the TipWizard

1. When the light bulb icon on the TipWizard button turns yellow, a new suggestion has just been recorded—based on your most recent action in Excel. Click the TipWizard button to display the Tip box.
2. If the Tip Help button appears to the right of the Tip box, click it for more information about the current suggestion.

3. If another icon appears to the right of the Tip box, the TipWizard is suggesting that you use this button as a shortcut next time you want to perform the same task. You can click it now—directly in the TipWizard—to see how it works.
4. To scroll through previous suggestions that the TipWizard has made during your current session in Excel, click the up or down arrows at the right side of the Tip box.
5. To close the TipWizard, click the TipWizard button in the Standard toolbar again.

NOTES At the beginning of each new session with Excel, the TipWizard presents a "Tip of the Day"—an interesting technique or description that may be new to you. To view the Tip of the Day, scroll up to the first suggestion in the Tip box.

See Also Help.

TOOLBARS

Excel has an assortment of built-in toolbars, each of which you can display or hide at any time. They provide dozens of different buttons that you can use to streamline your activities in Excel. Initially, the Standard and Formatting toolbars appear on the screen, but the other toolbars are just a mouse-click away. In addition, Excel has a collection of extra buttons that are not initially assigned to any toolbar. To use one of these buttons, you can add it to an existing toolbar, or you can create new toolbars of your own. Finally, Excel provides "custom" buttons to which you can assign your own macros.

To Display a Toolbar

Point to any toolbar with the mouse, and click the right mouse button. On the resulting shortcut menu, select the toolbar you want to display. Alternatively, choose View ➤ Toolbars, check the toolbars you want to display, and click OK. Note that the Toolbars dialog box contains the complete list of available toolbars, whereas the toolbar shortcut menu lists the most commonly used toolbars.

NOTES Once a toolbar is displayed on the screen, you can move it to a new position or change its shape. Some of Excel's built-in toolbars appear initially as *floating* toolbars, and others are located in toolbar *docks*.

A floating toolbar is displayed with its own title bar. To move a floating toolbar to a new place on the screen, drag its title bar with the mouse. To change its shape, position the mouse pointer over the window's border until you see a double-headed arrow; then drag the border into a new shape. To hide a floating toolbar, click the Close box at the upper-left corner of the toolbar window.

The toolbar docks are fixed locations at the top, bottom, left, and right sides of the Excel window. The Standard and Formatting toolbars are docked by default at the top of the application window; the rest appear initially as floating toolbars. You can change a docked toolbar to a floating toolbar by dragging it away from the dock. Conversely, you can dock a floating toolbar by dragging it toward the top, bottom, or side of the Excel window. (Toolbars that contain drop-down lists or tear-away palettes cannot be docked to the sides of the application window.) To hide a docked toolbar, click any toolbar with the right mouse button, and select the name of the checked toolbar that you want to hide.

In Excel 5, convenient ToolTips are available to identify buttons and describe their uses.

To View a ToolTip

Position the mouse pointer over any button on a toolbar. A small box appears beneath the mouse pointer, showing you the button's name. In addition, the status bar displays a brief description of the button.

NOTES If a ToolTip does not appear when you point to a button, choose View ➤ Toolbars, and check the Show ToolTips option. Conversely, you can uncheck this option if you do not want to see ToolTips.

To Add Buttons to a Toolbar

1. Display the toolbar to which you want to add one or more buttons.
2. Click any toolbar with the right mouse button and choose the Customize command from the resulting shortcut menu. (Alternatively, choose View ➤ Toolbars and click the Customize button on the Toolbars dialog box.) The Customize dialog box displays a list of button categories and a group of buttons corresponding to the current category.
3. Select a name from the Categories list. Then drag a button from the Buttons group to the toolbar where you want to display the button. Excel adds the button to the toolbar.
4. Repeat step 3 for each button that you want to display in a toolbar.
5. Click Close to close the Customize dialog box.

NOTES When you drag a button to a toolbar, a copy of the button remains in the Customize dialog box. Excel allows you to add a given button to as many different toolbars as you like.

You can remove buttons from a built-in toolbar. To do so, display the toolbar and then open the Customize dialog box. Drag any number of buttons from the toolbar to the Customize dialog box, and then click Close. To restore a built-in toolbar to its default status, choose View ➤ Toolbars, select the name of the toolbar you want to restore, and click the Reset button.

To Create a Custom Toolbar

1. Click any toolbar with the right mouse button, and choose the Toolbars command from the resulting shortcut menu. (Alternatively, choose View ➤ Toolbars.) The Toolbars menu appears on the screen.

2. In the Toolbar Name box, enter a new name for the custom toolbar you are about to create. Then click the New button. Excel creates and displays the new floating toolbar and also opens the Customize dialog box.
3. Select a button category from the Categories list, and then drag a button from the Buttons box to the new custom toolbar.
4. Repeat step 3 for all the buttons that you want to add to the custom toolbar.
5. Click the Close button to close the Customize dialog box.

NOTES As you add buttons to the new custom toolbar, Excel increases the size and changes the shape of the toolbar. After you close the Customize dialog box, you can move and resize the custom toolbar, or you can place it in one of the toolbar docks.

To delete a custom toolbar from the set of available toolbars, choose View ➤ Toolbars, select the name of the toolbar you want to delete, and click the Delete button. Excel displays a dialog box asking you to confirm the deletion. Click OK to delete, or Cancel to retain the toolbar.

To Assign a Macro to a Custom Button

1. Develop the macro that you will assign to a custom button. For maximum convenience, store the macro in the Personal Macro Sheet, PERSONAL.XLM. (See Macro Recording for details.)
2. Display the toolbar to which you want to add the custom button. You can use one of Excel's built-in toolbars or a custom toolbar of your own.
3. Click any toolbar with the right mouse button, and choose the Customize command from the shortcut menu.
4. In the Categories list, choose the Custom option. The Buttons box displays the custom buttons to which you can assign macros.

5. Drag one of the custom buttons from the Customize dialog box to the toolbar where you want to display the button. When you do so, Excel automatically opens the Assign Macro dialog box. This box lists the names of the macros available in all macro sheets that are currently open, including the hidden Personal Macro Sheet.
6. Select a macro from the Assign Macro box and click OK.
7. Click Close on the Customize dialog box.

NOTES After you assign a macro to a custom button, you can click the button to run the macro.

See Also Customizing Excel, Macro Recording, Shortcut Menus, TipWizard.

TRANSPOSING RANGES

You can use the Edit ➤ Paste Special command to transpose a range of worksheet data—copying rows of data to columns and columns to rows.

To Transpose a Range of Data

1. Select the entire range that you want to transpose, and choose Edit ➤ Copy. Excel displays a moving border around the range.
2. Select the cell at the upper-left corner of the location where you want to copy the transposed data.
3. Choose Edit ➤ Paste Special. In the Paste Special dialog box, click the Transpose option. An X appears in the corresponding check box.
4. Click OK.

NOTES If the data you are transposing contains formulas, Excel adjusts ranges in the formulas appropriately.

See Also Copying Data.

TRENDLINES

A trendline is a feature you can add to an existing chart to identify and clarify trends in selected data series. Trendlines are produced by a variety of mathematical algorithms, under the general category of *regression analysis*. In Excel 5, you can view a trendline almost instantly, without having to deal with the mathematical background. You simply choose the Insert ➤ Trendline command and select the trendline type along with other options. You can also extend the trendline backward or forward to follow a trend graphically to its logical conclusion, and—if you wish—you can examine the trendline's equation directly on the chart where you have displayed the line.

Trendlines are available for area, bar, column, line, and xy charts in Excel. For other chart types, the Insert ➤ Trendline command is dimmed.

To Add a Trendline to a Chart

1. Activate the chart sheet or double-click the embedded chart where you want to add the trendline.
2. Click the data series for which you want to develop the trendline. This action selects the data series, and displays the corresponding SERIES function in the formula bar.
3. Choose Insert ➤ Trendline. The Trendline dialog box contains two tabs, Type and Options.

4. On the Type tab, select the type of trendline that you want to create. The choices are Linear, Logarithmic, Polynomial, Power, Exponential, and Moving Average.
5. Click the Options tab. In the Trendline Name box, select the Automatic or Custom option for the trendline name. If you select Automatic, Excel will provide a name for your trendline, based on the data series that the trendline describes. If you select Custom, you can enter a name of your own choosing for the trendline. Either way, this name will appear in your chart's legend.
6. In the Forecast group, you can specify a number of periods forward and/or backward to extend the trendline. If you want the trendline to extend only within the current data series, leave these options set at 0.
7. If the Set Intercept check box is available, you can check it and enter a value in the corresponding check box. This is the value at which the trendline will cross the y-axis (the vertical axis on the chart.) The Set Intercept option is not available for all types of trendlines.
8. Check the Display Equation on Chart option if you want to see the trendline's equation directly on the chart. Check the R-squared Value on Chart option if you want to see the R-squared value directly on the chart. (This is a value from 0 to 1 that measures the validity, or "fit," of the trendline. An R-squared value near zero indicates a poor fit; a value near 1 indicates a good fit.)
9. Click OK. Excel adds the trendline to your chart.

NOTES Like other items in a chart, a trendline can be reformatted. Double-click the trendline in the chart to open the Format Trendline dialog box. The Patterns tab allows you to change the style, color, and weight of the trendline. The other two tabs in the dialog box—Type and Options—allow you to modify the definition of the trendline itself.

See Also Charting, Series.

UNDO

The Edit ➤ Undo command undoes the effect of your most recent action. Undo is available for many—but not all— operations in Excel.

To Undo the Most Recent Action

Choose Edit ➤ Undo immediately after the action that you want to reverse.

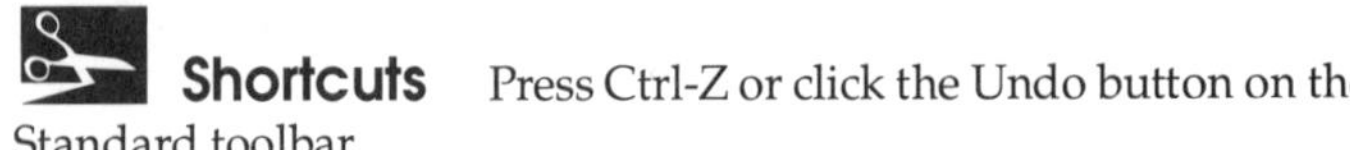

Shortcuts Press Ctrl-Z or click the Undo button on the Standard toolbar.

NOTES In the Edit menu, the Undo command identifies the action that will be reversed. For example, the command might be displayed as Undo Font or Undo Delete. If the command is dimmed or displayed as Can't Undo, the undo feature is not available for your last action.

After you choose Edit ➤ Undo, the first command in the Edit menu changes to Redo. Choose this command if you want to restore the effect of the action that you have just undone.

See Also Repeating Commands.

VIEWS

The View Manager is an add-in macro that you can use to define and save different views of a worksheet. A view consists of a variety of settings that affect the information you see on the screen and the format of the sheet you send to the printer. These include window settings—size, position, selection, panes, and frozen titles; sheet settings such as zoom percentage; and many settings you select in the Tools ➤ Options command. When you create a view, you also have the option of including print settings and hidden rows and columns as part of the view definition.

You use the View ➤ View Manager command both to create views and to switch to a view you have already created.

The View Manager works along with the Scenario Manager (Tools ➤ Scenarios) and the Report Manager (File ➤ Print Report) to give you detailed control over the content and appearance of reports you create from a worksheet. See Reports and Scenarios for further information.

To Create Views of a Worksheet

1. Open the workbook and activate the worksheet for which you want to create the views.
2. Prepare the worksheet in any combination of the following ways:
   - Adjust the zoom setting to display the worksheet scale that you want in the view.
   - Adjust the size and position of the worksheet window on the screen.
   - Add panes and frozen titles if appropriate.
   - Select display settings from the View tab of the Tools ➤ Options command.
   - Select print settings from the File ➤ Page Setup command.
3. Choose View ➤ View Manager. The resulting dialog box contains a list box for displaying the names of defined views, and a column of command buttons.
4. Click the Add button. The Add View dialog box appears on the screen. Enter a name for the current view in the Name box, and select any combination of the View Includes options. Then Click OK.
5. Repeat steps 2 to 4 for any additional views you want to create for the active worksheet.

NOTES When you next save your worksheet, the views you have defined are saved with it.

To Show a View of a Worksheet

1. Activate a worksheet on which you have defined views, and choose View ➤ View Manager.
2. In the Views dialog box, select a name from the list of views, and click Show.

NOTES If your view includes specific print settings, you can now print the worksheet without having to choose the File ➤ Page Setup command.

To delete a view from the view list, choose Window ➤ View, select the name of the view you want to delete, and click the Delete button. Excel deletes the view immediately, without asking for confirmation. (You cannot undo this deletion.)

See Also Page Setup, Panes, Reports, Scenarios, Window Operations.

WINDOW OPERATIONS

You can use familiar mouse techniques to adjust the size and position of workbook windows within Excel. In addition, several commands in the Window menu and the Tools ➤ Options command give you control over the appearance and organization of windows.

To Change the Size and Position of a Workbook Window

Drag any border or corner of the window to change the size and shape. Drag the title bar to move the window to a new position on the screen. Click the Maximize button to expand a window's size to the entire available screen space. Click the Restore button to return to the previous size and position. Click the Minimize button to reduce a window to an icon.

NOTES A window's Control menu shows a list of keyboard techniques for performing these same window operations. To pull down the Control menu, click the window's Control-menu box, or press Alt-hyphen.

To Activate the Window for an Open Workbook

Pull down the Window menu and choose the name of the workbook you want to activate.

To Open Multiple Windows for Viewing the Active Workbook

Choose Window ➤ New Window.

NOTES Multiple windows allow you to view different parts of a workbook at one time. When you open more than one window for a workbook, the title bar of each window displays the workbook's name, followed by a colon and the window number—for example, Book1:1 and Book1:2.

To Rearrange Two or More Open Windows

1. Choose Window ➤ Arrange.
2. Click one of the options in the Arrange group: Tiled, Horizontal, Vertical, or Cascade.

3. If you want to arrange only the multiple windows of the active document, click the Windows of Active Workbook option. An X appears in the corresponding check box.
4. Click OK.

NOTES The Tiled, Horizontal, and Vertical arrangements allow you to view multiple workbooks side by side or one above another.

The Window menu has other commands that affect the appearance of windows. These include Hide and Unhide for hiding and redisplaying windows, and Split and Freeze Panes for dividing windows into panes. See the Hiding and Panes entries for details.

To Close a Window

Activate the window and choose File ➤ Close, or double-click the window's Control-menu box (at the upper-left corner of the window). If you have modified the workbook since the last save, Excel asks you if you want to save the changes.

To Change the Display Options of an Active Window

Choose Tools ➤ Options, click the View tab, and select the Window Options that you want to apply to the active window:

- The Automatic Page Breaks option allows you to display or hide the page breaks that Excel sets for printing a worksheet.
- The Formulas option determines whether a sheet displays formulas or their resulting values.
- The Gridlines and Row & Column Headings options are for displaying or hiding a sheet's gridlines and headings. These settings are both checked by default. In addition, you can select a color for gridlines and headings by pulling down the Color list.

- The Outline Symbols setting is for switching the display of outlining symbols on or off in a worksheet that contains an outline.
- The Zero Values setting specifies whether Excel displays zero or a blank cell when an entry is equal to zero.
- The Horizontal Scroll Bar, Vertical Scroll Bar, and Sheet Tabs options are for displaying or hiding scroll bars and tabs.

In addition, the three option buttons in the Objects group determine how Excel displays graphic objects in the active worksheet. The default is Show All, but you can also choose to represent embedded objects with blank placeholders (Show Placeholders), or to hide all objects (Hide All).

Shortcuts Press Ctrl-' (left quotation mark) to toggle between formula-display and value-display on the active worksheet.

NOTES You can use the View ➤ View Manager command to define and save different sets of Tools ➤ Options selections as views. You assign a name to each view that you define. Then, when you want to look at your worksheet in a different way, you can simply choose View ➤ View Manager and select a view. See Views for details.

You can also record a particular arrangement of open workbook windows as a *workspace*. See the Workspace entry for details.

See Also Graphic Objects, Hiding, Opening Files, Outlines, Panes, Views, Workbooks, Workspace, Zooming.

WORKBOOKS

The workbook is the basic document type in Excel 5. A workbook may contain any combination of worksheets and chart sheets. If you make use of Excel's advanced programming capabilities, you'll also store macros, modules, and dialog sheets in workbooks. To activate any sheet in a workbook, you simply click the sheet's tab along the bottom border of the workbook window. Although each new workbook starts out with a standard number of worksheets, you are free to add or delete sheets according to the requirements of a particular document. You can use a workbook effectively to store and manage any number of interrelated worksheets, charts, and macros.

To Create a New Workbook

Choose File ➤ New. (If the New dialog box appears, select Workbook in the New list, and click OK.)

Shortcut Click the New Workbook button on the Standard toolbar.

NOTES A new workbook has a default name like Book1, Book2, and so on. Initially each new workbook contains sixteen worksheets, named Sheet1 through Sheet16.

If you want new workbooks to contain some other number of worksheets, choose Tools ➤ Options, click the General tab, and change the setting in the Sheets in New Workbook box.

To Activate a Sheet in a Workbook

Click the sheet's tab at the bottom of the workbook window. If the tab is not visible for the sheet you want to activate, click any combination of the four tab scrolling buttons at the lower-left corner of the window to move other tabs into view.

Alternatively, press Ctrl-PgDn to activate the next sheet in the workbook, or Ctrl-PgUp to activate the previous sheet.

To Insert a Sheet into a Workbook

Pull down the Insert menu and choose Worksheet, Chart, or Macro, depending on the kind of sheet you want to add to your workbook. (Before you add a new chart sheet, you'll generally want to select the data upon which the chart will be based; see Charting for details.)

Shortcut Click any tab at the bottom of the workbook with the right mouse button. The workbook shortcut menu appears. Choose the Insert command, select a sheet type from the Insert dialog box, and click OK.

To Rename a Sheet in a Workbook

1. Activate the sheet that you want to rename.
2. Choose Format ➤ Sheet, and then click the Rename command in the Sheet submenu. The Rename dialog box appears on the screen.
3. Enter a new name for the sheet and click OK. The new name appears on the sheet's tab.

Shortcuts Double-click a sheet's tab to display the Rename dialog box. Alternatively, click a sheet's tab with the right mouse button and choose the Rename command from the resulting shortcut menu.

To Move or Copy a Sheet

1. If you want to move or copy a sheet to a different workbook, open both the source and the destination workbooks. If you are moving a sheet to a new location within a workbook, only the target workbook need be open.
2. Activate the source workbook and click the tab for the sheet that you want to move or copy.
3. Choose Edit ➤ Move or Copy Sheet. The Move or Copy dialog box appears on the screen.
4. In the To Book list, select the name of the destination workbook. If you are copying or moving a sheet within one workbook, leave the name of the current workbook name as the To Book selection. To move or copy the active sheet

to a new workbook, select the *new book* entry in the To Book list.

5. In the Before Sheet list, select the name of the sheet that will be located *after* the sheet that you are moving or copying.
6. To copy the sheet, check the Create a Copy option; to move the sheet, leave this option unchecked.
7. Click OK.

Shortcuts To move a sheet within its workbook, drag the sheet's tab to a new position in the row of tabs. When you release the mouse button, Excel moves the sheet. To copy a sheet within its workbook, hold down the Ctrl key while you drag the sheet's tab to a new position.

To move or copy a sheet to a different workbook, arrange the source and destination workbooks so that both can be seen at once, and drag the tab of the sheet from one workbook to the other. (To move the sheet, simply drag with the mouse to move the sheet. To copy the sheet, hold down the Ctrl key while you drag.)

To move or copy a sheet to a new workbook, drag the sheet's tab into the blank background area of the Excel window. (Hold down the Ctrl key if you want to copy the sheet.) Excel creates a new workbook, and moves or copies the target sheet into the new book.

To Hide a Sheet

Activate the sheet that you want to hide, and choose Format ➤ Sheet. Then click the Hide command from the resulting submenu.

To Delete a Sheet from a Workbook

Activate the sheet that you want to delete, and choose Edit ➤ Delete Sheet. Excel displays a warning box; click OK to confirm the deletion.

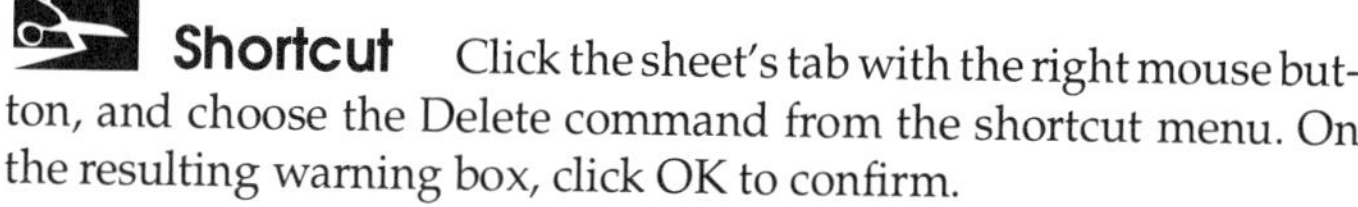

Shortcut Click the sheet's tab with the right mouse button, and choose the Delete command from the shortcut menu. On the resulting warning box, click OK to confirm.

See Also Charting, Group Editing, Links and 3-D Formulas, Opening Files, Saving Files, Window Operations, Workspace.

WORKSPACE

You can record a particular arrangement of open workbooks as a *workspace*. When you open a workspace file, Excel opens all the workbooks that are recorded in the workspace and displays them as they were arranged when you saved the workspace.

To Save a Workspace

1. Open and arrange the workbooks that you want to include in the workspace.
2. Choose File ➤ Save Workspace. Excel suggests RESUME.XLW as the name of the workspace file. Accept this name or enter a name of your own choosing.
3. Click OK to save the workspace.

To Open a Workspace

1. Choose File ➤ Open.
2. Click the drop-down arrow next to the List Files of Type box, and select the Workspaces (*.xlw) entry. The File Name box lists any workspace files you've saved in the current directory. (Use the Directories box to change the directory if necessary.)

3. Select the name of the workspace file that you want to open, and click OK.

NOTE If you want Excel to open a workspace automatically at the beginning of each session, save the workspace in the startup directory, XLSTART.

See Also Opening Files, Saving Files, Windows, Workbooks.

WRAPPING TEXT

When you enter a long text value into a worksheet cell, Excel initially displays the entry across adjacent cells to the right. You can use the wrapping option to display the entire text entry within the boundaries of a single cell.

To Wrap a Long Text Entry in a Cell

1. Select the cell that contains the long text entry.
2. Optionally, adjust the column to the width you want for the wrapped text.
3. Choose Format ➤ Cells and click the Alignment tab. In the resulting dialog box, click the Wrap Text option. An X appears in the corresponding check box.
4. Click OK to wrap the text.

NOTES Excel adjusts the height of the row in order to display the entire entry of wrapped text.

Alignment.

ZOOMING

You can use the View ➤ Zoom command—or the Zoom Control box on the Standard toolbar—to enlarge or reduce the viewing scale of a window.

To Change the Scale of a Worksheet

1. Activate the sheet whose scale you want to change, and choose View ➤ Zoom. The Zoom dialog box contains a group of Magnification option buttons.
2. Click one of the preset magnification or reduction options. Alternatively, click the Custom option, and enter a value from 10 to 400 in the % text box.
3. Click OK to apply the zoom scale.

Shortcut Click the drop-down arrow next to the Zoom Control box on the Standard toolbar, and select a percentage scale value from the list.

NOTES The Zoom command affects only the active sheet. Other sheets in the active workbook retain their current scale settings.

To Find the Best Scale for Displaying a Range Selection

1. Activate the worksheet and select the range that you want to display.
2. Choose View ➤ Zoom. In the Magnification group, click the Fit Selection option, and then click OK.

Shortcut Select the range that you want to zoom. Then click the drop-down arrow next to the Zoom Control box on the Standard toolbar, and click the Selection option.

NOTES When you select the Fit Selection option, Excel calculates the best scale for displaying the selection. For a small range of cells, this may mean increasing the scale; for a large range, Excel reduces the scale.

See Also Page Setup, Views, Window Operations.

Index

Boldface page numbers indicate definitions and principal discussions of primary topics and subtopics. *Italic* page numbers indicate illustrations.

SYMBOLS

& (ampersand), representing text operations with, 243–244

! (exclamation point), following range names, 133

; (semicolon), dividing custom formats with, 54

| (vertical bar), separating application names from document names with, 82

A

accessing Help, **119–120**

adding
- buttons to toolbars, **249**
- controls to a dialog box, **78**
- dialog sheets to workbooks, **78**
- graphic objects, **111–112**
- text boxes to worksheets, **239–240**
- text to charts, **241–242**
- trendlines to charts, **252–253**

add-ins, **4–7**
- creating new, **6**
- installing, **4–5**
- loading the XLQUERY.XLA add-in macro, **194**
- opening, **5**
- removing, **5**

Advanced Filter, 66, 90, 93, 95, 134

alignment, **7–10**
- breaking and realigning long text entries, **9**
- changing cell or range, **7**, 103
- centering across columns, 25
- changing label, **10**
- changing text, **240**
- changing title, **10**
- justifying long text entries, **8**

rotating entries within cells, **8**
ampersand (&), representing text operations with, 243–244
analysis tools, **4**, **10–12**, 85, 95
AND, 135–137
annotating cells, **156**
applying
names to formulas, **155**
shading to ranges, **176**, **219**
styles to ranges, **232**
arithmetic operations, **12–13**, **71**, 106
array formulas, 14–15
auditing, **16–17**, 107
AutoFill, **17–19**, 55, 216
AutoFilter, 2, 66, **90–93**, 134
AutoFormat, 2–3, **20–22**, 55
AutoSum button, **236–237**
AVERAGE, 43, 45

B

base conversion functions, **85**
bessel functions, **85**
Bookmark ➤ Define, 119
borders, **23–24**
changing the color of, **39**
changing graphic object, **176**
displaying cell, 103
buttons
changing the text alignment of, **9**
creating, **79**

C

cells. *See also* ranges
annotating, **156**
applying shading to, **176**
breaking and realigning long text entries in, **9**
changing the alignment of entries in, **7–8**
changing the color of, **39**
changing font size in, **183–184**
clearing worksheet, **35–36**
copying visible, **48**
creating series of, 18
deleting notes from, **159**
editing current entries in, **105**
editing directly in, **84**
entering dates and times into, 70, **73**, **244–245**
entering formulas into, **106**

entering functions into, 108, 135–136
entering numeric values into, **104–105**
entering text into, **104–105**
finding formulas that refer to selected, **107**
formatting, **103–104**
going to named, **154–155**
inserting, **126**
justifying long text entries in, **8**
protecting worksheet, **190–192**
rotating entries within, **8**
selecting, **213–214**
tracing, **16**
shortcut menu options for, 220
viewing notes attached to, **157**
wrapping long text entries in, **264**

characters, applying styles to, **101**

charts, **2**, **25–36**
adding text to, **241–242**
adding trendlines to, **252–253**
applying an AutoFormat in, **20**
changing the alignment of titles or labels in, **10**
changing the color of areas and items in, **40–41**
changing default formats of, **34**
changing the type of, *33*
creating charts from chart sheets, **35**
creating a custom AutoFormat for, **20–21**
creating embedded, **26–27**, **35**
creating new chart sheets, **27–28**
editing and formatting, **30**
printing, **186–187**
shortcut menu options for, 220
using the ChartWizard with, **28–29**

ChartWizard, 2, **26–29**

Choose Format ➤ AutoFormat, 20

circular references. *See* iteration

clearing
formats from a range, **50**
outlines, **168**
worksheet cells, **35–36**

Clear Outline, 168

Clipboard, copying ranges of worksheet data to, **37**

closing windows, **258**

colors, **38–42**
  changing border, **39**
  changing cell, **39**
  changing chart area, **41**
  changing chart item, **40–41**
  changing gridline, **40**
  changing graphic object, **113**
  customizing workbook color palettes, **41–42**
  displaying worksheet entries in, **38**
columns
  centering across, **25**
  changing series from columns to rows, **33–34**
  changing series from rows to, **33–34**
  changing the width of, **42–43**
  deleting, **75**
  hiding and unhiding, **120–121**
  inserting, **125**
  rearranging, **227**
  selecting, **214**
commands
  repeating previous, **201**
  selecting menu, **220**
comparison operators
  displaying logical arguments with, 136
  entering formulas into cells with, 106
  searching for patterns of text entries with, 67
  searching for records using, 59
complex number functions, **86**
concatenating text values, **244**
consolidating data, **43–46**
controls
  adding, **78**
  linking, **79**
converting
  between date and time formats, **71**
  formulas to fixed values, **52**
copying, **46–49**
  all the pages of a pivot table, **182–183**
  data using Copy and Paste commands, **47**
  data using the drag-and-drop technique, 48–49
  data to worksheets in a group, **116–117**
  formats, **49–51**
  formulas, **51–53**
  inserting data during copy-and-paste operations, **47**
  notes, **157**

only the cells that are visible, 48
pictures of data to the Clipboard, 37
ranges of worksheet data to the Clipboard, **37**
selected records to new locations, 95
selections to multiple locations, 48
sheets in workbooks, 261
style definitions, **233–234**
using Fill commands for, **89**

Count, 45
Count Nums, 45
customizing, **53–56**
number formats, **53–55**
toolbars, **249–250**
workbook color palettes, **41–42**
cut and paste, **47**, **149–150**

D

Data ➤ Consolidate, 43–44
Data ➤ Filter, 66, 91–95, 134
Data ➤ Form, 56–59
Data ➤ Get External Data, 194
Data ➤ Group and Outline, 166, 168
Data ➤ Pivot Table, 176
Data ➤ Refresh Data, 182
Data ➤ Sort, 58, 134, 225–227
Data ➤ Subtotals, 2, 234–236
Data ➤ Table, 60–63
Data ➤ Text to Columns, 172
DATA area, viewing source data in, **183**
database(s), **2**. *See also* lists
applying custom criteria to filtered, **92–93**
creating, **64–65**
creating criteria ranges for, **66–67**
creating pivot tables from, **177–178**
filtering, **90–94**
functions, **68–70**, 134
inserting subtotal lines into, **234–236**
performing calculations on matching records on, **68–69**
removing filters from, **93**
working with data from external, **194–195**

data forms, **56–60**, 134
- adding new records to lists in, **58**
- deleting records in, **58**
- editing records in, **57**
- opening, **56**

data tables, **60–63**
- creating one-input, **60–61**
- creating two-input, **62–63**

date and time functions, **70–74**
- entering dates, **70**, **73**
- entering current dates and times into cells, **70**
- finding the difference between two dates, **74**
- getting date or time information from serial numbers, **72**

DatePlus, 144
DATEVALUE, **71**
DAVERAGE, **68**
DAY, **72**
DAYS360, **71**
DCOUNT, **68**
DCOUNTA, **68**
default fonts, changing, **102**
default formats, changing, **104**
defining
- creating styles by, **232–233**
- names, **151–153**
- scenarios in worksheets, **209–210**

deleting, **75–77**
- columns, **75**
- custom number formats, **55**
- files, **76–77**
- notes, **159**
- ranges of cells, **76**
- records in data form, **58**
- rows, **75**
- sheets from workbooks, **262–263**

dependents, tracing, **16**, 107
DGET, **69**
dialog boxes
- adding controls to, **78**
- creating buttons that open, **79**

dialog sheets, 55, 77–80
directories, changing, **80**
disks, deleting files from, **77**
displaying
- cell borders, 103
- changing display options for active windows, **258**
- numeric values, 103
- TipWizard, **246–247**
- toolbars, **247–248**

worksheet entries in color, **38**
DMAX, **69**
DMIN, **69**
DPRODUCT, **69**
dragging
clearing data by, **36**
creating a series of cells by, **18**
inserting cells by, **126**
ranges, **150**
drawing borders, **23–24**
DSTDEV, **69**
DSUM, **69**, 134
Dynamic Data Exchange (DDE), **81–83**

E

EDATE, **71**
Edit ➤ Annotate, 119
Edit ➤ Clear, **35–36**, 50, 157, 159
Edit ➤ Copy, 35, 37, 47–48, 50, 52, 81–82, 112, 129, 131, 157–158, 162, 164, 192, 200, 251
Edit ➤ Cut, 149
Edit ➤ Delete, 59, 75–76
Edit ➤ Fill, 9, 89, 116, 215, 217–218
Edit ➤ Find, 99
Edit ➤ Go To, 15, 48, 107, 154
Edit ➤ Goto, 168
Edit ➤ Links, 83
Edit ➤ Move, 261
Edit ➤ Paste, 35, 47–48, 52, 112, 150, 192
Edit ➤ Paste Link, 81
Edit ➤ Paste Special, 49–50, 81–82, 129, 158, 200, 251
Edit ➤ Repeat, 201
Edit ➤ Replace, 202–203
Edit ➤ Undo, 36, 76, 125, 159, 254
Edit ➤ Undo Delete, 59
Edit ➤ Undo Goal Seek, 111
Edit ➤ Undo Sort, 227
editing
current entries in cells, **105**
directly in a cell, **84**
documents in a group, **115–116**
embedded objects, **163**
group, **115–117**
notes attached to cells, **157**
embedding
an Excel object into another application, **164**
objects in worksheets, **161–162**

engineering functions, **85–86**
entering
  data into entire ranges at once, **90**
  dates, **73**
  formulas, **90**, **106**, **215**
  functions into worksheet cells, **108**
  logical functions, **135–136**
  lookup functions, **138–139**
  mathematical functions, **148–149**
  statistical functions, **230**
  text functions, **242–243**
  a time into a worksheet cell, **244–245**
EOMONTH, **71**
error functions, **86**
event handlers, **77**
exclamation points (!), in range names, 133
exiting, **86**

F

FALSE(), 136–137
File ➤ Close, 123, 237, 258
File ➤ Exit, 86
File ➤ Exit and Return, 162
File ➤ Find File, 76–77, 97–98
File ➤ New, 164–165, 238, 260
File ➤ Open, 80, 87–88, 121, 147, 164–165, 174, 238, 263
File ➤ Page Setup, 117, 147, 158, 169–170, 201, 255–356
File ➤ Print, 34, 123, 158, 185–188
File ➤ Print Preview, 116, 184–185
File ➤ Print Report, 204–205, 210, 255
File ➤ Print Topic, 119
File ➤ Return Data, 195
File ➤ Save, 238
File ➤ Save As, 87, 174–175, 207–208, 237
File ➤ Save Workspace, 263
File ➤ Unhide, 120
file(s)
  deleting, **76–77**
  extensions, for add-in files, 5–6
  finding, **97–99**
  formats, **87–88**
  importing, **121**
  opening, **80**, **88**, **164–165**
fill handles
  creating a series by dragging, **18**

- inserting cells by dragging, **126**
- filling ranges, **89**
- fill patterns, changing, **176**
- filters, **90–95**. *See also* AutoFilter
  - applying custom criteria to filtered databases, **92–93**
  - filtering lists or databases, **90–91**
  - removing, **93**
  - using criteria ranges to filter databases, **94**
- financial functions, **95–97**
- finding
  - the best scale for displaying range selections, 265
  - the difference between time entries, **245–246**
  - files, **97–99**
  - formulas that refer to selected cells, **107**
  - worksheet data, **99–100**
- fonts, **100–103**
  - applying character, **101–102**
  - changing, **101–103**, **183–184**, **241**
- Format ➤ AutoFormat, 21–22, 33
- Format ➤ Cells, 7–8, 23–25, 38–39, 53, 55, 74, 84, 101– 103, 159–160, 176, 183, 191, 219, 246, 264
- Format ➤ Chart Type, 33
- Format ➤ Column, 42–43, 120–121
- Format ➤ Group, 113
- Format ➤ Object, 9, 79, 113–114, 162, 176–177, 240–241
- Format ➤ Row, 120–121, 206
- Format ➤ Row Height, 207
- Format ➤ Selected, 40–41
- Format ➤ Selected Axis Title, 10
- Format ➤ Selected Chart Title, 10
- Format ➤ Sheet, 261–262
- Format ➤ Style, 102, 104, 232–233
- Format ➤ Ungroup, 113
- formatting. *See also* formats
  - charts, **30–33**
  - numeric values, **53–55**, **159–161**
  - worksheet cells, 103–104
- Format Painter button, copying formats using, **50**
- formats. *See also* formatting

converting between date and time, **71**
copying, **49–51**
file, **87–88**
number, **53–55**, **159–161**
formula bar, **104–105**, **198–199**
formulas, **105–107**
applying names to, **155**
array, 14–15
copying, **51–53**
creating 3-D, **132–33**
creating data tables with, **60–61**
entering, **90**, **106**, **215**
pasting names into, **155**
pointing 3-D ranges while entering, **215**
remote reference, 161
types of references included in, **51**
using Goal Seek to change the results of, **109–10**
writing arithmetic, **12–13**
freezing panes, **171**
function(s), **108–109**
AND, 135–137
AVERAGE, 43, 45
Count, 45
Count Nums, 45
creating user-defined, **142–143**
database, **68–70**, 134
date and time, **70–72**
DATE, **71**
DatePlus, 144
DATEVALUE, **71**
DAVERAGE, **68**
DAY, **72**
DAYS360, **71**
DCOUNT, **68**
DCOUNTA, **68**
DGET, **69**
DMAX, **69**
DMIN, **69**
DPRODUCT, **69**
DSTDEV, **69**
DSUM, **69**, 134
EDATE, **71**
engineering, 85–86
entering text, **242–243**
EOMONTH, **71**
FALSE(), 136–137
financial, **95–97**
HOUR, 72
IF, 135–137
INFO, 123–124
ISNUMBER, 124
logical, **135–137**
lookup, **138–140**
mathematical, **148–149**
MAX, 43, 45
MIN, 43, 46
MINUTE, **72**
MONTH, **72**
NETWORKDAYS, **71**
NOT, 136–137
NOW(), **70**

OR, 135–137
Product, 46
SECOND, **72**
SERIES, 31, 131, 252
SQLREQUEST, **69**
statistical, 229–231
StdDev, 46
StdDevp, 46
SUBTOTAL, 235
SUM, 43–44, 46, 236–237
SVAR, **69**
text, **242–243**
TIME, 71
TIMEVALUE, **71**
TODAY(), **70**
TRUE(), 136–137
user-defined, **142–143**
Var, 46
WEEKDAY, **72**
WORKDAY, **71**
YEAR, **72**
YEARFRAC, **71**
Function Wizard, 85, 96, 108–109

G

Goal Seek, **109–111**
graphic objects, **111–115**, **176**, 220
gridlines, changing the color of, **40**
group editing, 1, **115–117**

H

headers and footers, **117–118**, 169
Help, **118–120**, **140–141**
Help ➤ Contents, 119
Help ➤ Lotus 1-2-3, 140
Help ➤ Search, 119
hiding data, **120–121**, **262**
HOUR, **72**

I

IF, 135–137
importing files, **121**
information functions, **123–124**
Info window, **122–123**
Insert ➤ Cells, 126
Insert ➤ Chart, 26–28
Insert ➤ Columns, 125
Insert ➤ Copied Cells, 47
Insert ➤ Function, 108, 230, 242
Insert ➤ Macro, 78, 142
Insert ➤ Name, 106, 151, 154, 155
Insert ➤ New Data, 31
Insert ➤ Note, 156–158
Insert ➤ Object, 161, 163
Insert ➤ Page Break, 189
Insert ➤ Remove Page Break, 189
Insert ➤ Rows, 66, 125–126

Insert ➤ Titles, 31
Insert ➤ Trendline, 3, 252
inserting, **124–126**
  data during copy-and-paste operations, **47**
  document files, **163**
  sheets in workbooks, **260**
  subtotal lines, **234–236**
installing add-ins, **4–5**
ISNUMBER, 124
iteration, **127–128**

J

justifying long text entries within cells, **8**

L

labels
  changing the alignment of, **10**
  creating lists of AutoFill, **19**
layout, changing pivot table, **180–181**
lines, inserting subtotal, **234–236**
linking. *See also* Dynamic Data Exchange (DDE); links
  controls to worksheet cells, **79**
  document files, **163**
links, **128–133**
  between two workbooks, **129–130**
  between worksheets on the same workbook, **131**
lists, **2**. *See also* database(s)
  adding new records to data form, **58**
  creating custom label, **19**
  creating pivot tables from, **177–178**
  filtering, **90–93**
  inserting subtotal lines into, **234–236**
  operations you can perform on, **134–135**
  removing filters from, **93**
  sorting, **225–226**
loading, the XLQUERY.XLA add-in macro, **194**
logical functions, **135–137**
lookup functions, **138–140**
Lotus 1-2-3 Help, **140–141**

M

macro(s), 56, **141–144**. *See also* macro sheets
assigning custom toolbar, 250–251
assigning graphic object, **114**
loading the XLQUERY.XLA add-in, **194**
recording, 3, 142, **145–147**
running command, **147**
macro sheets. *See also* macro(s)
replacing data in, **202–203**
searching for data in, **99–100**
margins, adjusting before printing, 169, 185
mathematical functions, **148–149**
MAX, 43, 45
measurement conversion functions, **86**
menus, shortcut, **219–220**
MIN, 43, 46
MINUTE, **72**
MONTH, **72**
moving data, **149–151**
sheets in workbooks, **261**
ranges by dragging, **150**
using cut-and-paste, **149–150**

N

names, **151–156**. *See also* renaming
book-level scope of, 1
defining, **151–152**
creating, **153**
pasting, **155**
range, **151–152**, **154**
renaming sheets in workbooks, **261**
writing field, **65**
NETWORKDAYS, **71**
NOT, 136–137
notes, **156–159**
attaching sound, **158**
copying, **157**
deleting, **159**
printing, **158**
NOW(), **70**
number(s). *See also* numeric values
accessing serial numbers for date and time entries, **74**, **246**
date entry, **72**, **74**, **246**
formats, **53–55**, **159–161**
numeric values. *See also* number(s)
displaying, 103
entering, **104–105**

O

object linking and embedding (OLE), **161–164**
opening
  add-ins, **5–6**
  data forms, **56**
  dialog boxes, **79**
  files, **80, 88, 164–165**
  the Info window, **122**
  multiple windows, **257**
  new workbooks, **165, 238**
  one or more Excel workbooks from disk, **164–165**
  password-protected documents, **174–175**
  workspaces, **263**
OR, 135–137
orientation, changing text, **240**
outlines, **165–168**
  clearing, **168**
  creating outlined worksheets, **166**
  focusing on selected levels of outlined worksheets, **167– 168**
  viewing levels of, *168*

P

page(s)
  breaks, setting manual, **188**
  scrolling to next or previous, 184
  setup, **169–170**, 186–187
panes, **170–172**
  dividing sheets into, **171**
  freezing, **171**
  removing, **172**
parsing, **172–173**
passwords, **173–174**. *See also* protecting
pasting, **149–50**, 155
patterns, **175–177**
  changing cell, 103, **176**
  changing graphic object, **113**
Personal Macro Workbook, 144, **145–146**
pivot tables, 2, **177–183**
  changing the layout of, **180–181**
  copying pages of, **182–183**
  creating, **177–179**
  developing, *180*
  with a PAGE field, *181*
  reorganizing, *182*
  updating, **181–182**
  viewing source data in, **183**
pointing to a 3-D range while entering a formula, **215**

point size, 183–184
precedents, tracing, **16**, 107
previewing, **184–185**
printing
- charts, **186–187**
- information from workbooks, **188–189**
- the Info Window, 123
- notes, **158**
- previewing documents before, **184–185**
- reports, **204**
- setup for, **185–186**
- worksheets, **169–170**, **188–189**

Product, 46
programming, **3**
protecting. *See also* passwords
- cells, 103, **190–192**
- workbooks, **192–193**

Q

Query, **193–196**
- modifying, **196**
- working with external database data using, **194–195**
- updating, **196**

R

ranges
- applying shading to, **176**, **219**
- applying styles to, **232**
- changing the alignment of entries in, **7–8**
- changing font size in, **183–184**
- clearing formats from, **50**
- copying, **37**
- creating criteria, **66–67**
- deleting notes from, **159**
- deleting, **76**
- dragging, **150**
- filling, **89**
- filtering databases with criteria, **90–94**
- finding the best scale for displaying, **265**
- going to named, **154–155**
- inserting, **126**
- protecting worksheet, **190–192**
- selecting, **213–215**
- shortcut menu options for, 220
- transposing, **251–252**

recalculation, **196–197**
recording macros, **145–147**
Record Macro, 146
Record New Macro, 142

records
adding new, **58**
deleting, **58**
displaying, **93**
editing, **57**
performing calculations on matching, **68–69**
searching for, **59**
viewing, **56**
references, 197–201
3-D, **128–133**, 198
absolute, **51**, 197–198
changing styles of, **199**
changing types of, **198–199**
circular, **127–128**
external, **128**, 198, 200
mixed, **51**, 197–198
relative, **51**, 197–198
remote, 161
regression analysis, 252
relational operators, applying custom criteria with, 92–93
removing
add-ins, 5–6
borders, **24**
cell protection, **192**
filters from list databases, **93**
panes, 172
repeating commands, **201**
replacing worksheet data, **202–204**
Report Manager, 4, 205–206
reports, 4, **204–206**
creating, **204**
printing, **204**
rotating entries, within cells, **8**
rows
changing the height of, **206–207**
changing series from columns to rows, **33–34**
changing series from rows to columns, **33–34**
deleting, **75**
hiding and unhiding, **120–21**
inserting, **125**
selecting, **214**
shortcut menu options for, 220
running command macros, **147**

S

Save File as Type list, formats included in, **87–88**
saving, **207–208**
files in selected formats, **87**

files with and without passwords, **174–175**
updating files after making changes in workbooks, **208**
workbooks to disk, **207–208**
workspaces, **263**
Scenario Manager, 204–206, 208–213
scenarios, **208–213**
creating summaries of, **210–213**
defining, **209–210**
viewing, **209–210**
searching and replacing
records in data forms, **59**
worksheet data, **99–100**, **202–204**
SECOND, 72
selecting
engineering functions, **85–86**
entire worksheets, **214**
information categories, **122**
menu commands, 220
multiple graphic objects, **112–113**
noncontiguous ranges, **214**
options for printing worksheets, **169–170**
ranges, **213–215**
rows and columns, **214**
semicolons (;), dividing custom formats with, 54
serial numbers
for date entries, **72**, **74**
getting date or time information from, **72**
Series, **215–18**
creating, **215–217**
creating trend, **218**
SERIES, 31, 131, 252
shading, applying, **176**, **219**
Sheet tab, 169
shortcut menus, **219–220**
Solver, 4, **221–225**
sorting, 2, **225–228**
in a custom order, **227–228**
rearranging columns of data, **227**
rows in a list, 134
sound notes, attaching, **158**
spelling checks, **228–229**
spreadsheets. *See* database(s)
SQLREQUEST, **69**
statistical functions, **229–231**
StdDev, 46
StdDevp, 46
styles, **231–234**
applying, **101**
changing, **241**

SUBTOTAL, 235
subtotals, 234–236
summation, **236–237**
SUM, 43–44, 46, 236–237
SVAR, **69**
switching
  to manual recalculation, **196–197**
  to manual updating, 83
symbols
  ampersands, 243–244
  exclamation points, 133
  hide detail, 165–168
  row and column level, 165–168
  show detail, 165–168
  semicolons, 54
  vertical bars, 82

T

tables. *See* data tables; pivot tables
templates, 237–238
text boxes, **239–242**
  adding, **239–240**
  changing the alignment of, **240**
  changing the font, style, or size of text in, **241**
  changing the orientation of, **240**
  changing the text alignment of, **9**
text functions, **242–243**
text operations, **243–244**
time entries, **244–246**. *See also* data and time functions
TIME, **71**
TIMEVALUE, **71**
TipWizard, 119, **246–247**
titles, changing the alignment of, **10**
TODAY(), **70**
toolbar(s), 56, **247–251**
  adding buttons to, **249**
  creating custom, **249–250**
  displaying, **247–248**
  docks, **248**
  floating, **248**
  shortcut menu options for, 220
  viewing ToolTips on, **248**
Tools ➤ Add-Ins, 4–6, 144, 194
Tools ➤ Assign Macro, 114, 162, 240
Tools ➤ Auditing, 16–17, 107
Tools ➤ Data Analysis, 10
Tools ➤ Goal Seek, 109–110
Tools ➤ Macro, 147
Tools ➤ Make Add-In, 4, 6
Tools ➤ Options, 19, 34,

40–41, 73, 122, 127, 141, 168, 196 n-197, 199, 228, 255–260
Tools ➤ Protection, 190–192
Tools ➤ Record Macro, 142, 145–146
Tools ➤ Scenarios, 204, 209–212, 255
Tools ➤ Solver, 221, 223, 225
Tools ➤ Spelling, 228–229
tracing, **16–17**
transposing ranges, **251–252**
trendlines, **252–253**
TRUE(), 136–137

U

undoing most recent actions, **254**
unhiding
 columns or rows, **121**
 workbooks, **120**
updating
 files after making changes in workbooks, **208**
 manual links, **83**
 pivot tables, **181–182**
 query, **196**
 switching to manual, **83**

V

Var, 46
Varp, 46
vertical bar (|), separating application names from document names with, 82
View ➤ Toolbars, 248–250
View ➤ View Manager, 204, 255–256, 259
View ➤ Zoom, 265
viewing. *See also* views
 the Clipboard, **37**
 levels of an outline, *168*
 notes attached to cells, **157**
 opening data forms for, **56**
 scenarios in worksheets, **209–210**
 serial numbers for date entries, **74**
 serial numbers for time entries, **246**
 source data in pivot tables, **183**
View Manager, 4, 204–206, 254–256
views, **254–256**. *See also* viewing
 creating worksheet, **255**
 showing worksheet, **256**
Visual Basic

basic uses of, **3**
creating user-defined functions in, 142–143
developing macros with, 141–143
Show method, 78, 79–80

W

WEEKDAY, **72**
wildcard characters, searching for data with, 59, 67, 100, 203
Window ➤ Arrange, 122, 129, 200, 257
Window ➤ Freeze Panes, 171–172
Window ➤ Hide, 146, 120
Window ➤ New Window, 257
Window ➤ Remove Split, 172
Window ➤ Split, 171
Window ➤ Unfreeze Panes, 172
Window ➤ Unhide, 120, 146
Window ➤ View, 256
windows, **257–259**
activation for open workbook, **257**
changing the display options of active, **258–259**
changing the size and position of, **257**
closing, **258**
opening multiple, **257**
rearranging two or more open, **257**
for viewing active workbooks, 257
workbooks, 1, **259–263**
activating sheets in, **260**
copying sheets in, **261**
deleting sheets from, **262–63**
dependent, **129**
hiding sheets in, **262**
inserting sheets in, **260**
moving sheets in, **261**
printing information from, **188–189**
renaming sheets in, **261**
saving, **207**
shortcut menu options for, 220
updating files after making changes in, **208**
WORKDAY, **71**
worksheets, **1**
adding text boxes to, **239–240**
changing the default font for all, **102**
copying data to, 116–117
copying ranges from, **37**
creating outlined, **166**

defining scenarios in, **209–210**
dividing, **171**
embedding objects in, **161–162**
entering text functions into, **242–243**
finding data in, **99–100**
focusing on selected levels of outlined, **167–168**
linking between, **131**
organized for outlining, *167*
printing, **169–170**, **188–189**
replacing data in, **202–203**
searching for data in, **99–100**, **202–203**
selecting entire, **214**
source, **131**
viewing, **209–210**, **255–256**
workspaces, **263–264**
wrapping text, **264**
writing, arithmetic formulas, **12–13**

X

XLQUERY.XLA macro, **194**

Y

YEAR, **72**
YEARFRAC, **71**

Z

Zooming, 185, **265**

Drawing toolbar

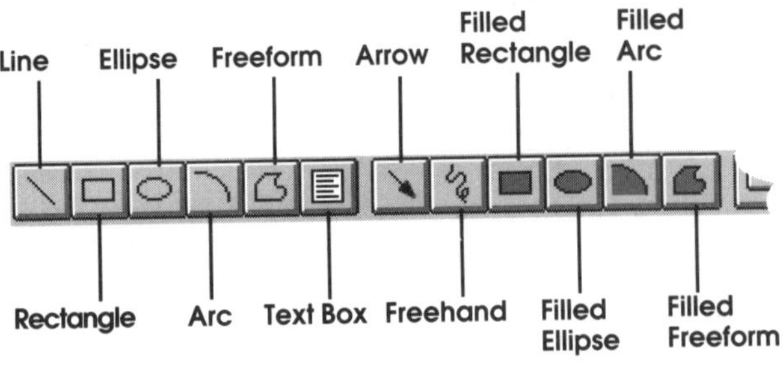
Line
Ellipse
Freeform
Arrow
Filled Rectangle
Filled Arc
Rectangle
Arc
Text Box
Freehand
Filled Ellipse
Filled Freeform

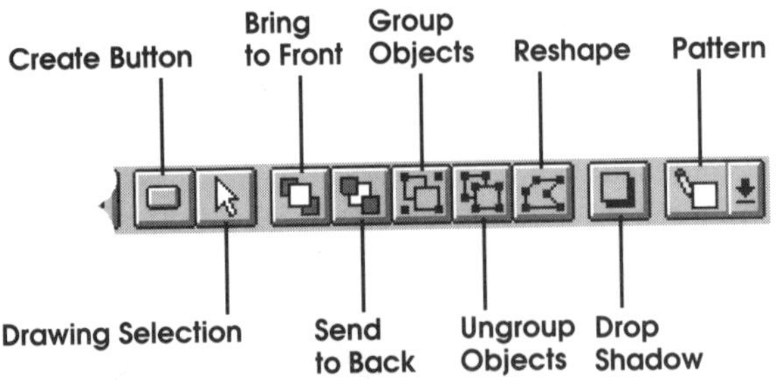
Create Button
Bring to Front
Group Objects
Reshape
Pattern
Drawing Selection
Send to Back
Ungroup Objects
Drop Shadow